Denver in Flames

Forging a New Mile High City

DICK KRECK

FULCRUM PUBLISHING
GOLDEN, COLORADO

The author is grateful to the following institutions to reprint the historical images from their archives: *The Denver Post*, the Denver Public Library/ Western History Department, the Colorado Historical Society, the Denver Fire Department, the Colorado Railroad Museum, and the Denver Firefighters Museum.

Library of Congress Cataloging-in-Publication Data
Kreck, Dick
    Denver in flames : forging a new mile high city / Dick Kreck.
        p.   cm.
Includes bibliographical references and index
    ISBN 1-55591-444-6
    1. Fires—Colorado—Denver—History.   2. Fire extinction—
Colorado—Denver—History.   3. Denver (Colo.)—History.
I. Title
    F784.D457 K74 2000
    978.8'83–dc21

00-009190

Printed in the United States of America
0 9 8 7 6 5 4 3 2 1

Editorial: Daniel Forrest-Bank, Jason Cook
Cover and interior design: Bill Spahr
Cover images: copyright © Kent Meireis; digital composite by Bill Spahr

Fulcrum Publishing
16100 Table Mountain Parkway, Suite 300
Golden, Colorado 80403
(800) 992-2908 • (303) 277-1623
www.fulcrum-books.com

For my children, Kevin, Valerie, Molly and Caitlin, so they'll have more than yellowing newspaper columns to remember their father by.

And for my wife, Victoria Gits, who learned far more about fires and firefighters than she ever wanted, or needed, to know.

"Funny thing about firemen. Night and day, they're always firemen."

—Actor Donald Sutherland in *Backdraft*

Contents

ACKNOWLEDGMENTS

This book, the research for which relied heavily upon eyewitnesses and contemporary accounts, would not have seen the light of day were it not for the following persons, especially the retired firefighters whose experiences and expertise I was fortunate enough to get on tape before they passed away.

Among the former Denver Fire Department firefighters who answered and reanswered my questions, many of which were absurdly elementary, were George Augusto, Terry Brennan, Dan Day, Frank Devine, Jack Franklin, Robert Hyatt, Jack Jaynes, Jim Jordan, Joe Keelan, Charlie Matty, Leroy Newton, Bob Nickerson, Frank Quintana, Stan "Smokey" Sorensen, Foy Wilkerson and retired fire chief Myrle Wise. Also of service was Carl Whiteside of the Colorado Bureau of Investigation, who filled in the blanks on the arson investigations. Tapes of those interviews that were recorded can be found in the oral-history collection at the Colorado History Society in Denver.

Thanks also to friends and associates who buoyed my flagging spirits from time to time, including David Halaas, Tom Noel, Clark Secrest, David Wetzel and my lifetime pal, Bob Rector. And to former *Denver Post* reporter Cindy Parmenter, whose precise printed accounts of the arson trials recounted in Chapter Twelve were vital; railroad historians Greg Lepak and Jackson Thode; and Kenton Forrest and the many others who ferreted out invaluable nuggets of information. A special thanks to Phil Goodstein, author of *Denver Streets,* for moving buildings back where they belonged in the list of notable fires, 1860–1999 (see Appendix E).

Finally, a million thanks to the staffs at the Colorado History Museum, the Colorado Railroad Museum, the Western History Department of the Denver Public Library, the Denver Fire Department, *The Denver Post* Library and the Denver Firefighters Museum for taking my bizarre requests and turning them into real information.

FOREWORD

Nothing so terrifies the human mind as the thought of death by flames. We live among fire — or its threat. Smokers are reminded to "Close Cover Before Striking," children learn the word "Hot!" early on, fire alarm boxes and extinguishers clutter the halls of buildings and every prudent homeowner installs a smoke detector in the kitchen. Faulty electrical wiring, oil-soaked rags, an errant match, a spark from a campfire — any of these can set a house or forest or city ablaze.

For nineteenth-century westerners, fire was never far away. Consider: Men smoked cigars constantly, at home, in saloons, as they worked in barns and stables; dwellings were illuminated by candles and lanterns and heated by wood- or coal-burning stoves and fireplaces; fire fueled forges and stamp mills and smelters; red-hot irons branded cattle and sheep; and live embers shot out of ash pits. City boosters defined the prosperity of their adopted community by the amount of smoke that belched from the town's chimneys and smokestacks.

Yet few frontier communities could boast anything like an organized fire department. A wide-awake boom camp or cow town was as likely to go bust as it was to prosper, and most residents considered themselves on the way to somewhere else. If the diggings played out or a cattle trail shifted to another town, people simply packed and moved on. Few were willing to spend time, energy and money on civic improvements. Churches, schools, libraries — and fire departments — had to wait until a community proved its permanence. In the event of a large blaze, volunteer "bucket brigades" were quickly assembled, but despite heroic vigor and determination they always seemed to be one bucket short.

Thus, nearly every frontier town suffered at least one catastrophic fire. Denver was no exception. In 1863 fire destroyed most of the town's business district. Through the next century and beyond, fires continued to erupt, destroying homes and buildings and forever changing the face of the city.

But *Denver in Flames* is more than a catalog of fires, and more than a history of the Denver Fire Department. It is the dramatic story of a people transforming a mining camp into a great American city. After the catastrophic 1863 fire, Denver's leaders enacted an ordinance requiring new buildings to be built of brick or stone. Other fires led to improved water systems, public safety laws and a professional fire department. In a sense, fire caused the city to reshape and redefine itself, over and over again.

Yet author Dick Kreck, a columnist for *The Denver Post*, never loses sight of those heroic men and women who willingly sacrificed themselves so that others might live. In the backdraft of the city's great fires—the 1863 conflagration; two destructive blazes in 1894 that tested the resolve of the state-imposed Fire and Police Board; a boiler explosion at the Gumry Hotel in 1895 that killed twenty-two lodgers, the largest toll to fire in the city's history; an acid spill in 1904 that pitted the city's bitterly rival newspapers against one another; the 1951 destruction of the Denver Athletic Club, playground of the city's prominent and wealthy citizens; the terrifying last minutes of a United Air Lines DC-8 during its emergency fireball landing at Stapleton Field in 1961; a series of union-related arson fires set along the Front Range between 1968 and 1974; and other major blazes—Kreck tells the compelling stories of Denver's firefighters, many of whom gave their lives to keep the populace safe. This book is a tribute to them and to those who will follow them into future infernos.

—David Fridtjof Halaas
Chief Historian, Colorado Historical Society

Chapter One

THE BOOMING OF
THE FLAMES

Every early western town fears fire, and Cripple
Creek faces this catastrophe twice in five days.
Mammoth fires ravage other towns and cities in
Colorado, including Denver, as well as Chicago, San
Francisco and tiny Peshtigo, Wisconsin, communities
where hasty construction, a shortage of water and
poorly trained volunteers form a deadly, and combustible,
combination. In Colorado, Cripple Creek, Central City
and Denver rebuild quickly.

I t seemed a small mishap. Finishing his lunch shift in the kitchen
of Cripple Creek's Portland Hotel, cook Frank Angel upset a
pan, splashing grease onto the hot stove.

In cruel reality, it was a prelude to disaster. In the span of a few
seconds, flames raced up a grease-soaked wall behind the stove,
exploded throughout the kitchen and sped up the stovepipe. A call
for help went out, but it was already too late. On April 29, 1896, the
fiery beast, the catastrophe residents of the mountain mining town,
any western town, feared most was set loose in their midst for the
second time in five days.

Caught by a vigorous wind riding a frigid winter storm, the fire
made quick work of the wood-frame structure that housed the hotel,
dismissed by one bystander as "a great rattle-trap (that) offered the
best of kindling for the beginning of a conflagration."[1]

Six shots, the gunfire signal for a blaze in a town lacking a traditional fire bell, rang out. Volunteer hose companies rushed to the scene, but they were helpless. Cripple Creek's volunteer fire department may have been the envy of many Colorado mining towns, but there was no water to play on the blaze.

Hydrants dotted the town, but the state of the water source — the nearby, creek-fed reservoir — was always precarious, being dependent upon spring thaws, scarcely half-full during the warm summer months and frozen during the winter. To make matters worse, a similar fiery outbreak just four days earlier had all but depleted the reservoir's meager cache.

Within fifteen minutes, hot embers and flames from the Portland Hotel, pushed along by the wind, had reached the Booth Furniture Store across Myers Avenue. Within thirty minutes, the fire had spread to both the El Paso Lumber Yard and the Harder Grocery Store. At the lumber yard, stockpiles of newly arrived material, acquired to help rebuild what had been consumed in the earlier fire, succumbed to the new blaze. At the grocery store, seven hundred pounds of dynamite in the basement exploded with a fearful roar.

The *Colorado Springs Gazette* reported:

> *So rapid was the progress of the flames that the people soon became panic-stricken and chaos ensued. Teams [of horses and mules] were lashed up and down the streets by excited men; people with bundles and papers were rushing pell-mell to the northward; shouts, the booming of the flames, the crashing of fallen timbers following the explosions of dynamite, all made one ominous, unintelligible roar.*[2]

Townspeople lined up wagons to haul fleeing residents and their meager possessions to safety on the outskirts of town. Some enterprising profiteers charged $100 a wagonload, but the normal charge was between $5 and $20. There was no shortage of desperate customers. Julie Luckraft, whose husband, John, was a mining engineer in Cripple Creek, wrote to her mother three days after the second fire: "How can I tell you of the terrors we have gone thru. The 1st fire [on April 25] was nothing in comparison with the 2nd &, ever since, the terrors of being burned up. Many men are now ill from fright. [John] looks ten years older. It was a terrible night knowing they were still setting places on fire & if the wind had changed we must

Residents of the booming Colorado mining town of Cripple Creek fled down Bennett Avenue to escape encroaching smoke and flame on April 29, 1896. Enterprising teamsters fetched as much as $100 to haul personal belongings to safety. (Courtesy of the Denver Public Library/ Western History Department.)

have gone."[3] Despite Julie's fears, she and her husband gave up their wagon to help transport those needing medical attention to a nearby hospital.

Ten saloons, including the colorfully named Blue Bird, Butte Burkel's, the Old Kentucky, the Thirst Parlor and the Hiawatha Club, as well as two banks, a harness shop, a restaurant, the newspaper offices, several rooming houses, a laundry, a livery stable and dozens of other businesses, burned to the ground. That night, looters finished off what the fire hadn't taken, choosing in particular to pilfer whiskey from the town's many saloons. One hundred fifty special police officers (deputized citizens) and members of the National Guard patrolled the littered streets. An outraged citizen shot and killed a would-be incendiary whom he had chased down.

Cripple Creek's first "Great Fire" had roared through town just four days earlier. Bennett Avenue, the mining town's main street, presented a picture of prosperous commercial establishments from east to west. But the prosperous appearance obscured a fatal flaw: Cripple Creek's hasty construction since its founding ten years earlier had produced a town consisting mainly of wood buildings with false fronts and roofs of wood shingles.

WORST FIRES IN U.S. HISTORY

OCTOBER 8, 1871—PESHTIGO, WISCONSIN, 1,182 DEAD
APRIL 18–19, 1906—SAN FRANCISCO, 700 DEAD*
DECEMBER 30, 1903—IROQUOIS THEATER, CHICAGO, 602 DEAD
NOVEMBER 28, 1942—COCOANUT GROVE, BOSTON, 491 DEAD
OCTOBER 12, 1918—CLOQUET, MINNESOTA, FOREST FIRE, 400 DEAD
APRIL 21, 1930—COLUMBUS, OHIO, PENITENTIARY, 320 DEAD
DECEMBER 5, 1876—THEATER, BROOKLYN, NEW YORK, 295 DEAD
OCTOBER 8, 1871—CHICAGO, 250 DEAD
APRIL 24, 1940—DANCE HALL, NATCHEZ, MISSISSIPPI, 198 DEAD
JULY 6, 1944—RINGLING BROTHERS CIRCUS, HARTFORD,
    CONNECTICUT, 168 DEAD
MAY 28, 1977—NIGHT CLUB, SOUTHGATE, KENTUCKY, 164 DEAD
MARCH 25, 1911—TRIANGLE SHIRTWAIST FACTORY, NEW YORK
    CITY, 146 DEAD
MAY 15, 1929—CLINIC, CLEVELAND, 125 DEAD
DECEMBER 7, 1946—WINECOFF HOTEL, ATLANTA, 119 DEAD
DECEMBER 1, 1958—PAROCHIAL SCHOOL, CHICAGO, 95 DEAD
MARCH 25, 1990—SOCIAL CLUB, BRONX, NEW YORK, 87 DEAD
NOVEMBER 21, 1980—MGM GRAND HOTEL, LAS VEGAS, NEVADA,
    84 DEAD
APRIL 5, 1949—HOSPITAL, EFFINGHAM, ILLINOIS, 77 DEAD
APRIL 19, 1993—CULT COMPOUND, WACO, TEXAS, 72 DEAD

*INCLUDES 503 KILLED IN EARTHQUAKE.
SOURCE: THE WORLD ALMANAC

About 1 P.M. on April 25, fire broke out on the second floor of the Central Dance Hall. How it started, exactly, was never determined. One version claimed a bartender and a prostitute got into a scuffle and a stove was kicked over during the fracas. Julie Luckraft was certain how it started: "It all came from one of these women being drunk & kicking over a gasoline stove. It was a sight seeing them rush out in their nightgowns all painted up & each one with a pug dog under her arm."[4]

Valiant volunteer firefighters controlled the blaze for a time, but, hampered by twelve-inch water mains, bursting hoses and gravity-fed water pressure, they ran out of water in less than an hour. Flames overtook the business district, consuming many of the parlor houses and gambling dens lining Myers Avenue. Explosions sent flaming material high into the air. Some were set off deliberately to create firebreaks, while others erupted haphazardly as the blaze ignited caches of dynamite and black powder stashed all over town.

When the fire was extinguished four hours later, more than three hundred buildings lay in ruin in a twenty-three-block area in the heart of Cripple Creek.

Reconstruction was well under way when calamity struck again on April 29. Lacking sufficient water to extinguish the blaze that had originated at the Portland Hotel, harried firefighters and citizens again used dynamite to try to clear combustibles from the path of the flames, effectively destroying what hadn't already burned.

The two fires caused an estimated $3 million in damage; leveled one thousand homes, forty blocks and countless businesses; and forced five thousand residents to seek shelter against the cold night air in blankets and tents on the hills above town. The refugees' campfires winked like stars on the dark hillsides as the town smoldered through the night.

Some said the destruction wasn't entirely a bad thing. After all, the two fires had destroyed dozens of saloons and brothels as well as most of the shanties that had stood in Cripple Creek since its founding. Construction of brick buildings began almost immediately.

It was a brave front, but the townspeople's worst nightmare had been realized. In western towns and cities, the threat of fire was ever-present. These communities were caldrons of barely contained combustibles just waiting to burst forth. Hay and rubbish littered the streets, wood-frame construction was the norm and cigars, black powder, candles and lanterns were omnipresent.

Nevertheless, the power and devastation of fire stunned those who witnessed it firsthand. One onlooker struggled to remember:

> In one awful instant, before expectation could give shape to the horror, a great flame shot up in the western heavens, and in countless fiery tongues struck downward into the village, piercing every object that stood in the town like a red-hot bolt. A deafening roar, mingled with blasts of electric flame, filled the air, and paralyzed every soul in the place.[5]

Where was this horrifying scene played out? Was it one of the two "Great Fires" most frequently associated with disasters of this kind—those of Chicago and San Francisco? It was neither. This flaming whirlwind took place far from the public's eyes and minds, in a small Wisconsin timber town called Peshtigo, located about halfway up the eastern shore of the state on Green Bay.

Four hundred bodies were found, but hundreds more were so badly incinerated, and so many drowned as they fled into lakes for refuge, that officials estimated the death toll at as many as fifteen hundred persons. An eleven-hundred-square-mile area of forests and small settlements was reduced to ashes and charred ruins. Peshtigo, a booming logging and economic center, was erased from the map and took years to recover. Today, a large part of the town's cemetery is dedicated to the memory of those lost in the catastrophe.

Perhaps worse still for those who were killed and those who lost all their worldly goods, the Peshtigo fire took place the same night, October 8, 1871, as a far better remembered blaze—the Great Chicago Fire. Not that there was anything puny about Chicago's stupefying blaze, or even San Francisco's equally renowned earthquake and subsequent fire on April 18, 1906. But numerous major fires, consigned to relative anonymity for lack of publicity, stalked the West in the nineteenth and early twentieth centuries. Seemingly, no city worth its weight in native lumber escaped untouched.

In the decades of America's westward expansion, beginning in the 1840s, fire was a constant demon, lurking in wait to devour ramshackle country towns or large, overcrowded cities. In their fervor to build, expand, move and build again, pioneers of the early West thought little about building codes or fire departments and oftentimes seemed philosophical about the inevitability of fire. Why not? Even the sidewalks in many "metropolitan" towns consisted of wood planks.

Expansion fever was everywhere, thanks to boosters bent on luring settlers and commerce. Consider Seattle, which grew from a population of 3,533 in 1880 to 42,837 by 1890. "The town's rapid growth during the late '80s," wrote historian Clarence Bagley in 1916, "developed conditions ripe for the conflagration which every American city apparently has to have at some early period in its history."[6] Two-story wood-frame buildings nuzzled up against mills, lumber yards and wooden sheds. Even Seattle's wharves were fashioned of wood. The city was proud of its volunteer fire department, but the city's water supply, as in many other western cities experiencing rapid growth, was woefully inadequate to the task of fighting large fires.

It was a scene repeated again and again. Hasty construction, a shortage of water and poorly trained or untrained volunteers formed a combustible combination. Volunteer fire companies were frequently little more than amateur athletic and professional drinking clubs whose members staged running competitions and fancy dress balls. They fought fire and each other for the glory of saving their towns. In Leadville, Colorado, in 1879, one historian noted that "when fires actually occurred, the scenes could become chaotic. Too often, each fire company dashed to the conflagration and attempted to upstage the others. The result was pandemonium."[7]

In the mid–nineteenth century, when vast blank spaces still covered the map west of the Mississippi River, fires and ill-prepared fire departments were a constant threat to the well-being of communities, just as they had been in the metropolises of the East, where blazes struck large parts of Philadelphia (1839); Albany, New York (1848); Brooklyn (1848); St. Louis (1849); Washington, D.C. (1851); Milwaukee (1856); and Charleston, South Carolina (1856).

Not even mighty New York City escaped the devouring element. On December 16, 1835, the city was struck by a conflagration that destroyed most of the city's best dry-goods stores, thanks to narrow streets, heavy winds and water hoses that froze in subzero temperatures. An even worse calamity occurred in the same part of the city at 3 A.M. on July 20, 1845, when flames broke out in a whale-oil store and spread to a storage facility for explosives. Three hundred buildings were destroyed and damages reached $6 million.

One of the country's most recounted fires was the blaze that roared out of Chicago's West Side at 1:30 A.M. on Sunday, October 8, 1871. The legendary tale of "Mrs. O'Leary's cow" continues to be debated, but there can be no argument that the fire was a devastating blow to the great city. The "Burnt District," as it came to be popularly known, covered an area four miles long and averaged three-quarters of a mile wide — an area of more than two thousand acres. It blanketed twenty-eight miles of streets and devoured eighteen thousand buildings. Total loss: two hundred fifty dead, ninety thousand homeless and $200 million in property literally up in smoke.

But few know that the night before the Great Chicago Fire a blaze scorched four square blocks barely a mile from the O'Leary

Refugees from the Great Chicago Fire in 1871 trudged toward Lake Michigan to escape the inferno. Two hundred fifty residents died in the fire. (Dick Kreck collection.)

Sightseers clustered at cross streets to watch the progress of fires savaging San Francisco following the Great Quake of 1906. Famed photographer Arnold Genthe used a borrowed camera to capture the view down Sacramento Street on April 18, 1906. (Courtesy of the California Historical Society.)

stable and nearly stormed the rest of the city. Or that Chicago, wracked by a yearlong drought and heat wave, had been hit by two fires a day for more than a year and had suffered twenty fires the week before its "Great Fire." The city's understaffed and underequipped fire department was exhausted and much of its fire-fighting gear was in disrepair because of the repeated burns.

In the blossoming American West, with its seemingly endless capacity for newcomers, fires raged with disheartening regularity. Incendiaries—firebugs—were a constant threat. They were adjudged "nocturnal deadbeats" and "floaters" and "bummers" by outraged newspaper editors. Drunkenness and disorderly behavior were commonplace and careless revelers set fires by accident or by design. Arson was a frequent tool of protest, political or otherwise. After the Civil War, onetime soldiers from the North and South poured into western cattle and mining camps, and old times there were not forgotten.

In San Francisco, the greatest of the city's "great" fires followed a devastating earthquake that came like a thief in the night at 5:12 A.M. on April 18, 1906. As the earth tore apart violently in opposite directions for 270 miles along the San Andreas rift, huge cracks opened on the city's thoroughfares and buildings toppled into tangled heaps of plaster and lumber, leaving thousands homeless to camp in the city's parks.

As terrifying as it was, the quake was a preamble to the fearful fires that followed. Before the last smoldering embers died away four days later, ten square miles of the city had been destroyed, at a 1906-adjusted price of $400 million. Seven hundred people had died and nearly a quarter million had been injured.

Arnold Genthe, a photographer living in San Francisco at the time, wrote in 1936:

> *The fire had started simultaneously in many different places when the housewives had attempted to get breakfast for their families, not realizing what a menace the ruined chimneys were. All along the skyline as far as eye could see, clouds of smoke and flames were bursting forth. The work of the fire department was badly hampered, as the water mains had burst.*[8]

Though San Francisco's 1906 earthquake/fire was, by far, the greatest catastrophe to strike the City by the Bay, fire was a frequent visitor. The first "Great Fire," fanned by high winds and fed by wood buildings that touched each other like children's blocks, swept through the city on Christmas Eve of 1849, at the height of the California gold rush. Another large blaze struck on May 4, 1850, and caused

$4 million in damages. Major fires also occurred on June 14 and September 17, 1850, and on May 4 and June 22, 1851.

No city—or town with big-city ambitions—was exempted from its own "Great Fire." In 1872 a small blaze in the rear of a hotel in Helena, Montana, seized the thriving mining community. Volunteer firefighters, though they had labored well against previous outbreaks, were no match for the fire, which tore through the hotel's roof and sent flames and hot embers raining down on the shingled roofs that surrounded it. "Human effort seemed utterly impotent to stay the ravages of the inexorable demon," wrote a newspaper reporter.[9]

Similar episodes savaged towns and cities in Oregon, Nevada, Washington and Utah. And in Colorado, the three deadly elements of tinder-dry building materials, lack of a reliable water supply and inexperienced firefighters—plus cramped topography—combined to make such disasters synonymous with mining communities.

On a warm, windy, dusty spring day in April 1863, it was Denver's sad fate to join the roster of western settlements that had been terrorized by fire. The struggling frontier town, which was then barely five years old and boasted a permanent population of just over five thousand residents, was attacked by a blaze that nearly strangled it in its infancy.

As was often the case, arsonists were suspected when a small fire began behind the Cherokee House, a saloon at F (Fifteenth) and Blake Streets, the center of the business district. While the city slept at 3 A.M. on a Sunday morning, a few well-meaning but untrained citizens turned out to fight the fire. Flames driven by a brisk, constantly changing wind consumed four square blocks of ramshackle buildings in just two hours. Although this was not much of a loss compared to the devastation of Chicago and San Francisco, it was a critical baptism by fire for Denver, which in the 1860s was part of the Colorado Territory. At that time, Denver was not linked to "the States" by railroad, and its supplies were frequently interdicted by Indians on the Plains and by the Civil War raging in the East. Many of Denver's precious stores of food staples, especially flour and pork, literally went up in smoke during the blaze, and every hardware store was destroyed.

Out of the flames came an ordinance requiring that all new structures be built of brick, a rule that even today gives downtown Denver its historic look. It also led to the establishment of an official volunteer fire department.

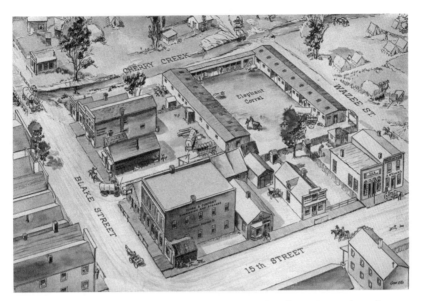

An aerial view of the area bounded by Blake, Wazee and Fifteenth (F) Streets shows the enormous Elephant Corral, which dominated the downtown Denver block. The "Great Fire of 1863" began behind the Cherokee House Saloon at lower left and swept four square blocks between McGaa (Market) Street and Wazee and from Cherry Creek to Sixteenth (G) Street. Following the fire, the city council designated a thirteen-block area the Fire District, where all buildings were required to be built of brick or stone. (Dick Kreck collection.)

Colorado's tinderbox mountain mining camps were ripe for destruction. In addition to being hastily constructed and protected only by volunteer fire departments, the camps were erected in confined spaces. Most of the surrounding hillsides bustled with mining and milling operations, and those living there were more concerned with striking it rich than with improving the towns' infrastructures.

The first of the great Colorado mountain fires broke out in the mining town of Central City at 10:30 A.M. on May 21, 1874. Long feared and expected by city fathers, the fire "tore madly down the street, consuming with the velocity of a whirlwind."[10] Unchecked, the fire blew up Spring Street to Bridge Street, crossed a gulch and attacked the rear of businesses fronting on Main Street. It swallowed up everything in its path along Nevada, Pine and Lawrence Streets.

Townspeople, led by Henry M. Teller, who later represented the state in the U.S. Senate, saved the Teller House by covering its windows with water-soaked blankets. But they could not do the same for the Rocky Mountain National Bank, where, reported the *Daily*

The heart of the thriving mining town was burned out of Central City, Colorado, by fire that "tore madly down the street" on May 21, 1874. The large building at the upper right today serves as the Gilpin History Museum. (Courtesy of the Denver Public Library/Western History Department.)

Central City Register, "every window sash and frame was burnt black and all the lights [were] broken or melted."[11]

In the aftermath, everyone looked for someone to blame. As frequently happened in the West, the finger was pointed at the town's Chinese population, who, some said, caused the fire during practice of "religious orgies." In the hours immediately after the fire, the *Register* pronounced that "it appears tolerably certain that the Asiatics were engaged with their women in some sort of heathen worship, of celebrations of rites known only to themselves."[12]

This charge was later withdrawn when Chin Lin Sou, a prominent member of Central City's Chinese community, complained that "the Chinese are too frequently made the victims of circumstances which any other nationality would escape without censure."[13] He had a point. After the 1872 blaze in Helena, Montana, an observer had noted, "A fire in these diggings is just one Chinaman away."[14] Ultimately, it was concluded that the Central City fire started in a defective chimney, whereafter the *Register* apologized to Chin Lin Sou and his fellows.[15]

Volunteers struggled to unload fire hoses when the Gold Coin Mill in Victor, Colorado, went up in flames on August 21, 1899. In three-and-a-half hours, the fire burned fourteen blocks of the mountain mining town. (Courtesy of the Denver Public Library/Western History Department.)

Thousands left homeless by the 1899 Victor fire milled around on hillsides above the town and guarded their possessions, including mattresses, trunks and household goods, from looters. (Courtesy of the Denver Public Library/Western History Department.)

On August 21, 1899, Victor's blazing number came up. As was often the case, the precise cause remains unclear. One story said the fire started when one of the Colorado mining town's soiled doves, an inhabitant of Jennie Thompson's 999 Dance Hall, was cleaning a

One year after fire destroyed its central business district, Central City was rebuilt with sturdier, multistory brick buildings. The Teller House, home of "the face on the barroom floor," is visible at the center. (Courtesy of the Denver Public Library/Western History Department.)

dress with gasoline while enjoying a cigarette. Another, more likely, version blamed a patron who carelessly tossed a cigar into a pile of rubbish behind the bar, igniting the bartender as well as the building. Still another version said the fire began in a "hop joint" (drug parlor) located behind the barroom.

Whatever the cause, it led to a fire that in an astonishing three and a half hours incinerated fourteen blocks of the six-year-old town, including two railroad depots and the surface buildings of the Gold Coin Mine. The blaze caused $1 million in damages and left three thousand residents homeless.

There was always fire. But there was also residents' spirit to rebuild, to make their communities whole again. It happened in Central City. The day after the 1874 fire had left the city in ruins, the town's newspaper declared, in disjointed fashion:

Not withstanding the desolation which now marks the spot where once our city stood and prospered, and the overwhelming calamities which have overtaken our businessmen, at a period when, with extensive new stocks, just opened and shelved for the summer trade[,] they were anticipating a harvest from the renewed activity of the mines, their spirits are not checked or dampened nor their ardor checked. Present appearances indicate a speedy rebuilding of the burnt district with more substantial structures than those that have gone. This will enable very many to resume business in a few days.[16]

In Cripple Creek, hours after the second of two fires had leveled the town in late April 1896, construction of substantial brick buildings in the business district commenced at a furious pace. At the same time, the town's founding fathers took a hard line with looters. The *Rocky Mountain News*'s man on the scene wrote that there was "no room in Cripple Creek for thieves, hold-ups or law-breakers of any kind, and a large number of obnoxious characters were given the quiet tip that they had only until the time the next train left to get out of the camp, and they got out."[17] On May 16, *The Denver Times* proclaimed in a headline, "Cripple Is Not Crippled," but reconstruction took more than a year.

In the first days after the Cripple Creek fires, donations of food, tents and blankets poured in by rail, particularly from Denver and Colorado Springs. Mining magnate and civic leader William S. Stratton, owner of Cripple Creek's opulent Independence Mine, donated a carload of goods to be shipped from Colorado Springs and promised $1 million in loans to business-people who would rebuild in the burnt district. A year later, fine brick structures stood where once there had been mostly wood buildings, the town's two main streets had been paved and the problems of water supply had at long last been addressed.

Denver, too, promised a glorious rebuilding after its April 1863 blaze. As one newspaper proclaimed, "One has only to stroll along

COBBLESTONE, UNPAVED STREETS AND SLIPPERY STREETCAR TRACKS MADE SPEEDING TO EARLY-DAY FIRES IN UNSPRUNG, HORSE-DRAWN WAGONS DANGEROUS BUSINESS. IN 1894, CHIEF JULIUS PEARSE WAS RUSHING TO A FIRE WHEN HIS BUGGY WAS STRUCK BY AN EXPRESS WAGON. PEARSE WAS THROWN TO THE STREET, UNINJURED, BUT THE CRASH DROVE THE BUGGY'S SHAFT INTO THE HORSE'S HEART, KILLING IT ALMOST INSTANTLY. THE SORREL WAS VALUED AT $150.

Blake Street any of these fine days and note the character of the improvements now being made."[18] Larger two- and three-story all-brick "fireproof" buildings, providing "a measure of prudence," sprang up in the central business district, leading the editors of the *Weekly Commonwealth and Republican* to brag, scarcely six months after the fire: "Never, in any period since the existence of the city of Denver, has she looked so thoroughly prosperous, and had more indications of true wealth displayed in her streets."[19]

Noted Denver gambling-house owner "Big Ed" Chase typified the attitude of those whose Blake Street businesses had burned. Reminiscing in 1921, he told an interviewer:

I was not idle long. The fire occurred on a Saturday night [actually Sunday morning] and by the next Tuesday I had another place going on the same spot. I bought a frame residence and moved it onto my ground. I had to tear out partitions in order to get room and in so doing destroyed my own bedroom, rendering it necessary to sleep on the tables until I could find another place to live.[20]

He was not alone in his optimism. Thanks to economic prosperity and the resiliency of the city's business community in the 1870s and 1880s, Denver grew to more than 106,000 souls by 1890 and became the economic heart of the Rocky Mountain West.

Though many towns and cities of the West were gutted by the fiery peril, a spirit of rebuilding prevailed. Julie Luckraft wrote to her mother from Cripple Creek on April 28, 1896, "We feel so disheartened we feel like giving up altogether," but she rebounded a few lines later and wrote philosophically, "It is terrible but many have lost everything. We have had a terrible lot of experience." She went on to describe with enthusiasm how men were building a new room on the family's cabin.[21]

The day after the second fire in Cripple Creek, rebuilding was in full swing. "The very air hums and throbs with the busy stir of carpenters and tradesmen," the *Rocky Mountain News* noted. "Those who were downhearted yesterday, today are enthusiastic and declare that Cripple Creek shall be the greatest camp in the world or they will know the reason why."[22]

No civic cheerleading, however, could match the grit of the owner of the town's English Kitchen restaurant. Although embers from that second fire were still warm, the diner—a temporary, flimsy wood-frame building with a canvas roof—displayed a sign promising, "Supper will be ready at 5 o'clock tomorrow." The English Kitchen served as promised.

Chapter Two

THE "GREAT FIRE"

*Many visit but few remain in barren, bleak, frontier
Denver. The business district, doomed by lack of a fire
department, is little more than a series of shacks
jammed together in the central part of town. After the
blaze, a new ordinance requires brick construction.
Businesses rebuild in a matter of days, and the new
construction gives Denver a more cosmopolitan look.*

D enver in the decade following its founding on November
22, 1858, was an inhospitable place. Perched on the western
edge of what some called the Great American Desert, the
Queen City was an island of the sparest kind of civilization, blasted
by Arctic winds in winter, roasted in hundred-degree heat waves in
summer.

The town made a bright beginning when thousands trekked from
the East and from the West, lured by the discovery of gold in Pikes
Peak country. An estimated thirty-five thousand gold-seekers passed
through the young town on their way to the gold fields. As is often
typical of the search for gold, most of the "Pikes Peak or Busters"
went home busted. Despite the surge of visitors, few chose to stay.
The first territorial census in 1860 determined that 4,759 residents
lived full-time in Denver City. A decade later, the 1870 census could
uncover only ten more residents than that.

In 1861, setting a trend that would be repeated throughout
Denver's up-and-down economic life, 25-by-125-foot lots could be
had for a dollar or two. Properties on the edge of town were held so
cheaply that they changed hands several times a night in the town's
plentiful poker games. The few surviving early-day photographs show

THIEVERY WAS RAMPANT AT EARLY-DAY DENVER FIRES. RUBBERNECKERS HAMPERED FIREMEN'S EFFORTS, WANDERING IN AND OUT OF THE FIRE SCENE. CROWDS ATTRACTED BY FIRES WERE FREQUENT VICTIMS OF PICKPOCKETS, AND LOOTERS FREQUENTLY SET BLAZES TO PLUNDER BUILDINGS AMIDST THE RESULTING CONFUSION. A COMMON TRICK AMONG JACKANAPES WAS TO CUT THE DEPARTMENT'S COTTON HOSES TO IMPEDE FIRE-FIGHTING EFFORTS.

streets barren of any vegetation and lined with ramshackle structures that provided little more than basic shelter.

Numerous visitors wrote disparagingly of the dusty village at the confluence of Cherry Creek and the South Platte River. One of the earliest pioneers to do business in Denver was Richens "Uncle Dick" Wootton. He noted after his departure in 1862, "When I left the place at the end of a four-years' stay, with about twenty times the population it had when I went there, the chances seemed to me that it would get smaller rather than larger."[1]

In 1864, visiting British clergyman William Hepworth Dixon found a town where men were "swearing, fighting, drinking, like old Norse gods. As you wander about these hot and dirty streets you seem to be walking in a city of demons. Every fifth house appears to be a bar, a whisky shop, a lager-beer saloon; every tenth house appears to be either a brothel or a gambling house; very often both in one."[2]

Jerome C. Smiley, who constantly boosted the glories of Denver, sniffed in his monumental 1901 tome *History of Denver* that Dixon must have been hanging out with the wrong crowd. But even he couldn't bring himself to say much nice about Denver in its earliest days, conceding that "the town was almost barren of any kind of verdure, besides being beset by dust-laden breezes. In the built-up parts, excepting in a few places on the Auraria side, there were no trees, no grass, no flowers." He added:

At this period [1861] in Denver's career the town in itself and by itself was not a pretty place. Its natural surroundings were magnificent, but no amount of local pride and patriotism, no stretch of partisan and partial enthusiasm, could make the town appear a thing of beauty. Its treeless, grassless, bushless condition gave it an

Larimer Street in 1860s Denver was typical of the crowded, ramshackle nature of the commercial center of town. One observer noted buildings "stood cheek by jowl without room for a yellow cat to squeeze between them." (Courtesy of the Denver Public Library/Western History Department.)

> *exceedingly uninviting appearance; its motley, irregular, ugly structures of brick, frame or log were calculated to cause nightmare in the brain of an unseasoned visitor. It is probable that nowhere else in the world were ever seen such architectural horrors, and combinations of architectural freaks and wretchedness as those presented in American frontier towns of a generation ago. It would seem that human ingenuity would be incapable of producing results so uniformly frightful—that the law of chance, if it may so be called, ought to and would have brought in an occasional something to vary the dreary monotony and relieve the ferocity of ugliness. But it never did so.[3]*

Writing in 1862, a reporter for Denver's *Weekly Commonwealth and Republican* newspaper gave a backhanded compliment to the town on the way it had grown up: "Time was, in the history of Denver, when a man or two shot a day was not considered remarkable, and when a stab from a bowie, or a shot from a revolver, were not uncommon occurrences."[4]

Though the town was remarkably peaceful in its early years, the arrival of con artists, hooligans and other societal lowlifes—along with plentiful amounts of bad whiskey—had a negative impact. The year 1860 was a particularly violent one, leading to the establishment of People's Courts and Vigilance Committees, which, in Smiley's words, "administered the only adequate remedies for conditions that had become intolerable. The evils with which they had to deal justified their methods and their applied remedies."[5] Said remedies included quickie trials and frequent necktie parties.

The town's physical appearance didn't improve much through the years. As late as 1873, Isabella Bird, a British adventurer who, remarkably, trekked the Colorado Territory on her own, observed the following on her first glimpse of Denver: "I looked down upon the great 'City of the Plains,' the metropolis of the Territories. There the braggart city lay spread out, brown and treeless, upon the brown and treeless plain, which seemed to nourish nothing but wormwood and the Spanish bayonet. The shallow Platte, shriveled into a narrow stream with a shingly bed six times too large for it, and fringed by shriveled cottonwood, wound along by Denver."[6]

In addition to being unattractive, pioneer Denver was an insurance agent's nightmare. The majority of the fledgling city's downtown area consisted of shacks built of logs or of native pine, a highly flammable, pitch-filled wood. Robert Perkin observed in his book *The First Hundred Years*:

> *A few of the "business blocks" towered to two stories. A lot more pretended to such architectural glory with false fronts. In the commercial district the structures stood cheek by jowl without room for a yellow cat to squeeze between them. Most of the homes still were log cabins. A few were frame, and some of these were prettied up with wooden fretwork lace at the eaves. As gestures to gentility the interior walls and ceilings of more pretentious homes often were hung with cheesecloth or sheeting in lieu of wallpaper. Roofs were of wooden shingles or rough-split shakes. Nearly everything was inflammable.[7]*

Since its earliest days, Denver's residents were aware of the danger of fire. In the ragtag towns of the West, fires were as regular as the seasons. The *Rocky Mountain News* and its editor, William N. Byers, were among the first to campaign for some sort of fire-fighting equipment and a trained force to operate it as protection against Denver's many "incendiaries." This category of firebugs included those who roamed the streets deliberately setting fires for moral, political or opportunistic reasons, as well as those who inadvertently set fires out of simple carelessness or drunkenness.

By 1862, the city council was empowered to prohibit the construction of wooden buildings. Ordinances provided for inspection of stoves and fireplaces and dictated that hay and straw could not be stored within forty feet of any structure. No tents could be erected. On July 15, 1862, the council took the first steps toward establishing fire-fighting facilities by approving the purchase of a hook and ladder and the hiring of two bucket brigades of volunteers. Still, the fire department existed only on paper. A full-fledged volunteer fire department lay four years in the future.

Denver experienced one of its periodic growth spurts in the summer of 1862. According to records filed by the U.S. Assessor for the Colorado Territory, approximately $8,000 in taxes were levied against new businesses that year. There seemed to be little chance the city would run dry—at least of alcohol. Among the 284 businesses issued licenses up to November 1, 1862, 10 were wholesale dealers in liquor, 54 were retail dealers in liquor and 3 were breweries. That there also were 5 bankers, 4 brokers, 13 lawyers, 11 physicians, 26 manufacturers and 10 hotels of varying degrees of elegance gave evidence to the city's astonishing growth. The *Weekly Rocky Mountain News* was moved to brag:

> *At no period since the founding of Denver have the prospects been more encouraging than now. At no previous time has the city been so full of people, or had so many actual residents. Every house is filled. Not even a cabin, fit for a stable, can be rented, and if there was a supply of lumber, building operations would be more brisk than ever before known. Denver is becoming more and more the entrepot of all commerce with the mountains and plains for hundreds of miles north, south and west.*[8]

Unabashed boosterism and civic pride aside, all was not rosy. One newspaper editor complained that Denver was as "dirty a town as any one of its size in the country" and berated public officials for allowing "old clothes, bones, and decayed vegetable matter" to litter the streets.[9]

A series of events conspired to seal the city's fiery fate. First, the ordinance requiring brick construction within certain districts was repealed in November 1862, leading to the construction of more flammable shanties.[10]

According to the *Weekly Commonwealth and Republican,* Alderman James A. Cook, a business owner, was fined $50 for violating the ordinance against frame structures when he put a roof from an old building on a new construction and tried to pass it off as an "old," and therefore exempt, building. Outraged by the fine, he refused to pay it, and even lobbied the city council to repeal the ordinance.

The council members, most of whom were, at the least, Cook's business associates, agreed, and even went one step further by remitting his fine. Under pressure from newspapers and the town's citizenry, the council reversed its decision and, in December, ordered Cook to pay the fine. A week later, the council reversed itself again and remitted the fine. Decrying the ordinance's repeal, the Commonwealth commented, "Many brick buildings have gone up in our midst [but] would have been built of [wood] frame if this ordinance had not existed."[11]

Only three days before the "Great Fire" of 1863 broke out, Alderman George Tritch, who would lose two businesses to the inferno, offered the council a resolution. He called on the street commissioner to instruct parties living along Blake and F (Fifteenth) Streets (where, probably not coincidentally, Tritch's two shops were located) "to repair broken sidewalks and also to compel parties throwing straw, dirt and other rubbish in the streets and alleys to remove the same, and that persons leaving wagons in the streets for sale or for any other purpose be required to remove same."[12] The resolution passed four to one.

In another sign of the disaster to come, a series of fires broke out in the city's "Riverfront District" late in 1862. Set by moralists outraged over the presence of brothels, the fires led the *Weekly Rocky Mountain News* to plead, "Will either the civil or military authorities take prompt and efficient steps to avert the danger and protect the lives and property of our citizens?"[13] And in a remarkably prescient bit of forecasting, the *Weekly Commonwealth and Republican* warned, "No very alarming results have been realized by the burning of these outside houses of ill fame, but we beg of those who have participated in those acts to remember, that if a house was set on fire in the city, on a windy night, or in fact if it occurred on ever so still a night, in the heart of the city, every house in Denver will be level with the ground in three hours."[14]

The *Commonwealth* reiterated its warning in February 1863 when a fire broke out near midnight at the Elephant Corral and only quick work by several hundred men prevented it from spreading to other buildings on Wazee and Blake Streets. "A light wind happened to be blowing from the south, which carried the flames from the buildings. If the wind had been blowing the other way, nothing could have saved the main portion of Blake Street. This is another warning to our citizens."[15]

The spring of 1863 was a dry one along the Platte. Warm winds frequently blew through town, raising dust. Sometime between 2 and 3 A.M. on Sunday, April 19, a small fire was discovered at the back of the two-story wooden Cherokee House, W. M. Keith's saloon and hotel on the southwest corner of F (Fifteenth) and Blake Streets, the epicenter of the town's business district. Later, some would claim the fire had been deliberately set by "bummers," roughnecks and troublemakers. The *Weekly Rocky Mountain News*, for example, offered that "it is certain that the fire caught from an ash box in the rear of the Cherokee House. It is equally certain that proper care was not taken to guard against fire about the kitchen and ash heaps of that house." The paper also advanced the opinion of some that "it was the work of an incendiary, and that its connection may be traced to the acts of the guerrilla bands and robbers that have for some time infested various portions of the Territory."[16]

However it began, a stiff, shifting breeze quickly spread flames in all directions. "The alarm was soon spread and the city aroused but all efforts to confine the conflagration to the neighborhood of its source were unavailing."[17]

Tradition in the Old West dictated that townspeople pitch in to fight fire, any budding town's worst enemy. This code was particularly strong among businesspeople, who obviously had much to lose. In Denver, a city ordinance provided that citizens present at a fire "shall be subject to and obedient to the orders of the fire wardens, the mayor and aldermen, city marshal and police officers."[18] Failure to comply could lead to a $5 fine and incarceration until the fire was put out.

Because the Denver fire broke out in the early-morning hours on a Sunday, few of the town's citizens were awake to answer the call to fight it, and those drawn by the flames did little to help combat them. Many residents were unaware of the fire until they awoke to find the heart of the city's business district reduced to charcoal and ash.

Those who roused themselves and left their beds to battle the fire were grossly untrained to deal with such an overwhelming blaze. Others, perhaps disconcerted by a sense of futility, chose to stand and watch. "About one-fourth worked—worked well, faithfully and heroically from the beginning," the *Weekly Rocky Mountain News* observed four days later. "The other three-fourths were mere spectators. For all the use they were[,] as many wooden men would have been as good, except that these would get out of the way of the fire and so not assist in spreading it. Want of system, a head and authority were painfully apparent."[19]

It soon became painfully apparent that whatever meager volunteer firefighters the townspeople could muster were woefully overmatched. At various points during the night, observers noted, a few well-placed buckets of water might have stemmed the flames. The fire, hurried along by gusting winds that kept changing direction, fed on the tinder-dry buildings crammed together in the heart of the business district. It blazed up F (Fifteenth) Street to McGaa (Market) Street, leaped to the east side of F Street, engulfing Cheesman's drugstore, and spread rapidly up Blake Street toward G (Sixteenth) Street before it was halted in that direction at Tootle & Leach's fireproof (brick) building.

The *Weekly Rocky Mountain News* detailed the fire's course:

> *Leaping Blake to Brendlinger's corner and the Elephant stable, the whole of that dense block was soon a mass of flames, west to Campbell & Jones' store, which was the last building destroyed in that direction. After a temporary check at Insley's on the south side of Blake, it leaped over that and enveloped the frame buildings beyond it, including the immense frame, formerly the Express office. An effort was made to check its course by tearing down the small frames next to Tilton's store, and with such success that it stopped at Tilton's.[20]*

On it raged, down F Street to Wazee Street. Up the north side of Blake Street it extended east and devoured one of the district's largest structures, the Kiskadden & Co. warehouse, before it was halted by efforts of volunteers. Luckily for the warehouse, its owners had shipped $24,000 worth of goods to Salt Lake City just ten days before the fire.

A sturdy outhouse (left) somehow survived Denver's "Great Fire of 1863." Burned-out ruins remained on G (Sixteenth) Street, but the city's business district was largely rebuilt of fire-resistant brick less than eighteen months later. (Courtesy of the Denver Public Library/Western History Department.)

The *News*'s enthralled reporter vividly recounted the scene:

There seemed to be no world beyond the little circle lighted up by the flames; all around and above was the blackness of darkness. In the center was a towering mass of flame shooting up in lofty columns, sweeping away to the right and left, leaping from building to building, sweeping them away like chaff, licking up the vast piles of goods that had been piled in the streets, seething, and surging, and rolling, in immense billows like a storm-tossed ocean, while upward and away on the breeze rolled the dense columns of smoke, uniting the lurid flames below with the pitchy darkness above.[21]

As it became apparent that destroying or moving smaller wood structures was having little effect on slowing the fire's progress, bystanders began hauling goods out of threatened buildings and carrying them to the sandy bottom of nearby Cherry Creek. It was an often chaotic and disorganized rescue. The *Weekly Commonwealth and Republican* commented dryly about one young man's efforts to help

*"In case of fire your loss was your own."
—Gambler "Big Ed" Chase. (Courtesy of
the Denver Public Library/Western History
Department.)*

empty a store on F Street. Leaving many more valuable items behind, he carried a pair of rubber overshoes a block away and carefully laid them on a pile of dry goods, then went back to the store, "probably after another pair, but found the building in flames."[22]

When daylight came, Denver's residents were shocked to view the devastation. "This dread catastrophe, so long expected, has at length fallen upon us," reported the *Commonwealth*.[23] Nearly all of a four-block area of the business district—McGaa Street to Wazee Street and Cherry Creek to G Street—had been reduced to heaps of smoldering ashes. Seventy structures had gone up in smoke in two hours, at an estimated loss (largely in inventory because most of the structures were little more than shacks) of $200,000 to $350,000 (accounts varied).

"Big Ed" Chase, a prominent saloon owner and gambler in the district, spoke for many of the town's business owners after his barroom on the south side of Blake Street went up in flames:

> *I moved once or twice and went broke just as often before I bought the old McNasser property which had been a hotel and was the original Planters' House. It just suited my purposes and I fixed it up so as to make it the finest and biggest gambling house in Denver. And then, what do you supposed happened? In less than three weeks and before I could get well straightened out, the cussed thing took fire and burned to the ground, going so fast that I did not save a thing. Insurance? Do you suppose that anybody would have insured anything here in those days? There simply was no such thing here then that I ever heard of. In case of fire your loss was your own.*[24]

The burned-out area became a hunting ground. Young boys reportedly reaped up to two hundred pounds of nails daily from the ruins, earning them $5–$10 a day in salvage. "All day yesterday crowds were walking about amid the ruins of the burnt district, searching for one thing and another that might have escaped destruction. Some found old gun locks, some found badly tempered jack knives and a good many found nothing. We saw one fellow who was looking for a roll of greenbacks which he said he had lost the night before the fire in Chase & Heatley's saloon. After carefully looking over the site of that establishment he was heard to exclaim, 'Well, now, this is nearly hell, ain't it?'"[25]

A boy named Charlie Scott was more fortunate. Digging amidst the ruins of Sherwood & Co.'s building, young Scott turned up a piece of metal in the shape of a ring. A jeweler determined the ring was gold and offered him $500 for it, but the boy refused to sell it or give it away, except to its rightful owner. "That boy ought to be well rewarded," said the *News*.[26]

Denver's "Great Fire" pales beside those that ravaged Chicago and San Francisco. For example, the 1871 Chicago fire covered an area four miles long and three-quarters of a mile wide, burned eighteen thousand buildings and caused two hundred fifty deaths; it also consumed Abraham Lincoln's personal copy of the Emancipation Proclamation. The 1906 San Francisco earthquake and fire killed an estimated seven hundred people and resulted in $400 million in property damage.

But Denver's conflagration was a crushing blow to the young frontier town. Because of sporadic Indian attacks on the Plains and the Civil War raging in the East, delivery of goods was often a hit-or-miss proposition. In addition, even though there were ample supplies of homegrown onions, potatoes, corn, peas and beans, area farmers suffered heavy crop losses to grasshoppers during the summer of 1863.

In the year prior to the fire, forty pounds of flour cost $18–$20, sixteen pounds of sugar cost $4, one hundred pounds of cornmeal cost $10 and a yard of muslin, used frequently for interior decoration in the town's simple shelters, cost $1. Prices of goods doubled after the fire. Clara Witter, a young homemaker who lived just across Cherry Creek with her husband, Daniel, recorded in her diary: "Flour was scarce, [we had] plenty of corn meal; ham and bacon [were] scarce and beef we never could get."[27] Ten groceries and three bakeries were listed among the 115 businesses lost to the fire (see Appendix B). Nearly half the goods in the city, particularly flour, bacon and sugar, had been stored in the burnt district, and every hardware and

THE CITY'S FIRST REGULAR COMPANY OF VOLUNTEERS, HOOK AND LADDER COMPANY NO. 1, WAS FOUNDED ON MARCH 25, 1866. THE FIRST ORDER OF BUSINESS: ORDERING 50 UNIFORMS THAT FEATURED A RED SHIRT WITH A BLACK NECKTIE, A BLACK LEATHER BELT WITH THE WORD "DENVER" IN WHITE LETTERS, AND BLACK DOESKIN PANTS. EACH MEMBER OF THE COMPANY WAS RESPONSIBLE FOR HIS UNIFORM, WHICH COST $12.

stove store in town had been leveled. Witter recalled later, "The hams you could smell for days after the fire and the flour also. It was a great loss—provisions were so dear."[28]

Townspeople were understandably jittery in the days immediately after the fire. Winds re-ignited embers in African American businessman Barney Ford's store on Blake Street, and the rekindled fire destroyed what little the initial blaze had not. False alarms were frequent. An anonymous tipster warned that Planters' House, a popular and well-known hotel, would be targeted. Attempts to set fire to Rohlfing & Co. on Ferry (Eleventh) Street and to the Cibola Hall dance house in Auraria were reported by the *Weekly Rocky Mountain News*, which vented its editorial anger on the perpetrators by offering that "if one of these infernal incendiaries was caught, and burned at the stake it would cure him at least, and not be a particle too severe either."[29] Both fires were extinguished quickly and caused little damage.

Recrimination over the lack of a fire department began almost immediately. "It is useless for us to expatiate on the lesson taught by this unfortunate event," wrote a writer for the *Weekly Commonwealth and Republican*. "Nor are we certain that it will not have to be taught again and again ere it is heeded. Yesterday morning the necessity of a properly organized fire department in the city was apparent to everyone."[30]

The *News*, which had campaigned relentlessly for the city's political leaders to organize a professional fire brigade, lost no time in going on the offensive:

One hundred men, properly organized, and equipped with hooks, ladders, chains, axes and buckets alone would have saved one

*hundred thousand dollars worth of property on Sunday morning;
and fifty so equipped, and knowing what to do and how to do it,
would have effected more good than all the three thousand who were
present, with their indifference or spasmodic or ill-directed efforts.
We suppose there is not a man in town who is so obtuse that he
cannot now "see it."*[31]

Among those calling most loudly for action in the days that followed the fire was the *Miner's Register* of Central City. "The Denver people had been very remiss in providing against a catastrophe of this sort," the paper chided. "They had been talking for some time of getting a fire engine, but had not done it. Whatever might have been done, it is now too late to talk about it. The most that they or we can do is to take warning and provide for the future, first by erecting buildings which will be perfectly safe against fire, and next by the organization of companies."[32] Ironically, eleven years after Denver's "Great Fire," Central City itself was almost destroyed by a devastating blaze in 1874.

Sixty years after Denver's inferno, Nathan A. Baker, who had worked as a reporter for the *Rocky Mountain News* at the time of the blaze, recounted that one of the few fire-fighting improvements made afterward—bizarre as it seemed—was the digging of two forty-foot-deep wells, one in the middle of Cherry Creek and the other at St. Louis (Tenth) and McGaa (Market) Streets. The wells were large enough for firefighters to descend to water level and pass up buckets.[33]

The *News*, which called for the appointment of a fire engineer "who understands his business and who should have full and absolute control of the Fire Department and its organization,"[34] was not alone in its demands. One month after the fire, the *Commonwealth* reminded citizens:

*The sum of fourteen hundred dollars was long ago set apart for the
use of the fire department, and is still lying idle in the City Treasury.
As yet, our city is mainly composed of wooden structures. The
lightness of the air and the very general dryness of things here make
it a very combustible city. A natural dread hovers over the community.
We of Denver have not only the prospect of being driven from our
comfortable beds at midnight, but of being utterly beggared and
rendered houseless and homeless. Our people demand that something
be done.*[35]

A horse-drawn steamer leaves Engine Company 1's house at Colfax and Broadway, present site of the Pioneer Monument. Primitive equipment, cobblestone streets and collisions with other vehicles took a high toll among early-day firefighters in Denver. (Courtesy of Denver Public Library/Western History Department.)

Reconstruction of the burnt district began at once. One day after the fire, the city council passed an ordinance forbidding all but brick buildings within what was declared to be the "fire limits" (see Appendix A, and map on page 34). The area was designated as follows:

> *Beginning in the centre of the alley between Wazee and Wynkoop streets, where the same intersects Cherry Creek; thence along the centre of said alley in a northeasterly direction to the centre of G [Sixteenth] street; thence southeasterly along the centre of said street to the centre of the alley between Larimer and Lawrence streets; thence along the centre of said alley southwesterly to its intersection with Cherry Creek; thence down to Fifth [Larimer] Street; thence westerly along the centre of said street to the centre of the alley between Ferry [Eleventh] and St. Louis [Tenth] streets; thence northerly along the centre of said alley to the centre of Second [Wewatta] street; thence along the centre of said street in an easterly direction and up Cherry Creek to the place of beginning.[36]*

Among other things, the ordinance required that outside and party walls be built of stone, brick or other fireproof material and that outside and party walls not be less than eight inches thick. A provision exempted privies, which could be constructed of wood if they weren't more than ten feet square and twelve feet tall. Violation of any of the many stipulations could result in a fine to property owners of $25–$100. Further, the city marshal was authorized to demolish, at the owner's cost, any wood structure deemed to be "a nuisance." Exceptions to any of the stipulations could be granted only by Mayor Amos Steck.[37]

Given the length and detail of the ordinance and the speed at which governmental bodies normally move, it is probable that work on this ordinance, which would have far-reaching effects on the safety and appearance of the city, began sometime before the fire broke out. In fact, the effort may have involved simply rewriting the ordinance repealed in 1862.

In the days that followed the fire, hard winds continued to blow off and on, raising dust and ash from the burnt district. But businesspeople had begun rebuilding almost before the last embers were dead. Only six hours after the fire had been extinguished, Dan Ullman, whose decimated meat market stood catercorner from the Cherokee House, leased a contract on a new brick building. The day after the fire, as work on his new market began, Ullman set up shop in a tent on his property. He was back in business by month's end.

As many as thirty buildings were hauled across Cherry Creek from Ferry (Eleventh) Street in Auraria and plunked down where burned-out shanties once stood. "In most instances they are poor concerns, and only put there temporarily to do business in until brick can be had. Our streets are almost blocked up with moving buildings, and old shanties that a week ago were not considered worth anything, are now selling at almost fabulous prices," the *Weekly Commonwealth and Republican* noted.[38] Under the city's new fire ordinance, all temporary or wood buildings in the district were to be torn down or removed by October 21, 1863.

Eleven days after the fire, the *Commonwealth* bragged, "F [Fifteenth] Street below Blake has opened up again nearly as lively as it was before the fire, and yet

Mayor Amos Steck. (Photo from Representative Men of Colorado, 1858–1902.*)*

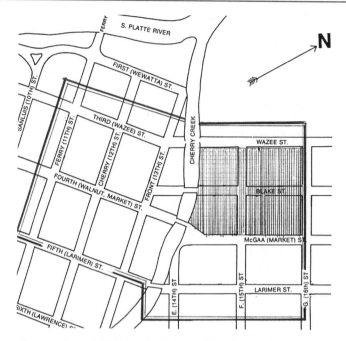

Only one day after Denver's 1863 fire, the city council passed an ordinance that required buildings in the new Fire District to be built of brick or stone. (Dick Kreck collection.)

the heaviest sufferers were in that neighborhood, but they were not to be beat, and therefore have moved buildings on and commenced business again."[39] George Tritch, Tom Lavin, J. H. Voorhies, Brannon & Mittnacht and J. A. Nye & Co. all were doing business on F Street only days after they had been burned out. Brendlinger's reopened almost immediately in a small shanty set up on the corner of F and Blake Streets to dispense cigars and tobaccos.

Other businesses whose goods were saved from the flames shifted their operations to Auraria on the west side of Cherry Creek, most of them along Ferry Street, while some establishments shared space with others. On Blake Street, Kountze & Bro. took an office in the Tootle & Leach building, and Campbell & Jones, whose building was leveled, relocated temporarily to A. E. & C. E. Tilton's. Whatever losses they had suffered, the city's businesspeople hadn't lost their sense of humor. Saloonkeeper Johnny Ruffner moved a building onto the site of his burned-out business and promptly dubbed it the "Fire Proof Lager Beer Saloon."

The reconstruction spawned a thriving new business in town — the manufacture of brick, a generally poor sun-dried product made from red clay found on the South Platte River at the foot of F Street.

W. W. Hull, owner of Planters' House, bought a brickyard previously owned by a Mr. Morrison and promised that he would be "burning brick at the rate of 100,000 a week." Kidder & Swartz advertised that their business would "soon be able to furnish nearly all the brick needed" for the season. They may have been overly optimistic though, as they also advertised for the employment of "fifteen good-working men. Good wages will be paid."[40]

Many thought the fire a blessing. "The late fire, in some respects, will be a benefit to Denver," was the opinion of the *Commonwealth*. "It will cause a better class of buildings to take the place of those destroyed. Brickmaking and laying will be a good business this summer. 'No great loss without some small gain,' is an old saying, and in this instance a true one."[41]

The optimistic spirit of the newspaper and of the city in general was restored to full cry by May. The *News* crowed on May 28, 1863, "We will wager an ironclad to a dugout that no city in the world less than four years old can boast as handsome women, as fast horses, as busy streets, as many churches, and as much genuine prosperity, as Denver. Who wants the bet?"[42]

The *Commonwealth* proclaimed proudly:

> *One has only to stroll along Blake street any of these fine days and note the character of the improvements now being made upon that*

IT WASN'T ALL FIGHTING FIRES IN THE EARLY DAYS OF DENVER. VOLUNTEER COMPANIES FREQUENTLY COMPETED IN ATHLETIC CONTESTS. THE FIRST STATEWIDE TOURNAMENT WAS HELD IN CENTRAL CITY IN 1875, TO MARK THE FIRST ANNIVERSARY OF THAT CITY'S DESTRUCTIVE FIRE.

AT A TYPICAL COMPETITION, TEAMS FROM VARIOUS DEPARTMENTS WOULD RUN 500 FEET TO A HYDRANT, LAY 200 FEET OF HOSE, BREAK COUPLING AND GET WATER THROUGH THE NOZZLE. THE WINNERS GENERALLY RECEIVED SEVERAL HUNDRED DOLLARS IN CASH AND CHAMPIONSHIP BELTS.

DENVER'S JAMES E. BATES COMPANY BECAME PARTICULARLY RENOWNED FOR THE SPEED OF ITS RUNNERS AND WON SEVERAL STATE AND NATIONAL COMPETITIONS IN THE LATE 1870S.

Two years after Denver's devastating 1863 blaze, F (Fifteenth) Street, looking north from Larimer Street, was lined with handsome brick buildings, giving the fledgling city a more cosmopolitan look. (Courtesy of the Denver Public Library/Western History Department.)

street in order to be thoroughly convinced of the extent and soundness of resources and the irrepressible energy of our business population. All these individuals who are now so busily engaged in forwarding these permanent improvements on Blake street have studied the future of this Territory with the best lights possible to any. The fire which swept over and desolated so large a portion of our city only hastened the undertaking of the work, not caused it. The intention of removing those frail tenements and substituting durable structures was entertained before the event. And in view of its having hastened the erection of these substantial structures, were it not for the loss of other property, we should not be disposed to regard the late fire as being, on the whole, very unfortunate for our city.[43]

By Christmas, the burnt district was nearly rebuilt. "A new era in building was commenced, and the structures erected and occupied were of that durable character befitting a city of such commercial importance as Denver had become."[44] Yet Denver would be tested again—and not only by fire: The legendary flood of 1864 lay only thirteen months in the future.

SAVING THE CITY

How Denver's leading businessmen, many of whom were wiped out in the "Great Fire of 1863," rebounded so quickly after the devastating blaze remains a mystery.

Larger, more elaborate brick and stone buildings replaced the ramshackle structures that crowded the city's main business district around Blake and F (Fifteenth) Streets. How did they finance such a resurrection, one which was nearly complete less than a year later?

One answer, which appeared in *The Denver Post* in 1920, fifty-seven years after the event, was supplied by Chauncey Thomas, a magazine writer and son of pioneer Denver newspaperman William Russell Thomas, who worked as a reporter for William Byers at the *Rocky Mountain News* and married Byers' sister, Flora.

According to the younger Thomas, who got the story from his father, the city's leading citizens simply looted gold and silver from the Clark, Gruber & Co. mint at G (Sixteenth) and McGaa (Market) Streets.

"If Denver was to remain and the men who had their all invested here were to continue to prosper, heroic measures were necessary," wrote *Post* reporter Joseph Emerson Smith in 1920. "To restore confidence, a building boom was decided upon."

The businessmen, according to Thomas' account to his son, simply "requisitioned" the precious metals out of the mint. "How and by what means it was gotten, by 'notes of hand' or by collateral or what not, there are no records," wrote Smith. However it was obtained, enough was extracted to save the city.

James D. Clarke, a young clerk at the mint, by all descriptions a solid, upright Christian citizen, took a cue from the borrowers. He embezzled more than $10,000 in gold bullion and galloped out of town on horseback but was captured a short time later near Laporte, Colorado.

The popular historic version of his capture was that he was returned to Denver and jailed to await trial but escaped, fled town and never was heard from again.

"The true story," according to the elder Thomas, as related by Chauncey, "is that young Clarke knew too much of the gold that had been taken out of the mint. The example around him was too great a temptation. If he should be prosecuted, the publicity would, of course, be disastrous. All the borrowers chipped in to make good the loss and he was let out and told to keep quiet."

— *The Denver Post*
February 29, 1920

Chapter Three

"GOOD GOD ALMIGHTY!"

As economic panic plunges Colorado into a deep recession, Governor Davis Waite takes control of Denver's corrupt police and fire departments. The massive Union Depot, pride of the city, erupts in flame. Four days later—heralded by an onlooker shouting, "There it comes!"—the Champa Block collapses ablaze into the street. Critics lambaste Chief Julius Pearse for his handling of these two devastating fires.

The period 1887 to 1893 was one of phenomenal growth for the Queen City of the Plains. Thirty years earlier, Denver had been just a dusty, treeless flat spot on the road to the gold fields, a meager settlement where the South Platte River and Cherry Creek came together and where less than five thousand souls survived.

In the words of historian Jerome C. Smiley, this period of growth was "the great era of wonderful activity in Denver real estate ... a time of much wild speculation and of quick accumulations of real estate fortunes." He noted that the annual value of real estate transactions in the city was $29 million in 1887 and rose to almost $66 million by 1890, the year the city's population soared to 106,713.[1]

In 1892, the Brown Palace Hotel was constructed at a cost of $1.5 million, the Equitable Building rose for another $1.5 million and work began on the state capitol, which ultimately cost $3 million. Farmers, buoyed by plentiful harvests throughout the rain-soaked 1880s, bought and planted more land. Assured by the Sherman Silver Purchase Act of 1890, which guaranteed the government's monthly purchase of $2 million to $4 million worth of silver, Colorado's mine owners dug fervently and mountain towns grew apace.

But the bottom fell out in mid-1893. The collapse—dubbed the "Panic of '93"—had been coming for some time and was as much psychological as economic. In 1890 the mints of India quit producing silver coins. When the U.S. government's reserves of gold slipped below $100 million, businesspeople and farmers, confronted with consecutive years of drought, began to retrench, creating an economic slowdown. Some fifteen thousand businesses closed and four million people were put out of work.

The Silver Act was a windfall of gigantic proportions for Colorado, which at that time produced 60 percent of the nation's silver. But bimetallism, with its strong bias toward gold, destroyed the demand for silver, plunging the state's industry into an economic crater from which it would not recover fully until the turn of the century. Repeal of the act in 1893 drove the final spike into the state's silver-mining industry.

By June of 1893, the price of silver, which had been as high as $1.05 an ounce in 1890, had skidded to 62 cents. Denver's banks closed one after the other, six of them in one day. Construction of new dwellings tumbled from 2,338 in 1890 to 124 in 1894. The closing of mines and smelters in mountain communities near Denver left many miners without jobs. They drifted down to Denver in search of employment, but work was nearly nonexistent. Early in 1894, the *Rocky Mountain News* reported that Georgetown mines shipped 56 cars of ore that year, compared with 104 the previous year. Miners' wages were sliced from $2 to $1.75 a day. "The outlook as far as production is concerned was never better [but] the miner gets very little for his ore nowadays."[2]

Auctioneers in Denver did a booming business peddling the furnishings of the city's once-thriving, well-heeled residents. A March 1894 classified ad in the *News* detailed the furniture and furnishings available from one particular house, "consisting in part of fancy rockers, nice chamber suites, Singer sewing machine in good order, dining table, B.B. and in-grain carpets, fine range, with water connections, dishes and kitchen utensils."[3] An estimated fifteen thousand citizens, unable to find work, fled the city within a few months. Publishers of the *Denver City Directory* explained in their May 1894 edition:

> *An eventful year has passed since the issue of the Denver City Directory for 1893, a year that will pass into history as being laden with depression in business, discontent and agitation of labor, shrinkage of values and great financial ruin covering our broad land. Our young state has suffered severely by legislation which has crippled and prostrated silver mining.*[4]

Into these economic doldrums came Populist governor Davis Waite, elected in 1892 to help rescue the state from its travails with what Smiley described as "many impossible remedies for all the ills to which the body politic is heir [which led to] the most disgraceful political episode in the history of the city and state."[5] Years of corrupt leadership had left the city's police and fire departments in disarray, and graft and dissolute behavior among police were commonplace. In *Hell's Belles*, a study of law enforcement, prostitution and gambling in turn-of-the-century Denver, author Clark Secrest noted:

> *The police department was so undisciplined that policemen while on duty were drinking free liquor and smoking free cigars in saloons; policemen were neglecting to arrest prostitutes and "low women" soliciting on the streets, from windows, and from the front steps of Market Street; the officers were winking at cases of indecent exposure; they were allowing saloons to run all day and night every day and night, even Sundays; on-duty the policemen were "frequenting houses of prostitution and dens of low resort, and participating in the advantages carried on in the same."*[6]

Finally, in 1889, the citizenry and political leadership could take no more. In a move to take control of Denver's police and fire departments, the state legislature created the Board of Commissioners of Public Works to run the city. Its members were to be appointed by Governor Waite.

The state legislature took a further step in 1891, when it created the Fire and Police Board to run two of Denver's most powerful departments. Its three members appointed by Governor Waite, this

Governor Davis Waite. (Photo from Representative Men of Colorado, 1858–1902.)

entity had significant power of its own. The sorry situation facing the board was so pervasive that it was compelled to issue various ultimatums regarding the behavior of Denver's firefighters and police officers, including this April 1894 directive: "policemen, patrolmen and detectives are prohibited from drinking in or entering or frequenting such saloons, dives, places and houses of prostitution, except to make arrests and detect crime."[7]

Drunkenness was frequent in the fire department, where firefighters were dismissed for a variety of violations, including insubordination, disobedience to commanders, profane language, reckless driving, absence without leave and "conduct in violation of the rules of the department." One captain who failed to answer three alarms was reprimanded for "the fact that he overindulged in his home too freely in drinking beer." In its directive, the board added, "Firemen are also prohibited to enter saloons while in full uniform and on active duty."[8]

The board blamed the fire department's lax discipline on Chief Julius Pearse, who was appointed chief of the paid department in 1883. In a letter to the chief on January 18, 1893, two of Waite's reform appointees, Jackson Orr and D. J. Martin, pointedly said of an incident at the department's station house at Twentieth and Curtis Streets: "The frequenting of saloons, profanity and coarse conduct indulged in by some of the men of this house deserve censure."[9]

Nevertheless, Governor Waite's handpicked three-person board was no better than its predecessors at cleansing the fire and police departments. Although the board had enormous powers, including the licensing of saloons and gambling halls, its members—even the new appointees—often yielded to the blandishments of the owners of such establishments. In addition, because firefighters and police officers were not subject to civil service, the board had free reign to hire and fire at its pleasure, leading to more abuses of power.

THE DESTRUCTION ON MARCH 18, 1894, OF UNION DEPOT, SYMBOL OF THE YOUNG CITY'S PROSPERITY, WAS A CRUSHING BLOW.

OWNED JOINTLY BY THE UNION PACIFIC AND THE DENVER & RIO GRANDE RAILROADS, THE $600,000 STRUCTURE WAS ERECTED IN 1880. THE MAGNIFICENT, 703-FOOT-LONG BUILDING WAS MADE OF ROUGH-HEWN LAVA STONE QUARRIED NEAR CASTLE ROCK AND TRIMMED WITH WHITE AND RED SANDSTONE FROM MANITOU.

THE TWO WINGS OF TODAY'S DENVER UNION STATION, WHICH STILL STANDS SENTINEL AT THE FOOT OF SEVENTEENTH STREET, ARE PART OF THE ORIGINAL STRUCTURE. THE MASSIVE CENTER SECTION WAS BUILT 1914–1918 TO EXPAND THE WAITING ROOM.

In March 1894, an impatient Waite named two new commissioners, Dennis Mullins and S. D. Barnes, to replace Orr and Martin. But Orr and Martin stubbornly declined to vacate their seats, a standoff that led to one of the most famous showdowns in Denver political history, known as the "City Hall War." Waite called out troops to storm City Hall at Fourteenth and Larimer Streets, if necessary, and eject Orr and Martin from their offices. Under threat of gunfire, the reluctant twosome yielded and Mullins and Barnes were put in power.

Despite the change in leadership, things did not improve for Pearse. Two fires four days apart in March 1894 were followed closely by his dismissal as chief.

The first blaze erupted about 12:30 A.M. on Sunday, March 18, 1894, when a fast-moving fire broke out in the west wing of the Union Depot, symbol of Denver's prosperity and importance in western commerce. As dawn brightened the sky, the elegant thirteen-year-old station was still standing but presented a sad shell of smoldering woodwork and blackened stonework.[10]

It was a crushing blow to the city's collective psyche. The depot epitomized Denver's astonishing growth since the arrival in 1870 of the first railroads, which made the Queen City of the Plains reachable in hours instead of weeks. Reputed at the time of its construction to be the largest building west of the Mississippi River, the depot was a

The Union Depot at Seventeenth and Wynkoop Streets, financed by some of the city's most prominent citizens, was a magnificent structure that dominated the downtown landscape when it opened in 1881. The two-story granite-and-stone structure was 703 feet long and crowned by a 180-foot-tall tower over its main waiting room. (Courtesy of the Denver Public Library/ Western History Department.)

showplace, the gateway to a rising metropolis where the Oxford Hotel and the Struby Estabrook Mercantile Co. buildings on Seventeenth Street impressed arriving visitors. And as with any magnet for the adventurous and the successful, the depot also attracted its share of con artists, cardsharps and mountebanks, who preyed on newcomers and tried to lure young women and girls into a life of vice at the city's brothels.

It was prominent Denver citizens, Walter S. Cheesman, David C. Dodge and Bela Hughes among them, who came together to raise funds for the depot, a station that would put all the railroads serving Denver under one roof. Built at a cost of $400,000 in 1881 on twelve acres of land at the foot of Seventeenth Street and facing Wynkoop Street, the Union Depot later was expanded with additions on either end at a cost of $100,000. The massive structure, 703 feet long, 65 feet wide and two stories high, was built in Second Empire style from granite and cut lava stone and showcased a 180-foot-tall tower at its center. The principal tenants and owners were the Union Pacific and the Denver & Rio Grande Western railroads.

The depot was an immediate success, drawing businesses from the commercial epicenter around Fifteenth and Blake Streets and serving as an anchor to one end of Seventeenth Street (with the Brown

Palace Hotel being at the other end). Buttressed by the depot, Seventeenth Street would become the city's financial center.

But architectural excellence, corporate power and public image could not save the Union Depot from what was popularly described in print at the time as "the consuming element." On March 18, 1894, ninety minutes before the fire broke out, two chandeliers suspended in the first-floor ladies waiting room at the west end of the station dropped suddenly. At the same time, lights flickered and went out elsewhere in the building and in businesses and residences around town. Electricity had arrived in Denver only a dozen years earlier and the city's streetlights had been converted from gas to electricity shortly thereafter, in 1885. Many residents were distrustful of the newfangled invention, but an electrician called to attend to the chandeliers made some repairs and declared the problem solved, though an electrical short ultimately was to blame for the fire.

Thirty minutes after the repair, smoke was discovered rising through the station's roof. The fire department responded, but with woefully insufficient force against a blaze that had already become almost too fierce to control. Within minutes, a call went out for a general alarm, and firefighters from Highlands on the north side of the Platte River joined the fight. The fire made great headway before a second line of hose could be run from a hydrant near the railroad tracks on the depot's north side, allowing firefighters to play water on the great station's roof.

Hoping to confine the flames to the western end of the depot, Chief Pearse ordered his men to flood the surrounding areas with water. At one point, five hoses were in play, but poor pressure, the bane of many early-day fire-fighting efforts in the city, left the company nearly helpless. The department's water-tower truck, purchased in 1891 for $4,000, also proved useless.

Early on, firefighters seemed to be winning the battle. "Good!" shouted depot manager Lon Pierce. "The boys have got it under control now."[11] But his elation was premature. A second fire, again attributed to an electrical short, broke out in the central section of the station, engulfing its great clock tower in flames. A reporter for the *Denver Republican* described the scene:

> *In the midst of the tumult raised by the great crowd which had gathered, a livid tongue of flames was seen creeping from the frame*

work of the tower in the building. There was a clamor and a shout from the men below to the firemen who were fighting the flames above. Attention was now turned to the fire raging in the tower. Every effort was put forth but the timbers burned like cinder and it was apparent that the entire building was doomed.[12]

As the fire grew in strength, bystanders and station employees began to carry luggage, papers and furniture from the structure. It was difficult, at times, to determine who was saving goods and who was stealing them.

Trying to be helpful, a group of railroaders broke into the office of William Deuel, general superintendent for Union Pacific, and began hurling out of windows papers that wafted away by the easterly winds. Another well-meaning group of volunteers carried Deuel's desk into the hall and heaved it over the banister to the floor below. "Three truck loads of [the desk] were removed yesterday in the forenoon," the *News* noted, tongue in cheek.[13]

The flames repeatedly appeared and disappeared near the depot's roof as firefighters doused them with water. Some of the firefighters, including John Dulmage, an assistant chief whose career was plagued by misfortune, battled their way to the depot's second floor and were about to enter the main hall when another assistant chief, Terry Owens, warned Dulmage that the floor was about to give way. As

An artist's rendering of the Union Depot in the Denver Republican *made the fire appear more destructive than it was. Estimates that damage would reach $1 million proved to be overstated. It turned out to be closer to $150,000, and the depot was back in operation within days of the fire. (Courtesy of the* Denver Republican/Colorado Historical Society.*)*

The great Union Depot presented a sorry sight after the fire on March 18, 1894. But the structure was declared sound and the railroads' ticket offices were back in business a few days later. (Courtesy of the Colorado Railroad Museum.)

the two men turned to leave, there was a loud crash. Dulmage had fallen through the weakened floor but had somehow managed to cling to a floor joist still attached to the wall. Despite the flames all around them, Owens grasped Dulmage's arm and pulled him to safety. The heat was so intense that both men's uniforms were scorched. Years later, Owens recalled the fire: "Oh, that was a bad one, and we had a hard time getting it out."[14]

At 1:10 A.M., as a growing crowd looked on from the nearby Sixteenth Street viaduct, the skeleton of the depot's clock tower began to weaken. Four minutes later, a large piece of the structure crashed to the ground. Four minutes after that, "Exactly at 18 minutes past 1 o'clock," reported the *Republican,* the tower "began to sway in the air. A freshening wind had started up from the east and this helped to agitate the motion of the now feeble block of timber. In an instant it had fallen through the air, hissing and seething as it went, and tumbled in a mass of furious heat immediately beneath the archway to the main entrance to the depot."[15]

Meanwhile, in the depot's east wing, the rapidly spreading flames burst through the roof. Firefighters turned their attention from the west wing, where the blaze had begun, and attacked the east wing, but the fire continued to burn sporadically until 3 A.M.

The Denver Times reported the following day that "one of the saddest sights" was the burning of an array of pies in the depot's lunch counter. When all was said and done, noted the paper's gastronomically minded reporter, dozens of pies had been consumed by the flames, but, he commented as an aside, "the sandwiches being of fireclay character positively refused to burn."[16] And although the barber shop and the dining and lunchrooms operated by the Barkalow Brothers were a total loss, many of the consumables were liberated by bystanders and the crowd on the inner platform enjoyed an ample free lunch.

Four days later, on March 22, 1894, a second major conflagration broke out downtown. At 6:30 P.M., the six-story Champa Block at Fifteenth and Champa Streets, as well as nearby businesses along Champa Street, caught fire and burned furiously for two hours. The fire department was on the scene in a matter of minutes, but only after mistakenly rushing to the St. James Hotel on Curtis Street, a block away, because of erroneous reports that the back of the hotel was on fire.

Although the Champa Block (also known as the Ware & Skinner Block) was a brick building, it was full of combustible materials, including lumber and furniture. By the time firefighters arrived, it was already engulfed in flames. The windows on every floor blew out and plumes of black smoke and fire poured forth copiously.

Estimated damage in the fire topped $185,000. Nearly every building in the vicinity of the Champa Block (erected only two years earlier and still unfinished at the time of the blaze) was damaged or destroyed, including A. N. Thompson & Co., furniture maker, which occupied the building's first floor; I. N. Rogers, undertaker, and Mrs. Farrell's lodging house, located upstairs at Rogers'; Weber's butcher shop; Johnson & Davis, plumbers; Diehl's notions; Bon Ton restaurant; Meek and Dodson Saloon; Baur's confectionery; Denver Watch & Jewelry; White's hardware; Joslins department store; the Oddfellows Hall; St. James Hotel and annex; Given Block; White Bear Saloon; Sunny Side Saloon; J. N. Corbin, carpenter; and A. B. Sullivan Block.[17]

At the White Bear Saloon, its owner surveyed the damage and invited bystanders to "drink and be merry, for it's all in a lifetime." Among those partaking of the gaiety were members of a suburban fire department, who were "conspicuous in the crowd which stood in front of the bar and drank at the expense of the owner. Many took bottles of whiskey away with them."[18]

Because of frequently disorganized efforts on the part of the Denver Fire Department, as well as repeated equipment failures, the handling of the Union Depot and Champa Block fires drew criticism of Pearse's leadership and competency. The ineffectual efforts of the department were made clear by the arrival at the Champa Block fire of the hose company from Twentieth and Curtis Streets, which immediately hooked up to a plug at Sixteenth and Curtis. Their strategy, said the *News*,

was a clear waste of effort as well as energy for the reason that even the stream never reached the fire. This was kept up for half an hour, and the same play was made by those in charge of the hose attached to engines No. 1 and No. 2 on the corner of Fifteenth and Champa. All these streams played on the front and sides of the building long after it was discovered that it was a useless move. The firemen seemed to lack generalship and moved from place to place as if dazed.[19]

Fifteen minutes after the fire began, the department determined once again that their water tower, lacking pressure as it had at the Union Depot blaze previously, was useless. Withdrawing it, firefighters instead trained their hoses on the blaze from buildings across Champa Street. The streets were awash in ankle-deep water, but the fire continued to burn at will.

After thirty minutes, the walls of the Champa Block began to collapse inward. The last wall to tumble was the six-story facade, which leaned toward the sidewalk and came down whole with a thunderous crash that shook Champa Street and sent onlookers scurrying to either end of the block for safety. Just before it fell, reported the *News*, someone in the crowd shouted, "There it comes!" Seconds later, there was silence, "save for the roar of the flames and the pounding of the engines, and then a yell of excitement that could be heard a mile away." When the wall fell, "it looked like the lid of a huge trap door closing over Champa Street."[20]

Despite intense heat and falling debris, only one firefighter, Lieutenant William Law of Steamer 4, was seriously injured. When I. N. Rogers's building collapsed, Law sustained a fractured wrist and cuts to his face and head. Nevertheless, he stayed on to continue fighting the fire.

The most ironic rescue of the Champa Block fire was the saving of the St. James Hotel and annex, 1528 Curtis Street, located

Chief Julius Pearse was criticized for his handling of the Denver Fire Department and resigned his position in 1894. (Photo from Representative Men of Colorado, 1858–1902.*)*

directly behind the Champa Block. Though the fire chased the hotel's eighty guests (including railroader Jim Rose, who had lost most of his personal belongings in the Union Depot fire days earlier) into the streets, damage to the St. James was held to a minimum. But on March 23, 1895, almost one year later to the day, the St. James caught fire again and four firemen were killed when they plunged through the hotel's lobby floor while fighting the blaze (see Chapter Four).

Criticism of Chief Pearse reached a new level among politicians and the newspapers. After the Champa Block fire, Pearse, who had been complaining for some time about the lean budgets forced on his department, exclaimed in the *News,* "Good God Almighty! I can't stand this sort of thing. If this keeps up I'll lose what little reputation I ever had. I expect to be roasted for the way I handled this fire but what can I do when they have cut down the force on me time after time and then made a political machine out of the department? I tell you if something isn't done, I shall throw up my hands and quit."[21]

He reiterated his complaints about the lack of adequate equipment and the pinchpenny city government. "Here are several hundred feet of hose under the debris [at the Champa fire] which are absolutely useless, and when I come to ask for new hose how they do shriek economy. Well, if they want to pay exorbitant insurance premiums and let the town burn down, all right, but I won't have anything to do with it."[22] Pearse also told officials that vandals, intent on robbing stores and spectators, cut the department's hoses at the Champa Block and other fires.

Four days later, an anonymous letter signed "A.B." and printed, at least in part, in all four of the city's newspapers, accused Pearse of bungling the department's efforts at the two fires. "In the case of the Champa street fire, dead and crippled hose were permitted to lay around in the streets long after the fire was out. Now supposing there had been another fire in other parts of the city, when thousands of feet of hose lay here on the streets?"

The writer, supposedly a firefighter with a suburban department, concluded, "There is no danger of Chief Pearse resigning unless he has to; there is too much in the office for him, and this is considered by many as only a big bluff to get politics that may not suit him and his pals out of the department."[23]

Pearse exploded in print the next day, branding the letter's writer a "sorehead": "I have been connected with the Denver fire department since 1872 and have been at its head for 12 years, and this is the first assault that has been made upon me in the newspapers. I decline to go into any explanations over this article and will simply say it is a lie in every line, nor is there a word of truth in it. That's all I'll say about this dirty attack."[24]

Pearse, a founder of the city's volunteer fire department in 1872 and its chief from 1875 to 1887, was worn down by annual budget cuts made necessary by the state's economic collapse. In 1893 he was twice ordered to "suspend" firefighters for indefinite periods to trim $1,000 a month in salaries. His requests for new equipment were frequently "filed" for later consideration by the Fire and Police Board, and appropriations for the police and fire departments for 1894 were "greatly reduced," in the words of the board. The fire department's appropriations slid from $192,000 in 1891 to $137,000 in 1894, and its staff declined from 124 people in 1892 to 116, only 102 of whom were firefighters, in 1894.

Pearse's complaints were met with derision. The Fire and Police Board's new president, Dennis Mullins, responded:

Pearse says Governor Waite is trying to make a political machine out of the fire department. Now, that's a good joke. Who has ever seen a more perfect piece of political machinery than the Denver fire department as it has been conducted by Chief Pearse for ten or fifteen years? Why, if I couldn't do better in keeping down fires than Pearse, I'd resign! When an alarm is turned in what is the result? The men are at the city hall playing cards instead of being at their posts of duty. The fire department is not what it ought to be, and if anybody is to blame it is Chief Pearse.

This talk of the chief is uncalled for and was in very bad taste.[25]

On March 28, 1894, the board announced:

Julius Pearse, chief of the Fire Department having been notified to appear before this board and receive his orders from it and having refused to receive his orders from it or recognize it in any way, stating that he should take orders from the old board and from it only, the said Julius Pearse is hereby removed from the office of chief of the Fire Department of the City of Denver to take affect [sic] at once.

William E. Roberts is hereby appointed chief of the Fire Department to take effect immediately.[26]

Even had he not refused to appear, Pearse likely would still have been fired as the city's fire chief, such was his low standing among the commissioners and the molders of public opinion. Also dismissed for refusing to obey the new board were two men who would later play prominent roles in the department—Terry Owens and John Dulmage.

In the fall of 1894, Davis Waite was voted out of office as governor, clearing the way for a new Fire and Police Board—one which promptly rehired Pearse, who apparently had been forgiven his incompetencies, to head the fire department in April 1895. Pearse did not forget his friends—but neither did he forget his enemies. Twenty members of the department who had remained loyal to the former Fire and Police Board were handed prewritten resignations. Pearse served until 1897, when he was again replaced by William Roberts.

Pearse, who founded a successful fire-equipment company after he retired from the department, died at age seventy in 1917 from blood poisoning following a fire-related injury. His obituary in *The Denver Post* remarked, "Julius Pearse was given much of the credit for the building up of Denver's fire department to its present high standard."[27] Buried in Denver's Fairmount Cemetery, he was survived by a widow, six daughters and two sons.

Despite the spectacular nature of the blaze at the Union Depot, and some overblown initial estimates that losses would reach $1 million, most of the damage was confined to the clock tower and the building's second floor. Within days of the fire, the business of the railroads was already returning to normal. In the cold dawn of day, the damage totaled out at around $150,000, about 80 percent of which was covered by insurance policies with ten different companies. The

1780. Union Station, Denver, Colo.

Freight wagons and pedestrians shared the parklike promenade in front of Union Depot in 1908. The tower was built to replace one destroyed by fire in 1894. The second tower was demolished in 1914 to make way for the present Union Station. (Dick Kreck collection.)

losses of paper and furniture to the railroads were minimal, although some ticketing functions were moved to offices uptown and waiting rooms had to be cleaned and dried.

Restoration of the depot began almost as soon the embers cooled and an inspection of the building showed that the main walls, made of stone, were blackened but sturdy. The center section of the depot was rebuilt and given a plainer roof line and a taller tower so that the depot would become "far more beautiful and convenient than the old," promised William Trufant, superintendent and secretary of the Union Depot and Railroad Co.[28]

In 1914 the depot was remodeled and the new tower demolished to make way for a larger waiting room. Today's Denver Union Station sees less passenger traffic—two regular Amtrak passenger trains a day and the Ski Train to Winter Park on winter weekends and some summer days—but it remains an architectural landmark and a focal point of urban renewal in the Platte Valley as well as in a revitalized lower downtown.

WAS IT ARSON?

By 1894, Chief Julius Pearse was a 22-year veteran of the city's fire departments, volunteer and paid, but a string of serious fires that year put him under the wrathful eye of the Fire and Police Board and ultimately led to his dismissal.

Pearse wasn't convinced that either the Union Depot or Champa Block fires, a mere four days apart in March 1894, were caused by electrical wires.

"Whoever did the work, provided it was a firebug, as I am now inclined to believe, knew his business," Pearse told the *Denver Republican* on March 14, 1894. "That Champa fire satisfied me there was something wrong soon after we got into the fight. The cutting of the hose, followed by the ringing of false alarms, raised the fear in my mind that there were bugs about."

The motive?

Thievery.

"That there are firebugs here may be true or may not be, but pipe cutters there certainly are," said Pearse. "The hose we use is cotton, and the work of the knife is most evident. There have been drawn to Denver within the past ten days more villainous fellows and cutthroats than we have ever had here. And all this for the sake of the little plunder they may get from burning buildings and the pockets they may pick during the excitement."

Even more mysterious was the *Republican*'s account of an unidentified stranger who approached cable railway flagman Thomas Barrett at Seventeenth and Welton Streets the night of the Union Depot conflagration and said, "I see there is going to be a fire at the Union Depot tonight."

Barrett thought it was a joke, but the man continued, "It's burning right now, I understand." Fifteen minutes later, the fire department was on its way.

—Denver Republican
March 14, 1894

Chapter Four

"Remember the St. James"

*Impenetrable smoke and intrusive crowds hamper
firefighters' ability to combat the blaze at Denver's
St. James Hotel. Captain Hartwell's cry of "Boys,
here's the fire, right over here. This is our chance.
Come on with the line!" leads the men of Company 3
to a fiery plunge. Despite universal praise of the
"colored" firefighters' efforts at the St. James, full
integration doesn't come to Denver's fire department
for another eighty-six years.*

"Come on, boys, lift on that hose and help me in there now!" were the last words the crowd milling outside the St. James Hotel on March 23, 1895, heard from Captain Harold Hartwell. Minutes later, Hartwell and three firefighters in his charge lay dead and disfigured in the smoke-choked basement of the St. James, killed by what they could not know lay directly in front of them.

Hartwell, 36, who was white, and Lieutenant Fred Brawley, 33; Richard Dandridge, 24, and Stephen Martin, 28, all of whom were African American, were the victims of what firefighters call a "blind" fire, one that produces huge amounts of smoke but one in which the fire itself is almost invisible. It was a deadly environment. One witness said the smoke in the hotel lobby was so thick that "a lantern could not be seen half a dozen feet away."[1]

The St. James Hotel at 1528 Curtis Street presented a handsome balcony to passersby. Built in 1872 as Everett House, it later became the Wentworth House. The five-story, 208-room addition at right was built in 1881. (Courtesy of the Denver Public Library/Western History Department.)

Located in the middle of the block on the south side of Curtis Street between Fifteenth and Sixteenth Streets, the St. James Hotel, 1528 Curtis Street, was at the time one of Denver's superior hostelries. Opened in 1872 as the Everett House, then renamed the Wentworth House, the St. James was rebuilt and enlarged in 1881. The five-story, 208-room hotel was set back from the noise of Curtis Street, one of the city's busiest thoroughfares, and featured elegant ironwork along its streetside verandas. Oscar Wilde, Eugene Field and a steady stream of prominent business and political leaders were among its guests. When it was remodeled with new carpeting, new furniture and new tile in its lobby in 1887, it was described by an observer as being "one of the finest houses in the West."[2]

Even before the remodeling, the hotel drew raves from a young midwesterner who in 1883 passed through Denver on his way to a job in Georgetown in the mountains of Colorado. Marion Cook wrote to his family in Nebraska:

> *The reason I put up at the St. James was I had seen a Denver paper with all the hotels advertised and this one had more guests than any of the rest. They set 15 tables and everything is carried on in the*

best style. A guest is not allowed to do anything. For breakfast there was 17 kinds of bread, four of potatoes, four of eggs, eight of drinks and 37 kinds of meat. My room was furnished with a very large bed, two marble top bureaus with keys for the drawers, wash bowl and pitcher, towels, two common chairs and a rocking chair, two gas lamps, a very fine mirror and a telephone. There is a bath room and a barber shop free of charge. I had my boots blacked. It costs nothing. My bill was $2.50.[3]

Hartwell, Brawley, Dandridge and Martin, the four doomed men of Hose Company 3, housed at what was then Twenty-sixth and Lincoln (Glenarm Place) Streets, were among the first to reach the fire, which because of the smoke billowing from the hotel's windows, looked to those gathered on the street as if it would consume the entire structure. One hundred fifty guests and employees, many clad in nightclothes, scurried through the lobby (directly across the spot where the four men from Company 3 would plunge to their deaths only minutes later) and out the front doors to safety on Curtis Street.

The fire began in a baggage storage area of the hotel's basement about 10:30 on a Saturday night. It was discovered by night manager S. P. Clark and night engineer Harry Morrow, who smelled smoke and descended a flight of basement stairs near the hotel's front door to locate the source. Morrow opened the storage-room door and was confronted by a barrage of flame. He quickly shut the door and the two men retreated upstairs.

When the first companies arrived, it was difficult to pinpoint the fire's location because smoke was spiraling up the elevator shaft and pouring from the roof. The assembled fire companies poured nine streams of water into the building, trying to keep flames from climbing to the upper stories. Several companies entered the building through the hotel's front doors. Three companies went around to the alley in back of the hotel and poured a torrent of water into the smoking basement through windows and the coal chute.

They made little headway in knocking down the smoke, and feared that the hotel's immediate neighbors, Kelly & Co., a coal dealer, and the offices of E. G. Wolff, who owned the hotel, would be incinerated as well. Employees of adjacent businesses carried furniture and documents to the sidewalk. A general alarm was called by Chief William E. Roberts at 10:50 P.M.

An artist for the Denver Republican *re-created the moment the fire-weakened floor in the lobby of the St. James Hotel gave way and swallowed four members of Company 3. (Courtesy of the* Denver Republican/*Colorado Historical Society.)*

Fire equipment clogged Fifteenth and Curtis. To make matters worse, the throng outside the hotel repeatedly hampered the work of the firefighters. "Until the lines were stretched the people persisted in crowding into the hotel and being in the way of the firemen and in danger of being smothered."[4]

Police set up barricades to keep the crowds at bay and to prevent thieves, frequently present at early-day Denver fires, from sneaking into the building. "The new regulation of having ropes at each end of the street to keep out the curiosity drawn crowds was tried for the first time and will be done regularly hereafter," Charles F. Wilson, a member of the city's Fire and Police Board, told *The Denver Times.* "In all the crowd there was not a single loss by robbery or pocket picking. Even the storekeepers who moved their stock into the street lost nothing."[5] Despite these new precautions and Wilson's enthusiastic support of them, one woman guest reported $13 taken from beneath her pillow, another said he had a ring taken from his room and a third guest claimed his overcoat had been pinched.

Into this chaotic scene rushed Captain Hartwell and his company, hurrying through the Curtis Street entrance of the St. James and dragging two lines of hose. They immediately aimed their hoses down the basement steps. Urging on his company, Captain Hartwell cried out, "Boys, here's the fire, right over here. This is our chance. Come on with the line!" Company 3 worked its way across the hotel's lobby rotunda as fellow firefighters, emboldened by their successes at knocking down the flames now visible from below, worked feverishly nearby. Company 3 soon approached an office amongst the check-in desk, elevator and cigar stand, not far from the front door. Suddenly, the tile beneath their feet collapsed. Untouched by the flames, the tile camouflaged the fact that the two-by-eight-foot wood beams and thin wood subflooring supporting the tile had been burned away.[6]

> THE MALTESE CROSS, THE TRADITIONAL FIRE DEPARTMENT SYMBOL, DATES TO THE CRUSADES. FIREFIGHTERS WERE VITAL TO THE CRUSADERS BECAUSE THE ENEMY FREQUENTLY TRIED TO TORCH THEM WITH NAPTHA AND BURNING LOGS. THOSE WHO RISKED THEIR LIVES TO SAVE OTHERS FROM BURNING TO DEATH WERE AWARDED A BADGE SIMILAR TO ONE WORN BY MODERN FIREFIGHTERS.

Hartwell, Brawley, Dandridge and Martin tumbled to their deaths in the flaming cauldron almost without drawing a breath. "Suddenly there was a hoarse shout of warning, and a swaying portion of the floor as the rolling of a wave, a great crash followed by a shriek like the wail of a soul; and four brave men had gone to their deaths amid broken stone and debris and the crackling of a thousand hungry tongues of flame," *The Times* reported two days later in the florid style of the era.[7]

Except for extraordinary luck, the death toll among firefighters might have been higher. William Mason fell through the floor to his armpits but was dragged out by a companion. William Curtis and Edward Whitney also narrowly averted a disastrous fate when they were grabbed by the clutching hands of their fellow firefighters. Captains James Kane of Company 4 and Daniel Ford of Company 7, working side by side, were pulled back from the edge of the fiery hole by their men, and Captain John Nalty of Hook and Ladder Company 2 was spared only by grasping a hose spanning the chasm until he could be pulled to safety. Some fighting the fire later recalled

Company 3's men brushing past them, but no one saw them fall in the smoke-shrouded lobby.

Because of the heavy smoke, the intermingling of the various companies and the generally chaotic conditions, it wasn't until thirty minutes after the fire had been subdued that the men from Company 3 were discovered absent. Chief Roberts, who narrowly avoided being pulled into the St. James's basement himself (and who later led rescue efforts at the fire and explosion that wrecked the Gumry Hotel and killed twenty-two on August 19, 1895), recounted the event:

As soon as I heard of the floor falling I began to count my companions. Some of the boys told me they had narrow escapes, which made me anxious. I could not find Hose Company 3. Someone told me 3's men were back there in the building so with Driver (William) Sullivan, I started with a torch to hunt for the missing company. We found their line and followed it to the edge of the hole. I came to the conclusion that the whole company was in the basement, but whether dead or alive I didn't know.

I called for volunteers and we began to dig. You know how we found poor Hartwell. Then I said, "Good God, my whole company is gone!"

It was such an awful thing, but it happened in such a way that nothing could be done. The company was one of the best in the department—splendid firemen, every one of them.[8]

Roberts immediately set other companies to searching the blackened, water-soaked debris in the basement below a twelve-by-twenty-five-foot hole in the lobby floor. Captain Hartwell's body was the first found, his hand protruding from the wreckage as if begging for rescue. At first, it was thought he might still be alive. A police surgeon who examined Captain Hartwell after he had been carried up to street level thought he detected "a faint flutter of the heart," but this soon stopped.[9] Because Hartwell's body wasn't badly burned, it was assumed that he suffocated in the choking smoke.

The discovery of Captain Hartwell's body caused the searchers to double their efforts. Fireman Dandridge was next to be found. "The body of [Richard] Dandridge was 30 feet from where it went down. The scalp was almost ripped from the skull and the body was in a position with both hands in the air, as if making a last clutch for air. For 30 feet this man must have slowly struggled with broken limbs and bare skull, struggling to get away from the torturing flames as well as to get a breath of precious fresh air. Finally, he reached the corner from which there was no possible chance of escape. Then he slowly drew himself up and threw both hands in the air as the end came."[10]

Shortly thereafter, Martin's body was found, his scalp missing from neck to forehead and his face grotesquely distorted. The arms, wrote the *Rocky Mountain News*'s reporter in grisly detail, were "burned to stumps and the body was crushed by the awful weight which bore it down."[11]

Finding Lieutenant Brawley's body took much longer, as he was partially buried by the collapsed floor. Because he was deeply buried and grossly burned and mangled, those who found him speculated that he may have been the first to plunge into the basement.

The funeral for the four brave men was unlike anything Denver had ever seen. Four hearses transported their bodies from the I. N. Rogers Mortuary at Fifteenth and Champa to the Coliseum Hall at Eighteenth and Champa. It was a brief but poignant journey, with hundreds of onlookers standing silently along Champa as the procession passed by.

The Coliseum Hall was jammed beyond its seating capacity and overflowing with standees. Amidst the floral pieces covering the platform, one arrangement stood out. "The most striking … was a great frame of smilax[12] resting upon an easel enclosing a floral bas relief of a red-helmeted fireman. It was the gift of colored citizens but they had ignored race distinction, and across the face of the emblem, in blue immortelles [dried flower arrangements], appeared the words 'Four Comrades.'"[13] Dozens of other arrangements crowded the stage, including one from ex-firefighters with the words "The Gates Ajar" made of smilax, violets and roses.

In front of the platform rested four identical caskets, sitting two abreast upon black-draped supports and surrounded by police officers and firefighters acting as pallbearers. Because the caskets were exactly alike, noted the *Denver Republican*, bystanders could not discern "which contained the white man and which his colored comrades. Thus were distinctions wiped out."[14] Each of the coffins was decorated with flowers — one with a harp of smilax and roses, another with a floral anchor surrounded by a white dove in flight and two with a floral cross and crown.

These four men (clockwise, from top left) —Lieutenant William Brawley, Richard Dandridge, Steve Martin, and Captain Harold Hartwell—all members of Company 3 stationed in Five Points, perished at the St. James Hotel. (Photos of Lieutenant William Brawley and Richard Dandridge, Gene Cassidy collection; photos of Steve Martin and Captain Harold Hartwell, courtesy of the Denver Republican/*Colorado Historical Society.)*

As the service, conducted by the Reverends Myron Reed and Kerr B. Tupper, began, the wails of Richard Dandridge's widow filled the hall. The Mendelssohn Club sang "One Sweetly Solemn Thought" and Reverend Reed told the gathering, "The fireman is the soldier of the city. All sorts of wagons pass us by and we heed them not, but we all stand still and look when the fire wagon goes by. Those men are going into battle; possibly they will come back dead. No work is so exacting as that which is irregular, intermittent; violent while it lasts. Of course, money cannot pay for this kind of work."[15]

The service concluded with the singing of the hymn "I Cannot Always Trace the Way." Then the four caskets were carried from the hall, through the large crowd outside, and placed one behind the other on the department's hook-and-ladder truck, which was draped in black crepe cascading from the overhanging ladder, and harnessed to four of the department's finest coal-black horses. The procession made its way slowly down Champa Street, up Fourteenth Street to Broadway and south on Broadway, past the state capitol, to Fourteenth Avenue.

Leading the funeral procession were Sigel's Military Band; forty police officers marching four abreast; a group of Masons (Hartwell was a member); seventy-two firefighters, representing all the stations in the city, marching two abreast and led by Chief Roberts; and a group of visiting and retired city firefighters. Behind the truck bearing the coffins came Company 3's hose wagon, driven by William Walton, the company's grief-stricken but lucky driver who escaped death at the St. James because it was his day off. More than thirty carriages behind the hose wagon carried city officials and relatives of the dead men.

When the solemn caravan reached Fourteenth Avenue and Broadway, the caskets were taken off the hook and ladder and each man was carried to his final resting place — Fred Brawley to his hometown of Cameron, Missouri, and the other three to Denver's Fairmount Cemetery. Richard Dandridge and Stephen Martin were buried side by side at the cemetery's Firemen's Memorial, and Hartwell was buried some forty yards away from his men beneath a four-foot-high obelisk that reads: "Harold W. Hartwell / Capt. Hose 3 / Denver Fire Department / who lost his life / at the St. James Hotel / night of March 23, 1895 / Aged 36 years, 10 ms & 8 days."

In the wake of the tragedy, the city's politicians and newspapers heaped praise on the men's performance. "No distinction could be made between the brave white captain and his equally brave negro subordinates," wrote the *Republican*. "The torrid smoke in that hole had wiped out the color line when it wiped out the lives of the four comrades."[16] Chief Roberts, among those who campaigned to integrate African Americans into the city's fire brigades, said, "What kind of firemen were they? We found the four, captain and all, dead together in the most dangerous part of the building when the fire was over. The three black men were farthest from the street. That's the kind of firemen they were."[17]

At the funeral, Reverend Tupper reminded the gathering,

> *There is a lesson to be drawn from this scene. We sometimes forget the worth and glory of our unknown heroes. We celebrate continually the deeds of the great heroes of history, and justly, too. But we should be equally mindful of the men whose names are not heard so far nor so long nor so loud. There are men and women around us every day who are doing brave things before our very eyes. It is sad that we must give these men up, but we may, if we will, learn a lesson from their death—a greater one, perhaps, than we could learn from their lives.*[18]

The *Rocky Mountain News* editorialized, "The tragedy connected with the fire brought tears to the eyes of many a strong man as he read the account of it yesterday. The four men whose lives were lost died at the post of duty. The black skins and the white covered the hearts of heroes. They died honorable deaths, and in them all thoughts of distinction of color and position vanished."[19]

The men were given a hero's sendoff. The city paid $482 for their services because the fire department, an independent entity at that time, had no funds for funerals.

Almost three hundred yards of black and white bunting were draped on the city's firehouses. Of the four men, only Captain Hartwell had life insurance, a $2,500 policy. All three of his subordinates canceled their policies months before the fire because they planned to leave the department. Hartwell, Dandridge and Martin, the last married only eight weeks before his death, left widows, but there was no official provision for the well-being of their survivors. The *Republican* organized a house-to-house fund-raising campaign for the widows, and the city's board of supervisors voted to donate $100 to each of the men's families.

The Denver Times wrote two days after the devastating tragedy: "Never in the history of Denver has such a willing sacrifice been made, and the whole city and state is mourning the loss of four brave men, whose very deaths demonstrated the full extent of their loyalty and usefulness."[20]

Though probably genuine, the wave of emotion was in sharp contrast to the racial attitudes prevalent at that time, attitudes evinced in the racial composition of the department itself. In 1888, an attempt was made to organize a "colored company," but it never entered service. Company 3 came into existence in the summer of 1894 only after a group of African Americans, led by Berry Foresyth, Ed Allison, Francis T. Bruce, Silas H. Johnson and Peter Joseph, demanded that an African American company be added to the city's roster.[21] Skeptics felt the company's presence was the result of the Populist movement sweeping the nation and dismissed it "as a bid for political effect."[22]

When residents of the wealthy Capitol Hill neighborhood complained to the city administration, some years before the St. James fire, that only the African American company was sent to fires in their aristocratic district, it was Chief Roberts who rose to the defense of the African American men, the *Rocky Mountain News* reminded its readers. Said Roberts, "I only wish every man in the department was the equal of those against whom these people complain, for then there would be a fire department without equal in the country."[23]

The fire at the St. James Hotel was initially attributed to an electrical short in the hotel's baggage storage room. Later, a coroner's hearing concluded that spontaneous combustion was the probable cause and that, in the opinion of building inspector Leonard Cutshaw, no blame could be attached to any person or persons for the deaths of the firefighters.[24]

After the blaze, the St. James continued on in declining elegance and prominence until 1927, when it closed its doors. For a brief time, 1901 to 1903, a space in the hotel's first floor housed the Nickelodeon Theater, the city's first commercial motion-picture house, which charged patrons 5 cents to sit on folding chairs and watch twenty minutes of movies projected on a bedsheet. The five-story building was demolished in 1961, and today, 1528 Curtis Street is a parking lot.

Despite the outpouring of praise and sympathetic words that followed the 1895 St. James fire and consequent funeral, things were to remain essentially unchanged for African Americans in the city's fire department for another six decades. The three deceased firemen of Company 3 were replaced by Wallace Martin, Silas Johnson (probably the same Silas Johnson who, among others, called for an African American fire company in 1894) and Charles Thomas, all African

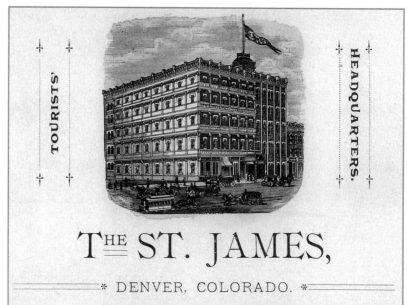

An advertisement for the St. James Hotel exaggerated its size, gave it a downtown corner to lure travelers and promised "superior location, excellent equipment and a careful attention to cuisine." In its early days, the hotel hosted many famous names, including Oscar Wilde and Eugene Field. Following the 1895 blaze, however, its fortunes began to decline. It was demolished in 1961, and the site remains a parking lot. (Nelson A. Rieger collection.)

Americans. Captain Hartwell was replaced by a white captain, H. M. Sauerwatch, "in line with public opinion," noted the *Republican*.[25] By 1906, Johnson was captain in charge of Company 3, which remained the department's official racially separate station until 1957.

In 1955, Denver city councilman Elvin Caldwell urged the city to stop "certain discriminatory practices" in the police and fire departments. The same year, sixty years after the tragedy at the St. James, a survey by *The Denver Post* found that African American firefighters were assigned only to Company 3, in the predominantly African American Five Points neighborhood.[26]

When the color line was broken citywide, it came almost as a fluke. In March 1957, a twenty-nine-year-old former plumber named Robert "Bob" Nickerson passed the city firefighter test. "I still believe that our chief at the time, [Allie] Feldman, didn't know there wasn't an opening for me,"

Robert Nickerson, the first African American hired to an all-white firehouse in Denver. (Robert Nickerson collection.)

Nickerson said in a 1998 interview when he was seventy years old. "He said there was one for me at the black firehouse (Station 3) but there wasn't. So, now that I had passed the exam, they had to put me somewhere so they went around to the firehouses in the East District at that time and asked [for approval from] the firemen at [Station 10], a chief's house, which was great because I'd be protected not only by the captain of the house but by the chief of that district. Being I had grown up where the schools were very well integrated, I had no trouble integrating into a white firehouse."[27]

Nickerson was placed in a previously all-white firehouse the same day another pioneer African American firefighter, Glen Davis, was transferred to Station 4, also an all-white firehouse. But because Davis had previously worked at Station 3, Nickerson became the first African American man to be hired for a previously all-white firehouse.

In a twenty-five-year career with the Denver Fire Department that ended with his retirement in 1982, Robert Nickerson spent time at Stations 1, 3, 9 and 10, and at Stapleton Airport. He recalled the long time between African American hires: "It was almost a 15-year span. From '57 until 1969, I was the last black fireman [hired].

The African American crew of Station 3 posed proudly in 1927. Captain George Brooks (at left in background) and James Simpson (far left, front row) died in a collision at Twentieth and Larimer Streets on July 17, 1938. (Robert Nickerson collection.)

There were some guys that came on before me — Fred Jackson, Tony Anthony and Junior Scales. The catch is they all went to [Station 3]. There was nobody [hired] after me until 1969."[28]

Councilman Caldwell complained to the Denver Civil Service Commission in 1969, "There are only seven members on the fire department from the black community and five of these are eligible for retirement." The city responded that it didn't keep exact records of the racial makeup of the department.[29]

Even nine years later, the battle for racial equality in the fire department was still being waged. In 1978, African American and Hispanic firefighters, led by Captain Frank Quintana, filed a lawsuit against the department, charging that they were discriminated against in promotions and assignments. In a fifteen-page ruling issued in September 1981, U.S. district judge John L. Kane ordered the department to reduce from nine to seven years the maximum amount of seniority for promotions; to reduce from four to three years the experience required before a firefighter becomes eligible for promotion to lieutenant; and to institute a sensitivity training class. "There was," wrote Judge Kane, "considerable uncontroverted evidence that minority firefighters are discriminated against in the assignment of

TOP—Station 3 at what was then Twenty-sixth and Lincoln Streets housed the crew, three African American firemen and their white captain, who perished in the St. James Hotel fire on March 23, 1895. (Courtesy of the Denver Public Library/Western History Department.) BOTTOM—Today, the building is the home of the Wallace Simpson Post #29 of the American Legion. (Dick Kreck collection.)

duties and in receiving on-the-job and other training opportunities."[30] Full integration had finally come to the Denver Fire Department eighty-six years after the St. James tragedy.

In 1997, the city righted an egregious wrong by posthumously declaring the much respected Captain Nathan Biffle an "honorary chief," a distinguishment denied him in life. Biffle served the department from 1925 to 1957, entirely with Company 3, and although he enjoyed status as unofficial mayor of Five Points, he scratched for advancement throughout his thirty-two years with the department.

In 1942, Biffle successfully petitioned the Denver Civil Service Commission to elevate him to the rank of captain, having been passed over for promotion three times and having been the only one of nine eligibles (the other eight were white) denied promotion that year. "From general appearances," he wrote to the commission, "it looked to me like a little matter of racial discrimination, a thing which our national President Roosevelt has begged to be eradicated."[31]

Fifty years before his death, Captain Biffle was promoted to assistant chief by Deputy Chief Cassio Frazzini, but the promotion lasted only until the department's chief, Allie Feldman, returned from vacation and ordered Biffle reduced back to captain.

Equal opportunity was a long time coming. On December 31, 1997, a report filed by the Denver Fire Department with the Equal Employment Opportunity Commission on the racial composition of its workforce showed that the department had 893 firefighters, 646 of whom were white, 173 Hispanic, 54 African American, 13 Native American and 7 Asian. The first woman firefighter, Heather Larson, was not hired until 1985. At the end of 1997, there were 30 women, including 4 Hispanics and 2 African Americans.

The 1895 death of the four men of Company 3 was not the last disaster to strike the company. On July 17, 1938, the company's pumper was "covering in"—moving to another firehouse to replace a company out on a call—when it ran a red light (passing a police car stopped for the light) at Twentieth and Larimer Streets at thirty-five miles an hour and hit Company 4's hook and ladder broadside. The collision caused Company 3's shattered truck to overturn, scattering firefighters from both trucks across the intersection.

The accident killed Captain George Brooks, 49, a popular man many said had a brilliant future with the department, and sent hoseman James Simpson, 42, to the hospital, where he died a short time later. As he was being rushed to Denver General Hospital in an ambulance, Simpson uttered his last words: "Thanks, fellow, for helping me. When we get there, if it's not too late, tell them to get me a priest—I'm through."[32] Two other members of Company 3, James Harrison and Sidney Frelow, were so seriously injured in the crash that they were forced to retire. All told, six firefighters and a bystander were injured in the accident, which was blamed on the driver of the Company 3 truck, who failed to observe a department-mandated ten-mile-per-hour speed limit when entering an intersection against a red light.

Company 3's firefighters had something of a reputation among other companies as being motorized "cowboys." In 1926, Company 3's truck banged into Company 10's truck in a serious accident at Twenty-sixth and Curtis Streets. The company was involved in another crash in 1937, although that collision resulted in no injuries.

The 1895 tragedy at the St. James Hotel, the only time in the city's history an entire fire company was killed in a single incident, reverberated for years. In 1966, then-chief Cassio Frazzini called the blaze "the worst ever" for the department. "For years afterward, there was a watchword among Denver firemen: 'Remember the St. James.'"[33]

Chapter Five

A PIT OF HORROR

*Denver's Gumry Hotel at Seventeenth and Lawrence
Streets blows up near midnight in August 1895,
killing twenty-two people—the greatest loss of life to
fire in Denver's history. Some are trapped in the
wreckage for hours. One man, entombed for nine
hours, is "mighty glad to get out." Young boiler
engineer Elmer Loescher denies the explosion was his
fault. Convened to determine the cause, a coroner's
jury spreads the blame around.*

S ome described it as the sound of a cannon. Others were sure it
was an earthquake.

Nat Burgess, out for a late-night stroll, suddenly found himself lying in the middle of Lawrence Street, his face and clothing covered by his own blood. For two blocks around Seventeenth and Lawrence Streets, windows were shattered. Lawrence and Larimer Streets were littered with broken glass. Awnings and doors were askew. Having been knocked unconscious briefly, Burgess was bleeding profusely, the fearful gash on his head and face inflicted by a peppering of sharded glass. He struggled to his feet and staggered toward Seventeenth Street.

Bystanders crowded the street, wondering what had happened. In the middle of the 1700 block of Lawrence Street stood the five-story Gumry Hotel, its stone facade intact but most of its windows blown out. Its tattered lace curtains, flapping through the holes, seemed to wave forbiddingly at onlookers.

The front windows at Ford's restaurant, 1746 Larimer Street, splintered with a crash. Patrons believed an earthquake had struck. The restaurant's cashier, thinking someone had dynamited the place as part of a robbery plot, grabbed the cash register and "ran at the speed of a scared wolf across the street."[1]

Residents of the Gumry Hotel crowded its windows, pleading to be saved. Some stumbled down the shattered stairs and into the street in their nightclothes. Partially dressed refugees described how the walls of their rooms had shook and how plaster had cascaded down on them as they slept. W. R. Logan, owner of the *Chaffee County Republican* newspaper in Buena Vista, was in room 6 on the second floor. "I was preparing for bed at the time I felt the explosion," he told bystanders. "I am a sufferer from hay fever and was taking a medical preparation at the time. I got on the side of the bed when I felt the bed move upward with a violent jerk. Before the bed righted itself a heavy quantity of plaster fell from the ceiling completely covering myself and the bed clothing. When I could see anything I saw that the walls of my room were torn asunder for several feet and that I was fastened tightly except for the window of the room. I lost no time in getting out of the building."[2]

Anna Schmittel and her two sons, Charles, 19, and Leo, 12, had lived on the fourth floor for a year after the death of her husband. "A peculiar feeling, I don't know what it was, came over me after I was in bed and prevented me from me going to sleep readily, as is my custom," she told *The Evening Post*. "When the crash came shortly after 12, I was awake. The building quivered, walls trembled and instantly the air in the room was filled with smoke and dust. With this came the plaster from the walls, particles of glass from the windows and transom. At first I thought it was an earthquake and then I looked into the street and saw the crowd and realized at this moment that we were all in imminent danger."[3] Anna and her sons were rescued by firefighters.

It wasn't until rescuers went to the back of the building that the full horror of what had occurred became apparent. At 12:04 A.M. on Monday, August 19, 1895, the boiler in the basement of the Gumry exploded with terrific force, tearing away the back of the hotel and sending tons of brick, mortar, wood and furniture plummeting into

the basement. All of the twenty-two who perished were registered in rooms at the rear of
the building.

"The hotel from the rear presented a
terrible sight," wrote a reporter for the
Republican. "Only about one-third of it,
that nearest Lawrence Street, appeared
to be standing. The remaining two-thirds
seemed to have been torn bodily from the
front part and had fallen in a mass that
reached to the height of the third story
and completely filled the alley. The place
had the general appearance of a crater,
where a mine had been sprung and hurled
what was over it high into the air. Tons
upon tons of brick filled in the crevices
between timbers and sections of flooring

Chief William E. Roberts. (Photo
from Representative Men of
Colorado, 1858–1902.*)*

and here and there splinters of furniture and shreds of blankets and
clothing were horrible premonitions of what might be found by digging into the ruins."[4]

Fire Chief William E. Roberts, who led firefighters in their efforts
to save those trapped in the wreckage, recalled the spectacle in a
1932 interview with the *Rocky Mountain News:* "It was a terrible scene.
There it was, after midnight. The building was wrecked. People inside
were screaming, couldn't get out. I heard those screams for months
afterwards in my sleep."[5]

The Gumry, which began life as a commercial building, then
served as a hotel, had become something of an upper-class rooming
house three years before the explosion. It led a star-crossed existence almost from the day it was built in 1887 by Peter Gumry. The
hotel's five-story stone facade came from the Clifford Building, which
stood on Lawrence near Sixteenth Street before it burned down in
1886. The Gumry's first tenant was the Eden Musee, a theater of low
repute with a counterpart 10-cent museum, but it was burned out in
February 1889. A short time later, a furniture store occupied the
building, but it too was destroyed by a fire.

Less than two months before its date with the 1895 fire, the rebuilt
structure, by now called the Musee Building, was purchased by
Frank Scott. He completed moving his hardware company from

An exterior view of the Gumry Hotel, 1725 Lawrence Street, before the explosion on August 19, 1895, which killed twenty-two people. The building experienced two more fires before being demolished. (Courtesy of the Colorado Historical Society.)

1621 Larimer Street into the first floor of the Lawrence Street property the day before the explosion.

In the early-morning hours of August 19, as a plume of dust rose silently into the night sky, moans and cries drifted from the rubble, which reached up twenty feet. Most of the estimated seventy or more people in the hotel that night were asleep or had just retired when the explosion erupted, trapping them in their rooms, or in their very beds.

Firefighters and police squads arrived within minutes and began tearing into the rubble to reach those trapped in the debris. Gangs of men, twelve to a squad, burrowed into the wreckage, but the work was so dangerous and difficult that a gang was allowed to work only ten minutes before being relieved by another crew.[6] "All day, from daylight until dark, sixty paid laborers aided by many willing hands of citizens and firemen, dug and pulled and worked upon the great heap of ruins to uncover the dead. It was a pitiful task, one that fascinated men and women onlookers and touched the heart of the rudest laborer with a thrill of pity."[7]

Eventually, the laborers uncovered a man, later identified as James Murphy, a burly contractor who supervised installation of plumbing in the Boston and Equitable Buildings and in many of the mansions on Capitol Hill.[8] Murphy, still alive, was held fast in the wreckage by a large beam lying on his legs. The laborers worked to free him, but as they were doing so, wisps of white smoke suddenly began rising from deep within the smoldering pile of debris. Already torn by the explosion, the Gumry was on fire.

In desperation, firefighters sprayed Murphy with water to ward off the encroaching flames. It was to no avail. A sword of flame snaked

The power of the boiler explosion at the Gumry Hotel is evident in the heap of rubble left behind. A fire that ignited after the explosion killed many of the twenty-two victims trapped beneath the wreckage. (Courtesy of the Colorado Historical Society.)

out of the debris, driving back Murphy's would-be rescuers. Aware that he probably was going to die, Murphy offered men in the crowd $1,000 to pull him to safety, but they were forced to stand helplessly by, even as Murphy then begged them to cut off his leg so he could be saved from certain death. Fatefully, the hotel's west wall collapsed, burying him in a crush of rubble. All was silent.[9]

Nearby, two unseen women pleaded weakly with rescuers to free them from the tomb that held them tight. Soon, as great clouds of smoke escaped the wreckage, they too were no longer heard from. "The cries for help had long since ceased. Out of the blackness and flickering lights there came no sound save the splashing of water and the hissing of steam. All life had long since gone out there," wrote the *Republican*'s man on the scene.[10]

The smoldering ruin attracted a tremendous crowd, which filled the alley between Lawrence and Larimer Streets and took up perches on surrounding buildings to watch the rescue efforts. Mayor Thomas McMurray arrived to oversee the rescue work and offered men in the crowd standard wages to help. Only three responded. McMurray then ordered police to clear the alley.[11]

Mayor Thomas McMurray. (Photo from Representative Men of Colorado, 1858–1902.*)*

There was no shortage of what *The Evening Post* called "ghouls," people scavenging the wreckage for coins, knives and forks, jewelry, bits of clothing and other flotsam. Some, witnesses said, were members of the city's police detective force. *The Denver Times* noted, "An unfeeling and gain-seeking storekeeper at 1728 [Larimer] Street, opposite the Gumry hotel wreck, stood in front of his place this morning shouting to the people who thronged the sidewalk: 'This way, good people, this way, to get the finest view of the ruins. Only 25 cents for a seat.'" Police arrived and ordered the storekeeper to desist, which drew "an insulting rebuff." Minutes later, Mayor McMurray asked the man, "Will you quit?" "No." Firefighters hosed the man down. He quit.[12]

Amidst the almost total destruction of the Gumry were few stirring stories of heroic rescues. M. E. Letson was one of the fortunate ones. Letson was just falling asleep in room 7 at the front of the hotel when his room began to shake and he and his bed followed the collapsing floor downward. He was trapped upside down in the basement, covered by layers of debris and wrapped tightly in his bedclothes, for nine hours.

Chief Roberts, walking atop the rubble, heard a man calling faintly but repeatedly, "I am burning! I am burning!" Fearing they could not reach him in time because he was buried so deeply, workers instead knocked a hole in the wall of the adjoining McMann Block. They found Letson alive but sealed up in a small space. He was given water and an occasional whiskey (one newspaper account described it as "medicine") as they dug to free him. Later, from his hospital bed, Letson said, "I was mighty glad to get out of that basement. You cannot have the faintest idea of my feelings as I lay there in the bottom of the basement, with all the ruins on top and round me. Everything I ever did or thought came to me."[13]

Thirty-seven years later, Roberts retold the horrifying rescue to a *News* reporter, "It took us six hours to get the timbers and beams cleared away to free him. He had been held there all those hours between two mattresses, and with one hand clamped down by a 20-foot beam. He was the only living person we got out of that building. We carried out twenty-two dead ones."[14]

Letson told *The Denver Times*, "It was a weird, uncanny, deathly experience to be in the mass of ruins for nine hours and have perfect consciousness and talk to Chief Roberts and the firemen and see them doing all that mortal man could do to release me. I feel as though I owed my life to them. I'm pretty badly done for but I'll be all right if I keep a stiff upper lip."[15]

There would be no other such rescues. Death came equally to all the building's tenants.

Peter Gumry, a noted builder and the man who supervised construction of the state capitol, was found in the wreckage,

Peter Gumry, proprietor of the Gumry Hotel, whose body was found at the bottom of the debris following the explosion. (Courtesy of the Denver Republican/Colorado Historical Society.)

his head and hands so terribly burned that identifying him was accomplished through a process of elimination once the other bodies had been found. Gumry's good friend Robert C. Greiner, a business associate and manager of the hotel, and Greiner's wife, Louise, died too. They had lived next to Gumry in rooms 30 and 31 of the hotel. Their bodies, among the first recovered, were found together, holding each other tightly as if they had realized that death was upon them.

Also among the dead were traveling salesmen, a young mother and her seven-year-old daughter, a conductor for the Rock Island Railroad, the hotel's twenty-year-old elevator operator, three German chambermaids, the treasurer of Gilpin County, Ferdinand French, and General Charles Adams, a prominent Coloradan who had been in the state since the Civil War. Adams, in his service as an Indian agent for the U.S. government, had negotiated with the White River Utes for the return of three captive white women after the Meeker Massacre. He was later appointed minister to Bolivia by President Rutherford B. Hayes.[16]

Numerous sad tales came out of the carnage. Some bodies were grossly disfigured. One of the first found was described in *The Evening*

THE TERM "FIRE PLUG" DATES TO THE 1660S WHEN WATER LINES IN LONDON WERE LITERALLY PLUGGED WITH WOODEN STAKES TO KEEP WATER IN THE LINES UNTIL THEY WERE RELEASED TO PROVIDE WATER FOR FIRE PROTECTION.

Post: "A large amount of debris had fallen on it, mashing it flat. The head also was flat and the eyeballs laid out upon the cheek bones. The entrails protruded from several places and hung down like ropes from the temporary stretcher and the stench that arose made many of the workmen ill."[17]

The body of young traveling salesman William D. Dodds was found with a letter from his wife in his vest pocket. The letter, said *The Evening Post,* was largely of a business nature but also noted that the writer "dreamed that papa had come home." Also in the envelope was a small note written in the hand of a five-year-old named Clara. Dodds's wife had labeled it as "Baby's first letter to papa."[18]

The hotel's three chambermaids had been close friends. One of them, Emma Muhlethaler, had worked at the hotel only eight weeks. Ironically, a week before the explosion, they had visited Denver's Riverside Cemetery, which one of them said "would be a nice place to be buried in." The three were laid to rest side by side in a triangular corner of the cemetery, although without a headstone to mark their final resting place.[19]

What could have unleashed such a powerful explosion? Former Colorado governor John L. Routt, a longtime friend to Peter Gumry, theorized it was dynamite. "In my opinion," he told *The Evening Post,* "the explosion was caused by dynamite instead of the boiler, and I think it was done to kill Mr. Gumry. You know he is superintendent of construction at the capitol building and lately discharged a number of men. These men have been heard to threaten the life of Mr. Gumry and I believe that they have accomplished their threat."[20]

Calmer heads believed it was a gas leak, and some said the hotel's boiler, used to operate the elevator, simply accumulated too much internal pressure. The city's head of boiler inspections, William Ensminger, who by the end of the investigation was referred to in newspaper stories as "ex-city boiler inspector Ensminger," came up with the unique and rather unscientific explanation that "when a boiler is ready to explode it will explode."[21]

But the most popular theory, one that continues to be espoused in many historical accounts, was that the young engineer in charge of the boiler, Elmer Loescher, got drunk during his watch and neglected to keep sufficient water in the boiler, then flooded it with cold water, causing the explosion. Newspaper accounts in the first days after the explosion mistakenly reported that he had been killed in the blast.

The most likely scenario: It was Gumry himself who touched off the explosion that demolished his namesake hotel. Several employees who survived said that Gumry frequently trudged down the basement stairs late at night to check that his engineer, the young and inexperienced Loescher, had adequately banked the fires for the night.[22]

After he had stepped off the Denver & Rio Grande train from the town of Antonito, Colorado, to which he fled following the explosion, Loescher told *The Denver Times,* "Mr. Gumry took a great interest in the boiler, even going so far as to help me with repairs after the elevator was stopped. The tubes frequently leaked and we would repair them.

"I believe that someone turned the cock connecting the mains of the water system direct with the boiler, and that flood of cold water in the tube caused the boiler to blow up."[23]

There is another indication that Gumry was very near the explosion when it occurred. He and the Greiners, his close friends, lived in adjoining rooms on the third floor of the hotel. The Greiners' bodies, blistered but not badly disfigured, were found the day after the blast. Gumry's remains, however, were not found until three days later, buried beneath tons of debris. Gumry's head had been torn from his body, and his hands were blackened and burned to the wrists. The only indication of his identity was a single cuff link found attached to a scrap of shirt cuff near the body.[24]

There is little doubt that Elmer Loescher was less than an ideal citizen. He drank heavily and "was a frequenter of cheap gambling houses." There also was some indication that he used drugs—a charge he admitted to, saying he had used opium once but didn't like it.[25] The night of the explosion, more than one man who knew him said that Loescher was on the street in the vicinity of Eighteenth and Lawrence Streets and that he was obviously drunk.[26]

The police and the newspapers were convinced that Loescher had perished in the crash. Still, detectives hunted for him throughout the city. "There were rumors that Loescher had been seen the day after the explosion, but these are probably no more than rumors. Nobody can be found to say, at first hand, that the young fellow is alive. It seems to be certain beyond question that he is down in the ruins, most likely blown to atoms."[27]

Not only was Loescher not to be found in the ruins, he wasn't to be found anywhere within in the city. Fearing he would be blamed for the explosion and possibly lynched by the crowd that had gathered at the hotel, the young engineer had fled town, headed for Southern California.

On August 23, 1895, he was arrested in Antonito, Colorado, by constable Harry Beardsley on charges of manslaughter and criminal carelessness, and remanded to the custody of Deputy Sheriff Tom Clark for transport by train back to Denver. Loescher, who stood a mere 5-foot-5 and weighed only 125 pounds, repeatedly claimed that he was not guilty, either of being drunk on the job or of causing the explosion. As he and the sheriff stepped off the Denver & Rio Grande train at Union Station, Loescher was met by his sister, Mrs. Martha Crook. "Don't cry, dear sister," he said. "I am not to blame; it wasn't my fault."[28]

He maintained that position through numerous police and newspaper interviews and at the coroner's hearing that followed. Shortly after his return to Denver, Loescher told police, "Yes, I drank a good deal and got full sometimes, but only when I was off duty. Sunday night [when the hotel blew up] I was sober. I cannot remember how many drinks I had through the day. Beer was what I drank. I remember being out at Kopper's Hotel on Twentieth Street twice that day to get beer. After 11 o'clock, when I had shut off the pump and put on the brake so they couldn't run the elevator, I went to Kopper's again and got more beer."[29]

Loescher was a frequent visitor to Kopper's saloon. In July, in fact, he had run up a tab of $12, but, he told the jury, "I treated a good deal." Otto Kopper, the saloon's owner, said he had never seen Loescher drunk, and Loescher's fellow employees said he was a dedicated worker whom they had never seen drunk on the job.[30]

A coroner's inquest of the Gumry tragedy brought together some of the city's leading citizens. The six-member jury consisted of *Denver Republican* publisher K. G. Cooper; real estate dealer Thomas B. Croke; architect Frank E. Edbrooke; hatter and furrier Charles W. Babcock; furniture-store owner Frank M. DeMange; and Robert

Elmer Loescher, the young boiler tender originally blamed for the explosion, was sketched in his cell by the Denver Republican, *executing a drawing of the layout of the Gumry Hotel's defective boiler. (Courtesy of the* Denver Republican/Colorado Historical Society.*)*

W. Speer, a former fire and police commissioner and soon-to-be mayor. For two days the jury heard testimony from boiler experts, from witnesses who were at the hotel at the time of the explosion and from Loescher himself.

In the course of the hearings, it was revealed that the forty-eight-foot-long Gumry boiler, used to power the hotel's elevator, had a history of poor repair, breakdowns and leaks. A week before the hearing, one of those living at the hotel who had survived the blast, machinist Bud Burns, told *The Times* that when he had returned to the Gumry after having been out of town, the desk clerk wanted to put him in a room at the back of the house. "Over that boiler of yours?" he said he announced to the clerk. "Not a bit of it. I'll sleep in the front of the house or not in it at all." When the explosion occurred, he said, he was not surprised.[31]

Loescher, his dark hair combed back in a pompadour, was a calm and careful witness on the stand. He described how he had begun

THE FIRST DECISION OF
THE NINE-MEMBER FIRE
DEPARTMENT PLANNING
BOARD, ORGANIZED IN
1932 TO IMPROVE THE
EFFICIENCY OF THE
DENVER FIRE DEPARTMENT,
WAS TO ABOLISH RED
SUSPENDERS AS PART OF
THE UNIFORM AND TO
ADOPT A NEW STANDARD
DRESS SHIRT.

working at the Gumry five years earlier at a salary of $17 a month, which eventually rose to $42 a month. He went to work at 7 A.M. and worked until 11 P.M. He described his duties in tending the boiler and recounted how Peter Gumry would descend the basement stairs at night to visit and to check on the boiler's tubes.

Loescher was an enigmatic figure. Born in Cincinnati as Hellmuth P. Loescher, he lost both his parents at an early age, his mother when he was six, his father when he was fifteen. He was unsure even of his own age. Asked at the coroner's hearing, Loescher said he was either twenty or twenty-two.

Loescher came from an abusive family background. His father was an alcoholic whose habit prevented him from supporting his wife and two children. A friend of the family recalled that when Loescher's mother was on her deathbed, Loescher's father arrived with two bottles of beer and forced his wife to drink part of one of them. Later, Loescher was sent to the state reform school. His father died in Denver.[32]

If Loescher was puzzling, Peter Gumry was no less so. Although he was never married and had no children, it was frequently printed in the local press that a daughter to Gumry was married to Robert Greiner. After Gumry's death it was discovered that his real name was not Gumry. A fanciful tale of being shipwrecked, rescued and renamed on a journey from Sweden turned out to be nothing more than that. Gumry's brother, Gustav Guneson, pointed out in a letter to Denver officials that Peter had lived in Minnesota, Wisconsin and Michigan before moving west.[33]

Once he arrived in Denver in 1862, Gumry began a career as a contractor. He built many of the city's more noteworthy structures, including the state capitol, for which he labored as construction supervisor.[34]

Gumry was reported to have amassed a sizable fortune in his lifetime, but no will could be found after his death. Several years of litigation were required to straighten out matters involving those claiming to be heirs. In one of the most bizarre claims, a woman turned up who said she and Gumry had been married in Omaha, Nebraska. Moreover, she brought along four witnesses who swore they had attended the ceremony. Frustrated, the attorney for the Gumry estate asked the woman to describe the late hotel owner. She did not hesitate, reported *The Times*. "She said her liege lord was a man about five feet six or seven inches tall, with a brown mustache and a bald head. She admitted that Gumry was not entirely unlike the attorney."[35] When it was revealed to the court that Gumry was approximately five feet tall, had a full beard and head of hair and was approximately seventy years old at the time of his death, the woman's claim was thrown out.

Ultimately, more than $200,000 in lawsuits were filed against Gumry's estate, which, it turned out, was only worth about $40,000. When all the cases were settled—all in favor of the estate—the undisclosed remainder was distributed among Gumry's brother and two sisters living in Sweden.[36]

In an absurd footnote that would be comic were the circumstances not so tragic, Robert Greiner's will, discovered two months after he was killed in the Gumry Hotel, dictated that upon his death, his right foot should be amputated four or five inches above the ankle and sent to the surgical department of the "Ann Arbor university." There, the will directed, the foot was to be displayed in a case labeled "Bob's Game Foot."[37]

Greiner wrote in his will that he had fractured the ankle several times, but that he still was able to walk twenty or thirty miles without fatiguing it. This remarkable feat, he felt, had earned his foot a place in medical history. Unfortunately, by the time the will was opened, Greiner's body (with the foot presumably still attached) had already been sent to Grand Rapids, Michigan, for burial. A spokesperson for the medical school at the University of Michigan–Ann Arbor said in 1994 that no record could be found of "Bob's Game Foot" having been received.[38]

On August 30, 1895, after deliberating its investigation into the cause of the Gumry boiler explosion, the coroner's jury decided that no one person was to be held accountable. A report signed by all six jurors said, in part:

We are unable to fix the responsibility ... but we believe the owners and managers, Peter Gumry and Robert C. Greiner, were blamable for requiring of the engineer sixteen hours work out of twenty-four, a requirement far beyond the ability of any man to endure and perform good work; also for employing an engineer whose habits were dissipated and unreliable, and whose experience did not justify them in placing him in such a responsible position, all of which were well known to them.

We find that the engineer, Hellmuth Loescher, had been drinking on the night of the disaster, and further he had not examined the safety valve to the boiler for two months, proving him to be unfit to occupy any position where security to life and property depends upon the faithful performance of duty.

We find that William E. Ensminger, late city boiler inspector, inspected the boiler on May 16, 1895, and ordered repairs thereon; that on May 21 he ordered a certificate issued by the city treasurer, allowing the boiler to carry 75 pounds of steam pressure. The repairs on the boiler were not finished until May 29, eight days after the certificate had been issued. The records of the city boiler inspector's office do not show that the boiler was ever inspected after repairs were made.[39]

The jury concluded its report with this advice:

With a view to preventing steam boiler disasters in the city of Denver in the future, we make the following recommendations to the mayor and City Council:

First, that the boiler inspector be allowed sufficient assistance to enable him to thoroughly inspect all the boilers in the city at least once a year.

Second, that an ordinance be passed containing the best known provisions for regulating the use of steam boilers in large cities ... and be rigidly enforced.[40]

The Evening Post commented editorially, "The primary responsibility for the cruel tragedy of death and desolation that might so easily have been avoided rests with the management of the wrecked building. [Peter Gumry and Robert Greiner] have indeed passed beyond accountability to any human tribunal. In the drear shadow of the cruel calamity that has brought to them so awful punishment for any fault with which they were justly chargeable it is hard to bring accusation."[41]

The precise time of the explosion was never established. Several contemporary accounts held that it happened shortly before midnight on Sunday, August 18; others held the time to be precisely midnight, a highly unlikely scenario. Fire Chief Julius Pearse testified that the first alarm was received at 12:01 A.M., August 19. A clock found in the hotel rubble, its nickel plate tarnished, had stopped at exactly three and three-quarter minutes past midnight.

The Gumry site stood empty until it was purchased in 1901 by F. W. Hubby.[42] On August 19, 1924, exactly twenty-nine years to the day after the Gumry Hotel tragedy, another fire erupted on the site and twenty-five women working on the second floor of Casey's Laundry had to be evacuated from the building.[43] Today, a thirty-two-story office building housing the offices of the Public Service Co. stands on the site at 1725 Lawrence Street. There is no trace, not even a plaque, of the tragedy that occurred there, one that snuffed out twenty-two lives.

"BOB'S GAME FOOT"

One of the most bizarre tales to come out of the Gumry Hotel tragedy was the story of "Bob's Game Foot."

Robert C. Greiner, co-owner and manager of the Gumry, was one of those who perished in the rubble. The bodies of he and his wife, Louise, were found together in bed, their arms wrapped around each other as if they had become aware of their awful plight in the final seconds of life.

Nearly two months after the tragedy, Greiner's will was filed for probate and it was, noted the *Rocky Mountain News*, "a very peculiar document."

First, Greiner requested that after his death his right foot be amputated four or five inches above the ankle and be "sent to the surgical department of the Ann Arbor university," presumably the University of Michigan. There, the will went on, the foot was to be displayed in a case and labeled "Bob's Game Foot."

Greiner had fractured the ankle "several times" but still was able, he wrote, to walk 20 or 30 miles without fatigue. This remarkable feat, he felt, had earned his right foot a place in medical history.

Unfortunately, by the time the will—which, by the way, had not been witnessed by anyone—was opened, Greiner's body already had been sent to Grand Rapids, Michigan, for burial. A spokeswoman for the university's medical school said in 1994 that no record of Greiner's foot having been donated could be found.

Equally peculiar was Greiner's request that his much-loved shotgun be given to the worst shot in the Crescent Gun Club, a local organization for shooting enthusiasts.

The final line of the will read, "God bless those who carry out my wish."

—*Rocky Mountain News*
October 8, 1895

REGISTERED AT THE GUMRY HOTEL

The following register of guests at the Gumry Hotel on August 19, 1895, the night it blew up, was compiled from lists that appeared in the Denver newspapers at the time. There were many contradictions, and many of the hotel's guests seem to have come·and gone without their whereabouts being known.

Some of the names may be fictitious. A. E. Irwin, the night desk clerk at the hotel, told investigators that names often were added to the register by the bell boy, who had nice handwriting, to make it appear as if the Gumry had more business than it actually did. Hotel employees would be housed in the empty rooms.

Registered (Room — Occupant)
3 — Bud Burns, Colorado Springs
4 — Charles D. Myers and William Sayce, Indianapolis (left Saturday)
5 — E. E. Clark, Black Hawk, Colo.
6 — W. R. Logan and wife, Buena Vista, Colo.
7 — M. E. Letson, Denver
8 — Unoccupied
9 — Unoccupied
10 — Unoccupied
11 — Gen. Charles Adams, Manitou Springs, Colo. (DEAD)
12 — Albert S. Blake, Pueblo, Colo. (DEAD)
14 — Ferdinand French and Bela I. Lorah, Central City, Colo. (DEAD)
16 — William J. Corson, Pueblo, Colo. (DEAD)
17 — Mr. and Mrs. W. G. Purcell, Broken Bow, Nebr.
18 — N. Carstens, Yutan, Nebr.
20 — Ethel White, Silver Plume, Colo.
21 — Mrs. O. H. Knight and sons, Lake City, Colo.
22 — Mr. and Mrs. Burgess and two others

23—A. Perry, Caribou, Colo.

25—A. L. Dallas, Denver

27—E. W. Edwards, Denver (DEAD)

28—Unoccupied

29—Herman Lueders, Manitou Springs, Colo.

30 and 31—Mr. and Mrs. Robert C. (Louise) Greiner, Denver (DEAD)

32—Peter Gumry, Denver (DEAD)

33—Alexander Groydon (Greydon?)

34—Peter Poss and daughter, Addie, Chattanooga, Tenn.

35 or 36—Mrs. F. P. Minton, Lake City, Colo.

37 and 38—Mrs. Anna Schmittel and two sons, Charles, 19, and Leo, 12, Denver

43—Louise Reinhuber (chambermaid), Denver (DEAD)

44—John Coleman and Eugene Hellen, New York City

46—Myron E. Hawley, Denver (DEAD)

47—Margaret Wolfe and daughter, Hannah, Lincoln, Nebr. (DEAD)

48—A. M. Monroe, Colorado Springs (DEAD)

49—Lizzie Laager and Emma Muhlethaler (chambermaids), Denver (DEAD)

50—Charles Gordon and M. G. Sleight, Denver

51—(?) Caldbeck

52—Mr. and Mrs. A. W. Roberts, Colorado Springs

53—Mr. and Mrs. W. C. McClain and child, Huron, Kans.

54—Mr. and Mrs. Henry Shaw (Sloan?), Huron, Kans.

56—W. R. McCormick, Chicago

57—T. G. Rowan (Brown?), Lake City, Colo.

59—E. F. McCloskey, Canon City, Colo. (DEAD)

62—Joe Munal, Peoria, Ill.

63—James Murphy, Denver (DEAD)

64—William Richards (bellboy), Denver (DEAD)

65—M. J. Baker, St. Louis, Mo.

66—George Burt, Colorado Springs (DEAD)

67—J. W. Peyton, Denver

Dead but Room Not Known
Fred Hubbold, Lisbon, Iowa
William D. Dodds, Albany, N.Y.

DEATHS IN THE
GUMRY HOTEL FIRE
August 19, 1895

Gen. Charles Adams, Manitou Springs, Colo.
Albert S. Blake, Pueblo, Colo.
George Burt, Colorado Springs
William J. Corson, Pueblo, Colo.
William D. Dodds, Albany, N.Y.
E. W. Edwards, Denver
Ferdinand French, Central City, Colo.
Louise Greiner, Denver
Robert C. Greiner, Denver
Peter Gumry, Denver
Myron E. Hawley, Denver
Fred Hubbold, Lisbon, Iowa
Lizzie Laager, Denver
Bela I. Lorah, Central City, Colo.
E. F. McCloskey (McClosky), Canon City, Colo.
A. M. Monroe, Colorado Springs
Emma Muhlethaler, Denver
James Murphy, Denver
Louise Reinhuber, Denver
William Richards, Denver
Hannah Wolfe, Lincoln, Nebr.
Margaret Wolfe, Lincoln, Nebr.

Chapter Six

SO THE PEOPLE
MAY KNOW

*A four-way newspaper war is ignited by the arrival in
Denver of Frederick G. Bonfils and Harry H.
Tammen. Papers trade charges and countercharges on
everything from politics to coal prices. When a nitric-
acid spill in the engraving room of* The Denver
Post *kills four firemen and leaves fourteen others
incapacitated,* The Post's *rivals have a field day. A
coroner's jury is convened to investigate* The Post's
*culpability in the accident, but suspends its
deliberations to await a key witness.*

W hen Frederick Gilmer Bonfils and his partner, Harry Heye
Tammen, put $12,500 and their dreams on the line to
purchase a woebegone newspaper on October 28, 1895,
one of the many things they agreed on was that their new enterprise,
The Evening Post, would give its readers local news.

"Nothing is too trivial to interest some reader," said Tammen, a
former bartender and curio-shop owner. "And never forget this: That
more people are interested in a man's falling and breaking his arm on
Curtis Street than are interested in a disaster in Egypt or China."
Bonfils, whose curious history as a real estate and lottery promoter
would play a major role in his life as a newspaper publisher, concurred. "A dogfight on Sixteenth Street is a better story than a war
in Timbuktu."[1]

Co-owners of The Denver Post *Frederick Gilmer Bonfils (right) and Harry Heye Tammen. (Photo from* Representative Men of Colorado, 1858–1902.*)*

Neither man knew the first thing about running a newspaper. But if a dogfight was what the people wanted, that is what they would get—and then some.

For the next thirty-eight years, until his death from complications of an ear infection in 1933, Bonfils (his partner and close friend Tammen would die of cancer in 1924) gave Denver and Colorado a slam-bang, no-holds-barred journalistic atmosphere that created one of the longest-running newspaper wars in the country's history. When Bonfils and Tammen took over *The Post,* it was a sorry fourth in a crowded field that included the *Denver Republican, The Denver Times* and the *Rocky Mountain News.* Within six years, *The Post* became the region's largest newspaper by outshouting, outmuckraking, outpromoting and outbragging its opposition.

Battling beneath an editorial flag that read, "So the People May Know," Bonfils and Tammen attacked the city's power structure, the owners and managers of the water company, the trolley system, politicians and, oftentimes, businesspeople who declined to advertise in their new venture. In the fiery eyes of *The Post*'s flamboyant owners, almost anyone in authority was "unsuited to the people." Nearly all governors "were bad for the state and unfit for office."[2]

There were promotions, most executed without cost to the newspaper, involving escape artists, children, all major holidays, food giveaways, birdhouses, fishing and hunting contests, rabbit shoots and automobile races. Anything that would get people to talk about the paper was fair game.

"*The Post* always spoke at the top of its voice," observed Gene Fowler in *Timber Line*, his sometimes fanciful but highly readable account of the paper's history. "As noise begets noise, the whole town took on a louder tone—just as the modern radio has made of each American home a place for conversational shouts. And if a man wanted publicity, all he had to do was perform some act of real or implied loudness."[3]

The shouting began almost immediately. Bonfils and Tammen, the latter a genius at dreaming up slogans for the pair's new mouthpiece ("The Paper with the Heart and Soul" and "*The Post* Is Your Big Brother" were just two of many used through the years), began employing bigger, bolder and sometimes red headlines to catch readers' attention. Divorces, suicides, sad stories of orphans and suicidal prostitutes and detailed accounts of grisly murders became standard fare. Accused of "yellow journalism," Tammen responded, "Sure we're yellow, but we're read, and we're true blue."[4]

The *Rocky Mountain News* was the city's first and largest daily but battled constantly with its rivals, *The Times* and the *Republican*. When the brash and brazen *Post* began attracting readers, it added turmoil to an already crowded field.

Each paper proclaimed itself the guardian of the people's interest. "From stem to stern *The Post* was loaded with silliness posing as wisdom, broad inconsistencies that wouldn't fool a prairie dog and bold statements that a certified idiot wouldn't believe—yet the people of Denver either believed these things or simply enjoyed the colorful manner in which they were served up."[5]

Edwin P. Hoyt wrote in *A Gentleman of Broadway*, his biography of onetime Denver journalist Damon Runyon: "One result of the newspaper war was a rash of self-congratulatory stories in all the newspapers, but particularly *The Post* and the *News*. The editors were constantly telling their readers how much they loved them and how much they were doing for them."[6] Only three days after Bonfils and Tammen bought their paper, they notified readers: "*The Post* is absolutely fearless and independent. It is always with the people. It is the sincerest friend the people have. It pleads every deserving cause. It is the home newspaper."[7] Those whom *The Post* loved (who in turn, of course, loved *The Post*) were referred to frequently as "prominent," while those with whom *The Post* took issue were merely "obscure."

The four papers began sniping at one another at once. There was a fierce fight for advertising, particularly from the city's four large department stores—A. T. Lewis and Sons, Daniels and Fisher, Joslins and the Denver Dry Goods Co. When David Moffat, the banker/developer/mine owner/rail tycoon who owned *The Times,* urged local merchants to boycott *The Post,* Bonfils retaliated in print:

> *Not content with boycotting* The Post *in a body, the big department stores are now sending their emissaries to all of the independent advertisers who still continue to patronize* The Post, *thus further showing their venom and hatred, and their desire to injure* The Post *and destroy it, if possible.*[8]

Charges and countercharges abounded. The *News* called *The Post* a "blackmailing, blackguarding, nauseous sheet which stinks to high heaven and which is the shame of newspapermen the world over."[9] Sometimes *The Post* was more simply referred to as "the Sixteenth Street mud dredge."

Bill Hosokawa wrote in *Thunder in the Rockies,* "The four newspapers proceeded, morning and evening, to belabor each other and the public with news stories blown up all out of proportion and an endless series of promotions and giveaways announced by bomb blasts, red ink and wailing of sirens borne aloft by that novelty, the airplane."[10]

The passage of time did nothing to quell the din. In 1899 the *Republican,* a staid voice of the GOP, began to wither. By 1913 it was defunct. *The Post,* not content to slug it out just with the *News,* took on *The Times,* and in a "So the People May Know" diatribe, called the paper "a paid hireling of the political corporations. Inane, hysterical, a poor suffering creature."[11] *The Times,* in turn, referred to Tammen as "editor of a disreputable evening newspaper." In 1902 *The Times* was purchased by the *News* but remained a separate publication until it folded in 1926.

Even the tiny pro-mining publication *George's Weekly* joined the donnybrook, labeling Patterson and his newspapers the "News-Times Riot Breeder," for Patterson's defense of the miners' unions.[12] In 1903 *George's Weekly* called Patterson "an unscrupulous old scoundrel, rotten to the core, who should be placed in a straightjacket and sent to the state mental asylum in Pueblo."[13]

Nothing was outside the bounds, particularly death. On September 20, 1904, the newspaper war opened on a new front after a nitric-acid spill in the engraving room of *The Post* at Sixteenth and Curtis Streets became a competitive focal

THE DEPARTMENT'S FIRST MOTORIZED TRUCK WAS PUT IN SERVICE AT STATION 8, SIXTEENTH AND MARION STREETS, ON AUGUST 25, 1917. THE LAST HORSE-DRAWN APPARATUS IN THE CITY WAS RETIRED ON JULY 24, 1924.

point. In a battle for circulation and advertising dollars, the ensuing printed volleys rode the shoulders of four firefighters who lost their lives battling the spill, as well as the long suffering of more than a dozen others.

The spill was heralded with lightning strikes and mighty booms of thunder from a late-summer thunderstorm that rattled downtown Denver. A woman walking at Fifteenth and Arapahoe Streets swooned to the pavement when a bolt of lightning struck nearby. A streetcar traveling on Fifteenth Street took a direct hit, but none of its thirty passengers was hurt seriously. A bolt struck a tree stump near the city's old jail, leaving a foot-deep hole.

At almost the same moment, shortly before 3:30 on that Tuesday afternoon, engraver Charles Prazak was working in *The Post*'s second-floor etching room at 1623 Curtis Street. As he was opening a sixteen-gallon glass carboy of pure nitric acid (used in making engravings of photographs and drawings), the bottle suddenly split, spilling the acid onto the room's wood floor and creating a haze of noxious brown gas. *The Post* would claim in its columns that the electrical storm caused the break. Later investigations, and stories in *The Post*'s own columns, proved otherwise.

The loosed acid spread quickly, contacting zinc plates on the floor and oozing beneath furniture. Engraving-room employees tried, without success, to counteract the chemical by throwing sawdust and copious amounts of soda on the spill, then called in an alarm to the fire department. Fire companies from City Hall (Fourteenth and Larimer), Nineteenth and Curtis, and Broadway and Colfax responded within minutes. Firefighters from Company 4, the first to arrive, ran a line of hose into the room while firefighters from Hook and Ladder Companies 1 and 2 used Babcock extinguishers, which contained soda, to suppress the acid fumes.

According to the *News*, all three companies believed they were fighting a fire, "only to stagger out a few brief moments later, their duty done, their lungs filled with a poison no human hand may stay."[14] Of those who entered the room, Captain Charles Eymann, Truckman John McGlade, Ladderman S. B. Wilcox and Lieutenant Charles Dolloff stayed the longest. Three of these four died within a month.

Post reporter Robert E. Harvey, who had called in the alarm, warned arriving firefighters that they didn't need hoses. "It is an acid fire — you need to use chemicals, not water."[15]

"There was no fire," said Captain John Nalty, one of the first firefighters to enter the etching room. He described the scene to the *News*:

When I entered the room blue flames were playing about the floor where the acid was spilled and had been covered by sawdust. And by no fire, I mean no complete combustion. From the floor rose fumes of every color, yellow, blue, brown and green, and so dense were they that it was almost impossible to distinguish objects across the room.

A line of hose was laid but no water was played into the room because there was no fire which threatened the building. A Babcock extinguisher was used, and this reduced the action of the acid to the extent of smothering the blue flames, but served to increase the noxious fumes.

It was impossible to remain in the room longer than an instant and the men would rush to the door for a breath of fresh air and then return.[16]

The Times gushed, "Bravely, they rushed into the thickest of the flames, and it was but a few minutes until all danger to the building had been averted, but at a cost such has never before been experienced by the department. Ten men, the pick and flower of Denver's splendid fire-fighting men, were almost unconscious from the effects of the fumes."[17] Several firefighters collapsed on the Sixteenth Street sidewalk afterward and had to be transported to their homes.

Assistant Chief John Dulmage, forty-nine years old and a twenty-five-year veteran of fighting fires in Denver, was acting chief at the time of the spill (Chief Terry Owens was away from the city on a honeymoon trip in the East). Dulmage helped push the smoldering carboy out of the engraving room and into a hallway, where Dolloff and McGlade assumed the task of carrying it out to Sixteenth Street. Later, firefighters reported that they could not recall Dulmage or anyone else connected with the department warning them that nitric acid was flowing freely in the room. However, some witnesses remembered hearing Dulmage warn his men, "Look out, boys. We had a man killed at the chemical works and we are not going to have any killed here."[18]

Warnings from others among the fifteen or twenty persons, mostly *Post* employees, in or near the etching room were ignored. "It isn't our custom to listen to bystanders for information," Captain Enos Patrick said. "We go ahead and see for ourselves. The only warning I heard regarding this fire was when something was said about, 'Look out—it will burn your shoes.'"[19] William Lewis, driver for Chief Owens, concurred: "If we followed the advice of outsiders at fires we should be driven crazy at every fire we go to. We were all careful to fight the fire lying on the floor, as is customary at [an] acid fire, or where the smoke is exceedingly thick."[20]

Like almost everything else done in the thirty minutes after the firefighters arrived, lying on the floor was the wrong thing to do. It came out later that throwing heavy amounts of soda on the fire created carbonic acid, which helped trap the nitric-acid fumes nearer to the floor. It was revealed during testimony at the coroner's inquest that the firefighters had little experience and virtually no training in fighting a nitric-acid spill, and had used soda extinguishers to quell the acid that leaked from the smoking carboy. One fireman commented that the men had "talked among themselves" about such an accident taking place.[21] There were no ventilator masks at the time.

A week after the incident, *The Post* and the *Republican* printed procedural guidelines from the Western Chemical Manufacturing Co., which had fallen victim to a fatal acid fire four years earlier. The company warned "all who use acids" that throwing sawdust on nitric acid increases the volume of poisonous gas and that soda makes carbonic acid, a heavy gas that creates a blanket over the deadly gas. Instead, the guidelines recommended immediate ventilation and pouring an abundance of water on the spill.[22]

The acid fire at *The Post*, which prompted a call to the fire department, turned out to be a small one. "Nitric acid does not burn of itself, nor does it cause anything else to burn with flame. It simply eats up anything with which it comes in contact, except glass, porcelain, beeswax, asphalt or parafine [sic]. In eating substances the acid forms chemical combinations and throws off a noxious smoke."[23] In its first story about the incident, *The Times* reported: "The fire was one of the smallest fought by the department for a long time, it being merely an incipient blaze, of a size usually handled without danger and little trouble. It was the acid which caused the damage and loss of life."[24]

The acid fumes were insidious. Edward St. Clair, an engraver at *The Post* and one of those in the room when the carboy burst, suffered no apparent ill effects from the fumes, probably, he theorized, because he was used to it. "It's a good deal like inhaling a cigar in that respect."[25] Others were not so fortunate. "The fumes were like ammonia," said fireman Peter Anderson, one of those hospitalized. "They were very sharp and caused me some little pain at first, but I thought nothing of it until today. None of us thought we were in danger at the fire."[26] Testifying at the coroner's hearing, James Ryan, a member of Company 4, concurred: "If someone had said it was nitric acid I don't suppose we would have gone in there."[27] Firefighters spent up to thirty minutes in the room where the spill took place.

When it was over, some of the stricken firefighters felt well enough that they finished their shifts and then went home, but only to fall ill during the night or the next morning and be carted off to Denver Emergency Hospital (later Denver General Hospital, now Denver Health Medical Center). Pipeman William Granger of Engine Company 2 resisted being kept in the hospital. "I'm not sick," he told doctors and nurses.[28] He waited until doctors attending him had left his room, then put on his clothes, slid down a column outside his second-story room and went off to parties connected with the state Democratic convention taking place in town.

Granger and others were advised, not by doctors, that large doses of alcohol would relieve the pain from breathing the acid fumes. The *Republican* reported, "Granger is a man of temperate habits and he drank only in hopes of curing himself. Hence, in the event of his recovery, no blame will be attached to him."[29] Granger recovered, both from the acid fumes and from his self-administered cure.

Four others were not so lucky. First to succumb was Charles Dolloff, 28, of Engine Company 4. Dolloff, a Boulder native, was among those firefighters sent home. He complained of feeling badly, drank half a cup of coffee and returned to work, only to become so ill that night—telling his comrades, "I feel pretty sore here, boys"[30]— that he was rushed to Denver Emergency. Surrounded by friends and members of his family, he was kept alive at the hospital for twenty-one hours by oxygen and drugs until his death at 1:45 P.M. on Wednesday, September 21, the day after the spill.

John McGlade, 35, known to his comrades as "Handsome Jack" from his matinee-idol appearance and large handlebar mustache that he curled up on the ends, was the next to perish. He fell unconscious early in the day on September 21, and was kept alive by massive doses of oxygen until approximately 6 P.M.

Autopsies on the two men revealed that they had suffered pulmonary edema—their lungs had filled with fluid—as the result of their air passages being seared by the toxic fumes. The symptoms were similar to acute pneumonia. One doctor noted that the acid withered the lungs of the firemen "like the sun would wither a leaf of lettuce."[31] Although the smell of the nitric-acid fumes was described variously as "rank" and "stinking," doctors who treated the ailing firemen explained that such fumes are easily inhaled, leaving no inflammation on the throat or the larger bronchial tubes. Dr. Walter S. Holmquist, one of the attending physicians, said the dead men's lungs were so affected that no remedy could have saved Dolloff and McGlade, not even the large doses of oxygen administered as a last-ditch effort shortly before they died. Today, drugs are available to combat the results of inhaling acid fumes, but the recovery process is long and slow.

The funerals for Dolloff and McGlade were the city's largest since the deaths of four firemen at the St. James Hotel nearly a decade earlier (see Chapter Four). The men's bodies lay side by side in the fire and police commissioners' offices at City Hall, Fourteenth and Larimer Streets, from 10 A.M. to 3 P.M. on September 25. More than eight thousand mourners passed by the coffins, which were heaped with flowers, including three dozen American Beauty roses sent for each man by *The Post*. Black and white bunting hung overhead.

"It was Denver's day of sorrow," intoned the *News*. "Denver's day to stop and meditate upon the calamity that has already sent two faithful men to eternity, brought others to the verge of the beyond and crippled the fire department as it has never been crippled before."[32] The *News* failed to mention the 1895 blaze at the St. James Hotel.

Services were conducted in City Hall, during which the Reverend John H. Houghton of St. Mark's Episcopal Church eulogized:

These noble men plunged into danger from a sense of duty. Their fate was like the fate of soldiers who give their lives for the country's sake. The lives of these men were not encompassed by long years. They did not have rich gifts of money or statesmanship to leave behind, but they give to their country the greatest gift that can ever go on record — their lives.[33]

The hymns "Lead, Kindly Light" and "The Lord Is My Shepherd" were then sung, after which visitors were again permitted to pass by the open caskets.

After the services concluded, an eleven-block-long funeral procession marched up Fourteenth Street to Broadway. It was led by twenty-four members of the fire department and followed by platoons of police, Mayor Robert W. Speer and other city officials on foot; two carriages filled with floral offerings; two carriages bearing the coffins; and a long line of private vehicles carrying relatives and friends of the deceased men. For several blocks up Fourteenth to Arapahoe Street, so many people had turned out to watch the procession that it found passage difficult.

For their final journey, the coffins lay on horse-drawn wagons, accompanied on either side by pallbearers — Captain Dan Delaney and firemen Franklin Johns, John Sullivan, Robert Geddes, Clarence McBride and John Duncan for McGlade, and firemen George Reynolds, George Geer, Victor Roberts, Stephen Keating, Raymond Griffin and John Hill for Dolloff. McGlade was buried at Mount Calvary Cemetery, on the site of the present-day Denver Botanical Gardens, but later was moved to the Firemen's Memorial in Fairmount Cemetery. Dolloff was buried in Fairmount.

Two more firemen who were present at the acid spill would die in less than a month. Frank P. Lunt, who entered the fire service in 1897, was a member of Hook and Ladder Company 2 and was thought to be improving from his run-in with the spill. On October 10, only two days before his death, the *Republican* reported that Lunt was "greatly improved" and that his chances for a complete recovery were "excellent." Ironically, Lunt had been burned in a similar acid incident, an explosion in the Denver Fire Clay Co. warehouse at Thirty-first and

Lieutenant Charles Dolloff

"Handsome Jack" McGlade

Frank P. Lunt

Captain Charles Eymann

Stricken by nitric-acid fumes, four firemen died and fourteen others became seriously ill at The Denver Post *in 1904. (Courtesy of* The Denver Post/*Colorado Historical Society.)*

Blake Streets earlier in 1904, and had rejoined his company only a few days before the incident at *The Post*'s engraving room.

Lunt was well enough two weeks after the accident to make an appearance at the coroner's inquest and testified that he and John McGlade carried the remains of the shattered carboy down the stairs from *The Post*'s offices and into the street. But Lunt later caught a

THE FIRST MOTORIZED APPARATUS, A SEAGRAVE COMBINATION HOSE AND CHEMICAL WAGON, WENT ON DUTY AT THE OLD CITY HALL, FOURTEENTH AND LARIMER STREETS, ON SEPTEMBER 1, 1909. IT WAS GUARANTEED BY ITS MAKER TO "GO UP A GRADE AT 25 MILES AN HOUR."

THE MOTORIZATION WAS COMPLETE ON JULY 19, 1924, WHEN THE DEPARTMENT'S LAST THREE PIECES OF HORSE-DRAWN EQUIPMENT WERE RETIRED.

cold, which worsened into pneumonia and resulted in his death on October 12, 1904. He was survived by a widow, a nine-year-old son and a stepson.

Captain Charles Eymann, one of the organizers of the Tabor volunteer company in 1880 and later a member of the Joseph E. Bates volunteers, became the fourth victim on October 21, 1904, despite having been released from the hospital after a ten-day stay. He never returned to his post with Truck Company 1 and died at his home, 1268 Tenth Street, in the company of his wife and two children.

His friend, Captain John Wilmot, visited Eymann's bedside the day before he died and recalled that the dispirited twenty-year veteran of the department was kept alive only by breathing oxygen through a tube. Eymann, he said, took the tube out of his mouth and said, "It's all off, Jack; my pipe is out." But Wilmot reinserted the tube and urged Eymann to keep up his brave fight.[34]

"Never was he known to flinch in the face of danger," reported the *Denver Republican* the day after Eymann's death, "and he was one of the first of the members of the department to run into the etching room where the carboy of nitric acid had broken."[35]

The fate of the four men's families was much improved financially from that of the families of the firemen killed at the St. James Hotel fire in 1895. The survivors of those men had received nothing from the department and had had to rely on donations raised by the *Republican.* The families of Dolloff, McGlade, Lunt and Eymann were the first to benefit under the city's new civil-service pension, enacted by the legislature in 1903. Lunt, for example, was earning $85 a month prior to his death; his widow received 50 percent of that amount monthly until she remarried and his son 10 percent monthly until he reached the age of fifteen.

In total, eighteen firemen and one civilian (*Post* reporter Robert E. Harvey) were affected by the fumes. Besides the four firemen who died, fourteen were taken ill but survived: Acting Chief John Dulmage, Assistant Chief John F. Healy, S. B. Wilcox, Vincent Davidson, R. B. Cooper, James Ryan, Captain Enos Patrick, William Lewis, Emile Normile, William Granger, William Alward, John Kelly, Peter Anderson and Ed Hollingsworth.

An inquest called by coroner W. P. Horan began on October 2 to determine whether carelessness by *Post* employees had caused the deaths of firemen Dolloff and McGlade and the serious incapacitation of sixteen others (Lunt and Eymann died after the inquest). The coroner's jury consisted of W. S. Fox, Charles Maltby, John H. Alton, Lawrence Murphy, George E. Tuck and Frank Swanwick.

The hearings continued for almost a week. In contradiction to *The Post*'s first account of the spill — that it had been caused by a lightning strike — engraver Charles Prazak testified that while he was taking the porcelain cap off the glass carboy with a file, the usual way it was removed, a triangular-shaped piece of glass came off with it, a crack ran down the length of the bottle and within seconds nitric acid was flowing onto the floor. He yelled, "I have broken the carboy!" and went for soda to throw on the acid.[36]

Among the city's always combative newspapers, the issue most intensely debated was whether the firemen had been adequately warned. While the hearings were being conducted in early October, during which time the ailing firemen were reported by the newspapers to be alternately wavering or regaining their strength, *The Post* maintained that there was ample warning to firemen of what lay before them. It defended itself in headlines daily: "All Knew Terrible Danger" (October 3), "Say Firemen Had a Double Warning" (October 4), "Fire Was Known to Be Acid" (October 5), "Firemen Had Due Warning" (October 6), "Everyone Was Warned" (October 7).

The facts as they came out in the hearings were less clear-cut. The consensus among witnesses was that the firemen had been told several times that there was an acid spill, but that the specific and very dangerous nature of the acid was never pinpointed. Some witnesses said they had been warned it was a "chemical spill," while others said they were told it was an acid spill. None recalled hearing the particular words "nitric acid."

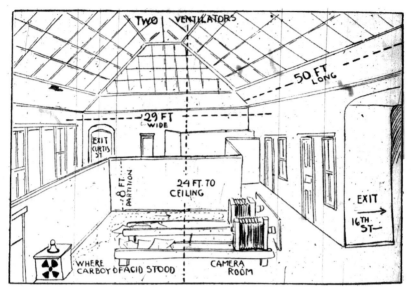

Stung by criticism of its handling of dangerous chemicals in its photo-engraving room, The Denver Post *responded by running a detailed diagram of the room along with one of its trademark page-one "So the People May Know" editorials, condemning as "lies" charges made by its newspaper rivals. (Courtesy of* The Denver Post/Colorado Historical Society.*)*

On September 22, Paul Thieman, writer of *The Post*'s editorial page, virtually dismissed the spill in an editorial headlined, "Plain Duty," part of which read:

> *The smallness of the accident in* The Post*'s etching department on Tuesday afternoon makes the loss of life all the sadder. In itself the incident was trifling, and there would be no occasion to speak of duty performed except that it cost the life of a brave man, Lt. Charles W. Dolloff of the fire department, and the suffering of many of his gallant comrades.*
>
> *A stranger would not have noticed anything unusual in the editorial rooms of the composing room.*
>
> *Denver always expects its fire department to do its duty. The city goes about its business, without thought of fire and death, because brave men are on guard who will do their duty, if it costs their lives. They accept the duty of dying, if need be. They do it. And Denver provides a pension for the disabled and the widows and the orphans of the servants whose duty may be to give their lives.*[37]

The *News* and *The Times* wasted no time in attacking *The Post* for its lax handling of the acid—and for its cavalier attitude about the deaths that followed. "Negligence on the part of someone is responsible," said *The Times*, adding that "the room itself was one of the worst death traps in the West. ... Gross carelessness is alleged."[38] The *News* charged that *Post* employees, "knowing the deadly character of the smoke and gases, ran from the room."[39]

Post management was so wounded that it felt compelled to run a page-one editorial under the paper's well-known "So the People May Know" banner: "The only truthful detail of the accounts of the extremely sad accident in *The Denver Post*'s etching department cheerfully printed by the *Rocky Mountain News* and *Times* is the names of the dead and injured," the editorial began. It then listed the claims by the *News* and *The Times*: that the carboy was kept in small, unventilated room ("THAT IS A LIE"); that there was no danger of fire and that *Post* employees cowardly ran away ("THAT IS A LIE"); that firemen were sent into the small room without warning of the dangerous vapors ("THAT IS A LIE"); and that *The Post* tried to give the impression that lightning caused the spill ("THAT IS A LIE").[40]

The Post's editorial was accompanied by a detailed drawing of the engraving-department quarters. The room, said the editorial, "is nothing less than Woodward's old stock exchange hall on the second floor of No. 1628, an arcade 29 x 50 feet in width and length, and 24 feet from the floor to the apex of the glass skylight. It is the place where William Jennings Bryan made a great speech and held a memorable reception, meeting thousands of people in 1897, and where many public meetings have been held in past years."[41]

The Times couldn't resist the opportunity to turn *The Post*'s own premiere weapon against it. A page-one editorial, mockingly titled "SO THE PEOPLE MAY KNOW" in capital letters, called the incident at *The Post* "the slaughter" and "gross—almost criminal—negligence" and "a catastrophe." It went on:

> *Readers may compare the [*Post's*] editorial with what* The Post *asserted* The Times *had charged, and settle that matter for themselves. But in view of* The Post's *unwarranted, and, under the circumstances, indecent denunciation,* The Times *will now call definite attention to the criminal neglect and equally criminal*

ignorance of The Post *that led to the horrible results, and in doing so take* The Post'*s own statement of the affair.*

The very worst feature of The Post's *defense is its unqualified effort to hold the firemen responsible for their own prostration and death.*

And to charge it upon their courage![42]

Two weeks later, *The Post* called its rivals' attacks on its acid safety and its handling of the spill:

a specimen of irresponsible journalism of the most degrading and dangerous sort, the kind which makes any man's word the target for the cowardly attacks of unprincipled newspapers[.] These attempts to deceive the reading public stand as shining examples of what one may expect from papers whose sole excuse for existence is to wreak personal spites of the editors at anybody's expense.[43]

A day later, following the third day of testimony by firefighters and others before the coroner's jury, *The Post* bragged in its news columns, "Thus far no evidence has been adduced to show that culpability of any sort attaches itself to anyone connected with *The Post* for conduct after the fire broke out."[44]

On October 7, 1904, coroner W. P. Horan suspended the inquest in hopes that Dulmage, a key figure in the incident, would recover enough to testify. He did recover but apparently never testified. A thorough check of Denver's four newspapers publishing at the time uncovered no evidence that the hearings ever resumed after October 6, 1904, and no results of the investigation could be found. In 1998 the coroner's office reported that its records for the period were missing.

The experiences of John Dulmage, who led his men into the poisonous atmosphere of *The Post*'s photo-engraving room, make for an interesting sidelight to the tragedy. Dulmage, among those who formed the city's first volunteer brigades in 1872 and one of the first six paid firefighters in the official fire department in 1881, remained with the fire department six more years after the incident at *The Post*.

His life as a firefighter was fraught with mishaps. While fighting the 1894 Union Depot fire (see Chapter Three), Dulmage barely escaped falling into the flaming basement when a section of floor he was standing on caved in. He had another narrow escape in 1895 when a business block at Nineteenth and Blake Streets was destroyed, and still another in 1908 at the Belmont Hotel fire (see Chapter Seven) when he fell through a burning floor while trying to rescue a hotel guest trapped in his room.

The evening of the disaster at *The Post*, Dulmage and his son, Robert, were racing in the chief's buggy to an alarm at Zang's brewery. As they crossed the railroad tracks at Seventh Street, their buggy was struck by a Colorado & Southern switch engine and young Robert was hurled to the ground. His father, already groggy from his encounter with nitric acid, was knocked onto the locomotive's pilot and the horse was tossed several feet from the track. None of the injuries was severe, but Dulmage was admitted to the hospital later in the evening because of minor injuries from the accident as well as complications from breathing the acid fumes. It was reminiscent of August 1883 when Dulmage's brother, David, was struck and killed by a train in Pueblo, Colorado.

Even Dulmage's dog suffered misfortune. During a fire at the Champa Block in March 1894 (see Chapter Three), the pet spaniel, which Dulmage once said he wouldn't sell for $100, charged down an alley ahead of a group of firefighters and was struck by falling electrical wires. The dog was injured so badly that it had to be shot. Afterward, Dulmage, then a second assistant chief, said, "I shall always think of [my dog] as dying in a good cause. He warned us and saved the life of fireman [George] Gifford."[45]

Though he never recovered his health enough to testify at the coroner's inquest in the matter of the acid spill—the newspapers described his outlook at various times in the weeks after the spill as "almost beyond hope," "in a dying condition" and "hanging to life by a single thread"—Dulmage was able to attend Eymann's funeral on October 22.

After his return to duty, Dulmage was injured twice in 1905 when his rig collided with other vehicles while en route to calls. The more serious of the two collisions occurred on September 16, 1905, when a streetcar clipped Dulmage's buggy at Thirteenth and Stout Streets, hurling the assistant chief twenty feet and knocking him unconscious for several hours.

Highly respected and "one of the most picturesque figures in the service,"[46] Dulmage retired in 1910 but was honored annually with a party by his friends in the department until his death thirteen years later. As doctors had predicted at the time of the acid spill, Dulmage and the others who lived through the accident at *The Post* suffered bronchitis and other respiratory ailments for the remainder of their lives. When Dulmage died at age sixty-eight on April 6, 1923, his obituary noted that he "retained his health and vigor, save for occasional attacks which came as the aftermath of a fire of many years ago in which he inhaled poisonous fumes."[47]

SHE WAS A MOTHER

Her gown bespoke the station of an humble toiler. Her rounded shoulders were wrapped from the autumn winds in a faded and tattered shawl. Her bonnet was plain. She was somewhere in the 50s.

In her calloused hands she clasped a bunch of dahlias. Long and wistfully she gazed upon the upturned face of Charley Dolloff, smiling, even though in death.

The procession behind pressed forward—gently, but firmly. She had to move on.

She dropped the dahlias into the casket. With them went a tear.

And as the unknown woman left the bier, she said, as if to herself:

"I didn't know him; but I did know another who died the same way—died on duty—and that one was my boy."

—Rocky Mountain News
September 26, 1904

Chapter Seven

"GOOD-BY, BILLY"

*Denver's Belmont Hotel becomes an inferno, offering
few escape routes to those trapped inside. Panicked
residents leap from the three-story building. A visiting
fireman risks his life to rescue ten guests. Although
the fire is attributed to arson by robbers bent on
looting the rooms, fire officials blame the antiquated
building and hamstrung ordinances.*

Onlookers fainted. When the Belmont Hotel, 1723 Stout
Street, exploded into flame shortly before 4 A.M. on September 8, 1908, panicked residents blocked from stairways and
the hotel's only fire escape leaped from windows in the three-story
building. Three of the four who died in the fire jumped to their deaths.

Some among the five hundred or so gathered on Stout Street
pleaded with those trapped not to jump, to no avail. Wrote a reporter
at the scene for *The Denver Times,* "Pressed closely by the flames which,
within less than five minutes, had eaten their way into every one of
the forty-one rooms of the hotel, men and women, unmindful of the
terrible chances they were taking, leaped from their windows to the
pavement forty feet below, filling the air with shrieks and cries for
help as they leaped through space."[1]

While some spectators fainted at the sight of falling victims, others
broke into tears. "The fire department will be here in a minute," one
cried out. "Don't jump! You'll get killed," begged another. Wrote a
reporter for *The Denver Post,* "The shrieks for help from these people
[trapped in the hotel] filled the air, and added to their appeals were
the cries from guests at the Albany Hotel, warning the people across
the street not to jump."[2]

Dense black smoke poured from a second-story window at the Belmont Hotel, 1723 Stout Street, on September 8, 1908. Smoke and inadequate escape routes forced three residents to leap to their deaths. (Courtesy of The Denver Times/Colorado Historical Society.*)*

The fire is believed to have begun in a linen closet on the second floor. Some, including city officials, theorized that the fire was set deliberately, aided by an accelerant sprinkled about the hallways. The *Rocky Mountain News* cited a source who claimed to have witnessed the landlady, Mrs. Louise Rahn, spraying the hallways with gasoline to get rid of bedbugs and rodents, a frequent source of irritation in summer.[3]

However the fire began, the fate of the Belmont Hotel, one of downtown Denver's numerous older lodging-house firetraps, was sealed. Once ignited, the fire and thick choking smoke raced through the upper two floors so quickly that escape became impossible because flames cut off egress to narrow stairs at the front and back of the hotel. For the more than fifty residents of the hotel, reaching the lone fire escape at the back of the house proved untenable. Many of them, most clad in nightclothes and some wearing almost nothing, looked frantically for a way out of the burning building but were forced to leap from windows or to dangle from windowsills, flames blistering their hands, until firefighters could raise ladders to them.

Once on the street, victims streamed to the Albany and Law Hotels nearby in search of clothing to cover their nearly naked bodies. One man pleaded with firefighters to let him return to his room at the Belmont so he could retrieve money to "buy drinks enough to forget his troubles." A bystander kindly offered to provide the drinks.[4]

Four men, three of whom leaped from windows prior to the fire department's arrival, died before the fire was extinguished at dawn two hours later. The devastation and the number of fatalities reminded many of the tragic explosion and fire at the Gumry Hotel on August 19, 1895, which took the lives of twenty-two people (see Chapter Five).

The first to perish at the Belmont was J. B. Moore, a sixty-two-year-old dealer in real estate who had moved to Denver from Philadelphia a year earlier and officed in the nearby Boston Building. Ignoring imprecations from the crowd, Moore hesitated at his third-floor window when an eighteen-year-old guest rushed into the room and begged him to crawl to safety in the smoke-filled hallway. Terrified of the advancing flames, Moore chose to dive to his death, his white nightshirt wafting behind him as he plunged into the gray smoke boiling up from below.

"A cry of horror went up from the crowd as it saw the figure shoot through the air and with a thud struck the brick pavement. The old man breathed his last in the arms of strangers."[5] The official cause of death was a fractured skull and internal injuries, which were more graphically described in the *Denver Republican*'s "extra" the morning of the tragedy: "He landed sickeningly on the pavement below and his blood and entrails were spattered over the cement. In his hand he carried a black leather notebook, which he had evidently snatched even in the frantic hurry."[6]

George Ott, whose roommate James Kelso became a hero by preventing a woman in a nearby room from jumping, also succumbed to desperation. Crazed with fear, Ott sailed to his death, despite Kelso's urgings to wait for the arrival of firefighters.

John D. Kane, a plaster contractor from Atlantic City, New Jersey, who lived in room 35 at the back of the third floor, was the only fatality who didn't die by jumping. Kane, who by some accounts had returned to his room the previous night intoxicated, was found lying beneath a window inside the hotel, one hand reaching up as if to grasp the sill. He died of suffocation from smoke inhalation.

Veteran assistant fire chief John Dulmage, who experienced many close scrapes in his career (see Chapters Three and Six), and police sergeant W. E. Sturges crawled on their hands and knees in an attempt to reach Kane's third-floor room but were driven back repeatedly by the flames. Dulmage rose from the floor in the hall and made a final attempt to kick in the door to room 35 but tumbled through a hole to the second floor. Dulmage and Sturges escaped with minor injuries.

One of the saddest and yet most graphic accounts of survival came from William E. Lewis, a brakeman for the Colorado & Southern Railroad. Lewis's roommate, George Bodle, a Pullman conductor with the same railroad, was another of the three jumpers killed. The two men were very close. According to *The Denver Times,* "They called each other husband and wife and were always cheerful and good-natured."[7] They were favorite boarders of the landlady, Mrs. Rahn, who had repapered and refitted their room a few days before the fire. As he lay in his hospital bed terribly burned from his own ordeal, Lewis recounted to *The Times* his perilous escape, and the loss of his friend:

> *I was awakened by the smoke which was pouring through the room, and called Bodle. We jumped up and ran to the door, but when we opened it were met by a wall of flame which forced us back into the room. We then wet towels and wrapped them about our faces, but they caught fire as soon as we opened the door, and we were again forced to return to the room, which had become ignited from the flames pouring in through the door.*
>
> *Bodle suggested we jump and I protested, trying to persuade him to wait until the arrival of the fire companies. He moved toward the window, though, and both of us climbed up on the sill and hung over the edge in order that we might get out of the flames and get air.*
>
> *Suddenly he looked at me, and I will never forget the terror in his eyes. Terrified as I was, I lost all my fear for the moment. He continued to look at me for a second without saying a word, and then he gasped out, "Good-by, Billy," and dropped.*[8]

Lewis clung to a windowsill awaiting rescue, flames searing his face, chest and hands and causing them to blister until the skin fell away. He thought briefly about following Bodle to the pavement but remembered a two-story building next to the hotel and, with the help of a stranger later identified as Patrick Treadwell, swung to safety. Bodle was taken to the hospital, where he died.

There were heroes galore, including members of the fire department and others who averted a greater loss of life. Miner James Kelso crawled out the window of his room and inched along a narrow ledge to the window of an adjoining room, where a terrified woman sat frozen with fear. Despite the fire at his back, Kelso held the woman until firefighters raised a ladder and took them down. Hotel guest Lena Mittlehauser, one of the first to notice the fire, ran screaming into the hall and banged on doors to alert sleeping residents of the danger. And among those who carried victims to safety were Captain Al Graeber of Hook and Ladder Company 1, Lieutenant William Martin of the same company, Captain Victor Roberts of Engine Company 5 and police patrolman Robert Smith.

The most remarkable rescuer was Patrick Treadwell, who was visiting Denver at the time of the blaze. A member of Cripple Creek's fire department, Treadwell was credited with saving at least ten lives in the Belmont fire. From his third-floor room at the hotel (which he shared with police patrolman Robert Smith), he quickly realized that the two-story rooming house located next to the Belmont was one of the few avenues of escape. Clad only in trousers and rubber boots, Treadwell stationed himself on the edge of the nearby roof, across a five-foot alley, and pulled escaping men and women to safety, including the very fortunate and very burned William Lewis. The heroic Treadwell later joined the Denver Fire Department.

Investigations by the coroner and by the city's building inspector clearly showed that either the city's building ordinances were inadequate or enforcement of the ordinances was lackadaisical. The *Rocky Mountain News* pointed out in a page-one story that the Belmont's only fire escape was virtually unreachable and that even if victims had been successful in getting to it, the metal stairs were thirty feet short of reaching the ground. "This same condition of neglect exists in nearly every structure in the downtown section of the city," warned the *News*.[9]

A coroner's inquest failed to answer the question on everyone's mind: Was arson the cause? The jury, consisting of John Bauer, Samuel Morgan, James Pierce, Robert Ward, J. M. Thomas and A. L. Gardiner, was unable to say, precisely, what caused the fire. But police and city officials, armed with ample evidence of incendiary activity, were convinced that arson was to blame.

The hotel's operator, Mrs. Rahn, was sure of it. "Someone set this hotel on fire, and burned men to death."[10] The day after the fire, she told *The Post:* "I hope it will never fall to my lot to again witness such scenes. I don't care for my own loss, which is almost complete. Money can be made again, but life cannot be brought back to those poor souls that perished."[11]

Fire Commissioner Darius Barton told investigators after the tragedy, "I do not think fire escapes are much benefit in any fire. People usually are unable to find them in the excitement . . ." (Courtesy of the Denver Firefighters Museum.)

There was plenty of circumstantial evidence to support her belief that an incendiary was afoot. One of those who died in the fire, J. B. Moore, confided to friends a few days before the blaze, "Don't be surprised to hear of my being burned up in that hotel. An effort was made to burn it down a few days ago."[12]

Since summer, numerous fires had been set in downtown Denver—at Eighteenth and Stout, at Sixteenth and Larimer, and, only thirty minutes before the fire at the Belmont, at the rear of the St. Regis Hotel, a rooming house at 1544 Welton Street. Midnight blazes had been lighted in piles of trash in downtown alleys. A fire had been reported in a stack of boxes at the back of Martin's restaurant in the 1700 block of Lawrence Street. And a series of small fires had ignited at the Toltec, Manhattan and Ferguson Buildings, all at about the same time of night, leading authorities to believe that a firebug was to blame. Noted the *News*, "Scarcely a night has passed in the last three weeks when a mysterious alarm has not been turned in from some quarter in the central part of the city."[13]

Frank Theddick, a prescription clerk and a roomer at the Belmont, told police that, just six weeks before the hotel's tragic blaze, he had come home late one night to hear someone on the back stairs. He gave chase but couldn't catch the intruder, instead finding a can partially filled with kerosene at the bottom of the stairs. A maid later testified to a coroner's jury that at least two fires had been set in rubbish behind the hotel. Smaller fires had been extinguished in the basement on two occasions. Theddick commented, "The hotel appears to have been marked."[14]

A possible motive: burglary. "I am firmly of the opinion that the fire was of incendiary origin and I know that thieves looted the place," said Mrs. Rahn, who operated the hotel for owner Mrs. Lorinda Babcock.[15] Later, she spoke about "the thievery that went on during that awful fire," declaring, "My God! Have men no hearts? They robbed the dead, they crawled over the bodies of the injured to rifle trunks and dressers."[16] She reported to police that $1,600 worth of jewelry and $325 in cash hidden in her second-floor apartment had vanished. Another guest, Mrs. J. L. Hole, said she lost a gold watch, a gold chain bracelet, a pair of pearl opera glasses, two opal rings and a diamond starburst. In all, half a dozen rooms were looted of watches, cash and clothing.

Damage to the hotel, which occupied the building's two upper floors, was assessed at $14,000, much less than the $40,000 originally estimated. Also destroyed was the first-floor business of Hendrie–Stephenson, a rubber supply company, as well as the Centennial School Supply company and Denver Title Co. All suffered severe smoke and water damage.

The fire and its consequent deaths set off a series of charges and countercharges in the city. Finger-pointing was epidemic, particularly concerning Denver's numerous turn-of-the-century hotels and lodging houses, of which the Belmont hotel, though decidedly a firetrap, was typical.

Like many of the city's older buildings, the Belmont, built in 1893, was exempted from "modern" fire ordinances, plus the hotel did not enjoy the best of reputations—for its accommodations or its clientele. "It is a beehive of industry about election times," said *The Post*, "and it is one of the places where ghosts are said to live because the names of men and women, long sleeping in the cemeteries, have been registered from that place."[17]

Whatever its social standing, the Belmont was no better or worse than many similar structures. Stairwells to its upper floors were only sixty-one inches wide, and the stairwell from the second floor to the alley, specifically for use in case of fire, was a mere thirty-three inches wide. Moreover, the escape stairwell ended at a heavy steel door that opened inward.

The *News* thundered editorially, "Just why it is that these things are never probed till they get to the coroner stage is a thing we have never been able to understand. But the fact is plain. With rare exceptions the only time a building gets any efficient inspection in this country is after someone has been killed in it."[18]

But building inspector Robert Willison despaired of ever strengthening the city's enforcement of ordinances. He told *The Post*: "Our ordinances in references to buildings apply only to buildings to be built after the passing of the ordinance. There are many fire

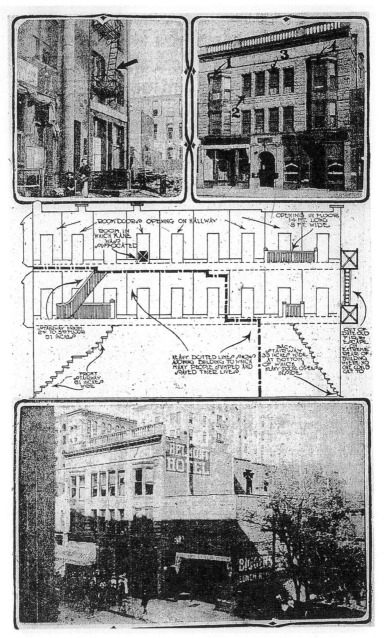

A photographic montage from The Denver Post *shows how residents of the three-story Belmont Hotel were trapped by smoke and fire. The antiquated fire escape (upper left) was thirty feet short of reaching the ground. "X" (bottom) marks the window where several people escaped by leaping to the roof of a building next door. The cross-section of the hotel shows a back stairway only thirty-three inches wide, with a heavy door that swung inward. (Courtesy of* The Denver Post/Colorado Historical Society.)

traps in Denver and in nearly every instance they are owned by men and women of wealth, but when it comes to making these places a little less dangerous, more commotion is aroused than anything else. The Belmont Hotel catastrophe is just one of a hundred others that would be, if anything, worse in case of a fire getting started in them."[19]

Willison also defended the city's fire safety:

> *The building laws of Denver are as stringent, if not more so, than in any city of its size in the United States and the inspectors and fire wardens see that they are complied with. That lives were lost in the Belmont fire is due to the hour of the fire and the fact that the dense smoke shut off the approach to the fire escape.*
>
> *Suffocation was the cause of death in most cases and when breathing smoke men become stupefied and are unable to reach fire escapes. It would probably have been the same if there had been a dozen escapes on the building. It is a most unfortunate affair and the fire will be investigated thoroughly.*

He added, with pride, "I believe there are fewer so-called fire traps in Denver than in most cities."[20]

Willison also explained his office's efforts in dealing with reluctant landlords. "The few rich men and women who own these buildings refuse to comply with our demands. They declare that they will not spend money at the beck and call of every city administration, and it was actually months before we could get the ordinances requiring red lights at exits and fire escapes and fire hose placed in hallways."[21]

The Post proposed that the Belmont was not the worst of the lodging-house firetraps in the city:

> *There are half a hundred 10-cent lodging houses in the lower parts of the city — Larimer, Market, Blake and Wazee Streets. These lodging houses consist of a big room with wooden partitions inclosing [sic] spaces seven feet long and about four feet wide. The beds are double-decked and scarcely a night goes by without every bed being occupied.*
>
> *At one of these numerous places on Market Street below Seventeenth bunks are so arranged that five men sleep in each bunk, reaching from the floor to just under the ceiling.*[22]

Fire Commissioner Darius A. Barton, criticized for not enforcing fire-escape rules more stringently, told the *Republican*, "I do not think fire escapes are much benefit in any fire. People usually are unable to find them in the excitement and in the meantime are either suffocated or burned to death."[23] Challenged to explain why the Belmont had only one fire escape, Barton responded:

> *I have looked over the ordinances thoroughly this morning in regard to fire escapes. I find the word "may" instead of "must" in the ordinances in reference to fire escapes on buildings. We have absolutely no backing whatever by the laws to force modern, up-to-date fire escapes on old buildings.*[24]

In addition, hotels with less than fifty rooms were not required to have more than one fire escape.

Shortly after the fire, Barton told *The Times*, "I would hate to tell you what I think of Denver's buildings and building ordinances. Neither myself nor the fire and police board is responsible for the buildings which are erected in Denver."[25] Nevertheless, he promised to propose changes in the ordinances, including the requirement that every room have a rope so occupants could let it down and slide to safety.

The Post would have none of it. It mocked in an editorial:

> *Fire Commissioner Barton of Denver is wrathful and there is a fine splendor in his anger.*
>
> *But Fire Commissioner Barton is a genial soul who hates the turbulence of reform, and he affirms that his department is doing all that can be done under existing ordinances. The idea of the council adopting another ordinance to more adequately cover the case is a thing that he ignores.*
>
> *It seems, by the way, that Fire Commissioner Barton contemplates one immediate innovation. He is going to compel hotels and rooming houses to provide a rope and staple in every room so that in case of fires the occupants could cast the ropes out and—we quote the sanguine commissioner—"slide to the ground." We contemplate with interest the figure Fire Commissioner Barton would present "sliding down a rope to the ground" from the eighth story of a burning hotel. And we suggest that jumping would be more rapid and less painful.*[26]

Colorado, the scene of many major conflagrations since the "Great Fire" of 1863 wiped out half the structures in Denver's business district, was not unmindful of the dangers of fire to its citizens. In 1883, the legislature, fearful of just such a catastrophe as the Belmont fire, passed a law requiring hotels more than two stories tall to provide a rope or rope ladder (later amended to metal ladder) for lodgers; lodgings more than three stories tall were to provide iron balconies with iron stairs for escape. The legislation, based on an existing law in Missouri, also required every hotel or lodging house with more than fifty rooms and standing more than four stories tall to have a watchman on each floor between 9 P.M. and 6 A.M., as well as an alarm bell near the building's office.

Though the ordinances were in place, they frequently went unenforced. Even some forty years after the Belmont tragedy, little had changed in the way of enforcement. Following a fatal fire at the Denver Athletic Club in 1951, the city's building inspector, George McCormack, reflected on the complaints made by his predecessor in 1908: "There's nothing we can do about the older structures except gradually to enforce a program of eliminating such hazards as open stairwells and other factors that might contribute to fire."[27]

It wasn't until the 1960s that Denver finally began to embrace the idea of developing a fire code instead of relying on building codes for its regulations. Myrle Wise, who was working in the department's fire prevention division at the time and who later would become the department's chief from 1970 to 1986, recalled leading the fight to create that first code. It took him four years to get it adopted. "In the 1950s, we fought for getting two means of exit from every floor of a building. All those safety features you see now are directly traceable to that fire code. It is probably one of the safest in the country."[28]

In 1973 the state legislature finally repealed its 1883 fire law. It had become so antiquated that it was unenforceable, and other, stricter laws governing building construction and fire suppression had since taken precedent. The city had come a long way.

When the Belmont Hotel fire was over, a proprietor of one of Denver's large hotels asked an assistant fire chief, "My God, chief, what would we do if our place caught on fire?" The chief replied, "Nobody would get a chance to do anything, for everybody in that place would be burned up before we could get there."[29]

VICTIMS IN THE
BELMONT HOTEL FIRE
September 8, 1908

The following list was compiled from newspaper accounts.

Killed

George Bodle, 30, Pullman car conductor, Colorado &
Southern Railroad brakeman, internal injuries sustained
jumping from third story

John D. Kane, 25, plaster contractor, suffocated

J. B. Moore, 62, real estate agent, fractured skull, internal
injuries sustained jumping from third story

George Ott, 27, collector, Singer Sewing Machine Co.,
internal injuries sustained jumping from third story

Injured

F. J. Bowden, city clerk, Silverton, Colo., scalp wounds
sustained jumping from second story

Lottie Cobbey, chambermaid, lacerated feet, hip sprain

Joseph David, waiter, Albany Hotel, hand and arm lacerations

Katherine Duff, waitress, Oppenheim's, fractured ankle,
internal injuries

Frank Gilman, hotel employee, bruises

Frances Hoffman, waitress, Oppenheim's, both legs badly
bruised from jumping

Mrs. J. L. Hole, Minneapolis, bruises, possible internal
injuries

O. E. Klinger, printer, back injury sustained jumping from
third story

W. A. Lanham, Colorado & Northwestern Railroad brakeman,
left hand badly burned

Mrs. Dora Lanham, burns, internal injuries sustained in
fall from third story

William E. Lewis, Colorado & Southern Railroad brakeman,
   badly burned on head, arms and body
William Louk, chest lacerated sliding down wood on
   outside of building
Mrs. Lena Mittlehauser, New York City, internal injuries,
   bruises sustained jumping from building
James O'Hara, slight burns
Mrs. James O'Hara, slight burns
Melvin Parker, Hillsdale, Mich., hands, face and arms
   burned
William N. Rahn, left forearm and head badly burned
Mrs. Louise Rahn, landlady, right forearm and right leg
   burned, cut across hip
Charles T. Stewart, soda dispenser, Trunk's, broken left
   hand sustained jumping from third story
Thomas Taylor, fireman, ankle fractured in fall
Patrick Treadwell, internal injuries
W. Weicks, bruised heel sustained dropping from fire
   escape
A. Williamson, waiter, Albany Hotel, sprained ankle, minor
   burns

Chapter Eight

"GET OUT, DAMN IT!"

*America gears up to win the war. Guava jelly is
exempt from rationing. Buy a bond, buy a bottle.
Critical to the war machine are the country's railroads,
linking East to West. When a tunnel fire near Boulder
closes the main line of the Denver & Salt Lake
Railway, the Denver Fire Department responds —
and three of its firemen perish inside the fiery
passage. Nine weeks pass before the tunnel and
line reopen.*

T hings were swinging America's way in World War II in September 1943. Allied troops, all the papers said, were driving the Germans to defeat in Italy and soon would take Naples from the Nazis. Victory surely could be only weeks away.

The Denver Post, in a page-one "Dear Adolf" letter accompanied by tiny American flags, warned sternly:

*You must realize now, if you haven't known it before, that your
defeat and the complete destruction of your whole Axis combination
are inevitable.*

   *You have been licked in Africa. You have been whipped in Sicily.
Slowly but surely, American and British forces are occupying Italy.
You shot your wad at Salerno. You couldn't stop them there. You
won't be able to stop them anywhere else.*[1]

Sixteen million American men and women in active military service were involved in the effort to win the war, and millions more pulled together on the home front. It seemed that everybody, overseas and at home, was part of the war machine.

Drives of all kinds—for aluminum, rubber, tin, fats and iron—were never-ending, all designed to fuel the war effort and boost the spirits of those at home. Newspapers, under strict rationing for newsprint, shrunk their daily papers and filled their columns with stories about the war—military victories, bond drives, Victory gardens, pictures of those promoted and pictures of those killed.

Rationing was everywhere. Although the economy was booming—men and women were working six days a week and getting paid time-and-a-half for Saturdays—there were few consumer goods to be had with the surplus money. Ration coupons ("red points" for meats, fats and oils; "blue points" for processed foods) were obtainable, but meat, butter and gasoline frequently were not.

The Daniels & Fisher department store in downtown Denver urged homemakers to "stretch your menus with tasty non-rationed foods," including guava jelly, kippered snacks, olives, gelatin and whole clams in bouillon. In Boulder, a Hi-Way Liquor Store advertisement cried, "This Whiskey Goes to War!" It linked bonds and booze. Customers who bought a $100 war bond were entitled to purchase two quarts or fifths of rye, bourbon or scotch, "unless sold sooner."

The war also brought about great changes in American society, particularly for women. By 1944, half the 206,000 jobs in the metro Denver area were filled by women.[2] That same year, married female workers outnumbered single female workers, representing 72 percent of the increase in employed women since 1940.[3] Women took a majority role in office jobs, such as secretarial work and typing, but they also stepped into other roles as meatpackers, cab drivers, grave diggers, tool and die makers and engine wipers for the railroads.

It was an era of change for the country's railroads too. Between the bombing of Pearl Harbor in December 1941 and V-J Day in August 1945, the railroads carried 97 percent of all domestic troop movements. In those forty-five months, 113,891 special troop trains moved 43.7 million members of the armed forces.[4]

Wartime meant good economic times for railroads, which had suffered severe losses during the Great Depression of the 1930s. A war demanded two things railroads were very good at delivering over

America's railroads were vital to the nation's efforts during World War II. A propaganda poster put out by the Union Pacific Railroad reminded citizens, "They're ALL Engines of War!" The Tunnel 10 fire caused the Moffat Road, an important East–West rail link, to be closed for nine weeks. (Courtesy of the Union Pacific Museum collection.)

long distances—people and freight. "One of the most favorable aspects of wartime rail traffic was the prosperity it brought to the rail industry," wrote John F. Stover in *American Railroads.* "Business was so good that the operating ratio for the five war years (1941–45) averaged only 67.7 percent, the lowest five-year average in the 20th century. The average rate of return on the net property investment

Notice to the Public

PROMPT MOVEMENT of armed forces of the United States is a responsibility the *Rio Grande* gladly assumes.

If we cannot supply you the Pullman or Coach space you desire, or if your train runs behind schedule, please understand that you are being inconvenienced so that Uncle Sam's men and material may get where they'll do the most good **Right Now.**

We will appreciate your co-operation.

Denver and Rio Grande Western Railroad

A sign posted by the Denver & Rio Grande Western Railroad reminded civilian travelers that a war was going on. Millions ignored suggestions to stay home. (Dick Kreck collection.)

during the war years was 4.97 percent. The industry [retired] nearly $2 billion of funded debt."[5]

Freight and passengers jammed the nation's rail systems. In 1944, the peak year of the war, railroads carried almost one and a half billion tons of freight. Although the government encouraged citizens to make only necessary trips, nonmilitary Americans traveled millions of miles anyway—three times as many miles in 1944 as they traveled in 1941. Standing room in coaches was frequently filled to capacity. An advertisement for the Atlantic Coast Line Railroad warned would-be travelers, "You'll be more comfortable at home."[6] Joseph R. Rose noted in *American Wartime Transportation,*

> *None of the voluntary measures served to mitigate the rising tide of civilian traffic during the war. People traveled on their vacations, during holidays and weekends. They were not even restrained by the overcrowded conditions of the trains and the resulting discomforts.*[7]

Unlike World War I, when almost all the soldiers and material were shipped to East Coast ports, World War II fronts in Europe and in the Pacific required long journeys cross-country, making lines

The rugged, almost verticle terrain of the Rocky Mountains dictated construction of thirty tunnels built between 1902 and 1913. The route is still an important link in modern railroading. (R. C. Farewell collection.)

like the Denver & Salt Lake Railway's serpentine route through the rugged Rocky Mountains critical. Construction of the Denver & Salt Lake route, popularly known as the "Moffat Road," was a herculean example of railroading deep in an area where almost everything is vertical. Built between 1902 and 1913, the track from Denver to Craig in northwest Colorado belonged, in succession, to the Denver Northwestern & Pacific, the Denver & Salt Lake Railway, the Denver & Rio Grande Western, the Southern Pacific and, in 1997, to the Union Pacific.

Dotting the route like a string of black pearls were thirty tunnels, built to overcome the precipitous terrain of the mountains. One of the bores, Tunnel 10, lies in an isolated location in the Rockies in South Boulder Canyon, twenty-seven miles west of Denver. Originally 1,561 feet long, it was lengthened by another 12 feet with concrete lining in 1937. It was, said R. C. Farewell in *Rio Grande Secret Places*, his volume on the railroad's tunnel district, "a hole in the wall" blasted through a vertical mass of Precambrian metamorphic rock.[8]

Much of the shorter tunnel work on the line was done by hand by men using horse-drawn carts. These laborers worked for 15 cents a yard for moving earth, 35 cents a yard for loose rock and 68 cents a yard for hard rock. "The line was literally blown out [with blast-

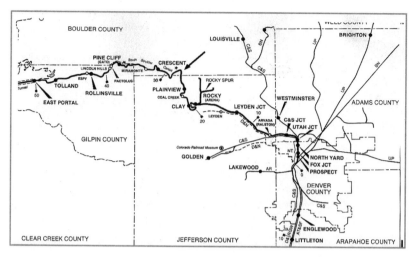

Tunnel 10 (arrow) is 27 miles west of Denver in Clear Creek Canyon. A pumper truck and four Denver firemen were transported to the remote site by flatbed railcars. Railroad crews backed trains down the line to Plainview to refill water tanks used in fighting the fire. (Courtesy of the Colorado Railroad Museum.)

ing powder], and the cans the powder came in are still rusting along the right-of-way."[9] The longer tunnels were dug by heavy machinery. At Tunnel 10, five electric drills were used to bore through its 1,561-foot length. More than 1,100 feet of the tunnel was lined with twelve-by-twelve-foot timbers.

Coal-burning, steam locomotives produced an abundance of red-hot cinders. It was not unusual for these cinders to start fires on the right-of-way or to ignite the creosoted timbers used to support tunnels. Speculating about the fire discovered in Tunnel 10 on September 20, 1943, Sheriff Arthur T. Everson of Boulder told the *Boulder Daily Camera* that the volume of rail traffic caused by the war had forced railroads to recommission older locomotives, ones without spark-arrester shields over their smokestacks,[10] but railroad workers, skeptical of Everson's knowledge of railroading, believed he was "talking out of turn," that it was doubtful there were any such engines on the rails.

At approximately 11 A.M. on Monday, September 20, locomotive No. 302, with engineer Ralph Vaughn at the throttle and pulling three-car passenger train No. 1, passed westbound (uphill) through Tunnel 10. Discovery of the fire happened in an almost offhand manner. Vaughn reported to his conductor, J. A. Pierson, in passing that he thought he had smelled smoke as his train went through the tunnel. The message was relayed to Bert Schneitman, a foreman in charge of a railroad bridge and building gang. At 12:20 P.M., Schneitman put a call in to general superintendent Al Johnson, a twenty-six-year veteran with the Denver & Salt Lake, telling him, "Mr. Johnson, this is Bert Schneitman at Quartz. Tunnel 10 is blazing like fury!" Johnson immediately ordered all trains on the main line halted.[11]

Schneitman also requested permission to dynamite the tunnel at both ends to smother the fire. Johnson and others, realizing that the railroad's route was the quickest way through the Rockies and a major link between vital shipping ports on both coasts, reacted quickly. "No! What do you want to do, shut the line down?" asked Johnson. The movement of wartime freight was vital; "the job of avoiding delays in the emergency was monumental."[12]

Closure of the line meant that trains would have to be routed to the Denver & Rio Grande trackage to the south through Pueblo and the Royal Gorge, adding 175 miles to the journey. The circuitous rerouting also would slow movement of livestock, including 110,000 head of sheep, which were unloaded from trains, penned near Rollinsville, west of Tunnel 10, then trucked to Denver.

Instead, Johnson ordered a stream of workers with tank cars, fire hose and other equipment, much of it from the tenant Denver & Rio Grande, to the site, but the fire had already made great headway and crews couldn't get close enough to be effective in extinguishing the flames. At the western end of the tunnel, which was thirty-one feet higher than the east end, the rising heat was so intense that workers couldn't get within two hundred feet of the tunnel mouth.

Schneitman, in desperation, made a second request to close the tunnel. Again he was turned down. A. E. "Al" Perlman, assistant to the president of the Denver & Salt Lake and chief engineer of the Denver & Rio Grande, denied the request because he believed the tunnel could be saved and the line kept open.

The railroads turned to the Denver Fire Department for help. Because the tunnel was inaccessible by road in 1943, Chief John F. Healy dispatched a pumper truck, one of the city's newest, from Engine Company 4 via a special train, which included a flat car for the pumper and four tank cars carrying eight thousand gallons of water each. Volunteers were enlisted to accompany the train to the scene. It was never made clear why the department took on such a task more than twenty-seven miles outside the city, but passing mention was made in *The Denver Post* that the fire was burning in an area near Gross Reservoir and could threaten the city's water supply.[13]

Four Denver firemen were chosen to accompany the pumper. Oldest among them was Douglas Parrish, 48, superintendent of the fire department's repair shops. Some of his fellow firefighters commented later that they were unsure why Parrish was selected other than for his skills as a mechanic. He was not an active fireman; his job at the fire was to pump fresh air in to the three men who entered the tunnel and to make sure the fire rig functioned properly.

Also chosen were firemen Jim Williams, 39, personal driver for Chief Healy, and Jack Kennedy, 37, both stationed at Company 8, and Captain William Parry. Only Parry came back alive.

Kennedy was a former Moffat Road employee. Andy Pitt, who worked as a fireman on the locomotive that hauled the pumper truck and water cars to the site, said:

> One of the Denver firemen (Kennedy) had worked on the Moffat and knew the engineer. He asked if he could ride the cab and help fire. I was kind of annoyed because I was young and liked to fire but I figured if he wanted to work I would have an easy trip. When we got to the tunnel it was just filled with smoke and fire. I had to stay on the engine because we were going to start making trips back to the Coal Creek tank to refill the water cars. We only made one trip because by then the firemen were dead.[14]

Shortly after it started, the fire was burning furiously, fueled by shifting winds blowing flames and acrid smoke through the tunnel. Sam Kusulas, section foreman for the Denver & Salt Lake stationed at Plainview, three and a half miles east of Tunnel 10, attempted without success to run a motor car through the tunnel from east to west in the first hours of the blaze. "The fire was ferocious," he told the *Rocky Mountain News.* "In some sections it spread to the ties supporting the track and warped the rails."[15]

Confined within the walls of the tunnel and fed by creosoted timbers and the changing mountain winds, the fire burned with a white-hot intensity. "Firemen were further handicapped by heat within the tunnel, so intense that rock was reduced to molten lava

*Firemen James Williams, Douglas Parrish and John Kennedy were trapped and died trying
to extinguish the blazing Tunnel 10. Kennedy's body was not recovered until November 21 and
Williams' on November 24. (Courtesy of* The Denver Post/Colorado Historical Society.)

and slag. Workmen were compelled to fight the blaze in 10-minute
shifts day and night, due to the blistering temperature of the tunnel's
rock walls."[16]

Because it had taken a while to round up equipment and crews,
the firemen and their equipment didn't leave Denver until 1:25 A.M.
on September 21. When they arrived at the tunnel about ninety minutes later, they found railroad workers seven hundred feet inside the
east portal, according to an account given by Parry the next day. He
told the *News:*

> *The air was clear and none of the men was wearing a mask.*
>
> *As the firemen prepared to take over, in an effort to prevent
> spread of the fire inside the tunnel—about five minutes after we
> arrived—the wind changed. Smoke began moving to the east tunnel
> entrance.*
>
> *Kennedy and Williams put on fire department masks, the only
> two we had with us. They took the hose inside the tunnel. Parrish
> and I fitted two old railroad masks and started into the tunnel. It
> was evident, immediately, that the masks were leaking and we came
> outside and refitted them.*
>
> *We went into the tunnel again but the masks didn't do the job.
> We tried to fix them with tape and started in again. Parrish and I*

were in about 100 feet or more when I said, "These masks leak, let's get out." Parrish said he wanted to stay a minute or two more. "Get out, damn it," I said, "or we won't make it." I staggered out into the air, but Parrish stayed behind.[17]

Parry's story didn't ring entirely true with his colleagues. Jack Jaynes, who joined the department in May 1941, said Parry became a pariah within the department after the Tunnel 10 incident. According to a story that circulated among firefighters, Parrish and Parry were close enough to their companions that they could see they were down, but Parry insisted on leaving the scene while Parrish pressed on in an attempt to rescue them.[18]

Williams and Kennedy were veterans of the department. Williams was hired on July 16, 1929, and Kennedy on October 16, 1928. To colleagues who knew them, that Williams and Kennedy waded into the dark, smoke-filled cavern, carrying hoses, was not a surprise, said ninety-four-year-old fireman Charlie Matty, who was hired by the department in 1927 and personally knew the men who died. Interviewed fifty-five years later, he said the two were competitive, particularly with each other. "Williams and Kennedy, it seemed like there was a little friction between the two, in this manner: If one thought he could do something, the other one says, 'I can do better.' One says, 'We'd better be going out,' the other says, 'Nah, we'll stay in, we'll go a little bit farther,' and that's what happened. They got in there too far and the air wasn't good enough for them, they passed out."[19]

As time went by and the two men didn't reappear, concern grew among those waiting outside the tunnel. "I think they was wanting to find out how far in anyone could go and work, and be safe," said Matty. "They were phoning back to Parrish, who was pumping the air [into] them through a hose and when they didn't come out, he called for help and went in."[20]

When Parrish didn't come out, G. E. Hamilton, a railroad worker, grabbed a mask and ran into the tunnel to find him. When Hamilton failed to return, other workers ran a short way into the smoke-filled tunnel to find him. Once inside, they stumbled across Hamilton, who was trying to make his way to fresh air. He said he had tried to drag Parrish from the tunnel but was forced to give up the rescue about one hundred feet from the entrance. Others found Parrish's body.

By midday on Tuesday, the day after the fire was discovered, rescue workers had given up hope of finding anyone alive in the tunnel. The fire, feeding on creosoted timbers, burned almost to the east portal, and workers reported that they could hear sounds of crashing timbers and rock as the tunnel fell in on itself. Beginning 306 feet from the east portal, debris fell from the sides and roof of the tunnel when the supports

THE FIRST NATIONAL FIRE PREVENTION WEEK WAS DESIGNATED OCTOBER 4–10, 1925, BY PRESIDENT CALVIN COOLIDGE. THE PREVIOUS YEAR, 15,000 LIVES WERE LOST TO FIRE IN THE UNITED STATES. NATIONAL FIRE PREVENTION WEEK IS STILL CELEBRATED EVERY OCTOBER.

burned away, creating heaps of rubble six to twenty feet deep.

In addition to severing the rail line, the cave-in entombed Kennedy and Williams. Kennedy's body was not recovered until 6 A.M. on November 21, two months after the fire. He was found 350 feet from the east portal, lying face down in water in a ditch along the tunnel's south wall. *The Denver Post* reported, "Although he was in a caved-in part of the bore, his body was not crushed. The clothing on his back was scorched by fire. Identification was established through papers found in his bunker trousers."[21]

Lying nearby was a helmet belonging to Williams, but no trace of his body was uncovered. It wasn't until three days later, at 5 P.M. on November 24, that workers discovered his body buried under tons of debris and rock in a ditch only ten feet from where Kennedy's body had been found.

A coroner ruled that Kennedy, Williams and Parrish all died of carbon-monoxide poisoning. Kennedy was survived by his wife, Marie, and three children: Jack, 10, Patricia, 8, and Larry, 4. Williams left behind a former wife, Martha, and a daughter, Joanne, 8. Parrish was survived by his wife, Adeline. Kennedy was buried at Mount Olivet Cemetery, Williams and Parrish at Fairmount Cemetery.

In an unseemly postscript to the tragedy, the families were denied survivors benefits because the Colorado State Industrial Commission ruled that the men had been killed outside the jurisdiction of the Denver Fire Department. Chief Healy, an irascible but popular head of the department, argued on behalf of the widows and their children.

After a series of hearings, William Reilly, chair of the commission, declared that the benefits would be paid "without further contest. Such denial was interposed pending a full investigation of the circumstances under which these firemen left Denver." A subsequent investigation, Reilly said, had determined that the men were "within the performance of their duties with the city and county of Denver."[22]

Joanne Williams was awarded $5,294 in a trust. Her mother, divorced from Williams, was paid $25 a month "for the sole use and benefit of Joanne." Adeline Parrish was awarded $60.76 a month and Marie Kennedy was awarded $43.31 a month. Each family also received $125 for funeral expenses and $500 for medical and hospital expenses. But Reilly warned, "This does not mean that in every case where firemen go outside the city limits of Denver to fight a fire that they, or their dependents, would be entitled to such benefits."[23]

Despite hopes that the railroad line could be kept open—repair estimates ranged from a few days to a few weeks—railroad officials reluctantly admitted defeat. Traffic of the Denver & Rio Grande was diverted via the Royal Gorge route to the south, and Denver & Salt Lake freight, passenger and mail service was trucked from Rollinsville to Denver. "In normal times," Edward T. Bollinger recorded in *Rails That Climb*, "the blockade would have been serious; in the middle of World War II it was an emergency."[24]

Cleanup crews dispatched to the scene two days after the fire began, including one hundred men called in from the Adams Tunnel on the Big Thompson Water Diversion Project, were hampered by lingering smoke and the colorless, odorless carbon-monoxide fumes from smoldering timbers that still glowed red-hot. Once they were able to enter the tunnel, workers found a major cave-in blocking the way about two hundred feet from the east portal. Generators, mucking machines and other equipment were obtained from construction firms, mines and municipalities in Colorado, Utah, Idaho and New Mexico.[25]

It was extremely dangerous work. A. E. Perlman, who later became president of the New York Central, wrote in his diary on October 27, 1943:

Slab of rock came down and broke five 3x10s on guniting platform [used to spray concrete on walls] immediately in front of operator;

cleaning off the entire platform except for the plank on which he was standing. No one injured. Later in day, Dumptor truck had stopped to allow another truck to pass, killed engine, and operator got off to crank machine. Just before he got back on, about a half-ton of rock came down from side wall of tunnel, demolishing operator's seat and steering wheel.[26]

A week after cleanup began, twelve workers narrowly escaped death when carbon monoxide, pushed by shifting mountain winds, swept over them. Two were transported to St. Joseph Hospital in Denver and the others were sent home after examination. All survived. From his oxygen tent at the hospital, Albert Neff, supervisor of work equipment for the Denver & Rio Grande, related what happened:

We were working about 275 feet from the east portal of the tunnel when an extreme shortness of breath warned us that the deadly carbon monoxide was in the air. We streaked for the east portal and had almost reached it when we found that two of the men had been overcome and left behind.

We went back after them and found them within a hundred feet of the [mucking] machine, luckily, because that was just about as close as you could get to the scene of operations and come back on your own legs.

We got the men who had been overcome out, half dragging, half carrying them, and brought them into St. Joseph's. I guess we're all all right now, but it was pretty close, and I guess we're just lucky.[27]

Cleanup continued via blasting and conveyor belts to haul the collapsed shoring, rock and other debris out of the tunnel. As part of the repair efforts, the walls of the tunnel, with the exception of six hundred feet of solid rock, were lined with concrete.

Predictions that the line, crucial to America's war effort, would reopen within two weeks proved wildly optimistic. A pioneer bore was dug through the debris on November 3, but it wasn't until December 1, 1943, nine weeks after the fire began, that the tunnel received its first train, which entered the east portal at 4:53 P.M. and emerged from the west portal at 5:07 P.M. That train was Denver & Salt Lake passenger train No. 1, the last train to pass through the tunnel before its closure. Normal service resumed the next day and "the worst crisis in the history of the line" was over.[28]

The former Denver & Salt Lake line, subsequently merged into the Denver & Rio Grande Western, now owned by the Union Pacific, continues to serve an important role today. It is used by UP and BN-SF freight trains, by The Ski Train to Winter Park and by Amtrak's California Zephyr. Travelers, tourists, skiers and railroad crews, however, find no memorial, no reminder of the deadly day in Tunnel 10, when Denver firefighters risked, and lost, their lives to keep America's war supplies moving.

NOT THE MOFFAT TUNNEL

Tunnel 10 of the Denver & Salt Lake Railway ... is not to be confused with the famous 6.2-mile Moffat Tunnel which pierces the Continental Divide 49.6 miles west of Denver.

Tunnel 10 is [1,573] feet long and is located at milepost 27.42 on the D&SL, which is commonly referred to as "The Moffat [Road]." The Moffat Tunnel is concrete-lined and reinforced with steel.

— *Trains* magazine
February 1944

"It Looked
Like Hell"

*A rescuer remembers how the victims of Elitch's Old
Mill ride looked as if they were sleeping. After the
blaze at the Denver amusement park, a fire inspector
brands the ride a fire hazard. A woman who saw the
fire first has no doubts about how it started. Still, a
coroner's jury can't pinpoint the cause.*

As their white American-LaFrance rescue truck turned the
corner at Twentieth and Curtis Streets, firemen Robert Hyatt
and Tom Kevil saw heavy grayish brown smoke billowing
150 feet into the air over Denver's northwestern skyline. They knew
something at Elitch Gardens was burning furiously, but as their rig
roared over the Twentieth Street viaduct, they argued about what
exactly it was.

"It's the Trocadero," offered Hyatt. "No, it isn't," returned Kevil.
"It's the theater." As the truck, driven by Sherwin Terry, reached
Thirty-eighth and Tennyson, just outside the historic amusement park,
it was directed by police and bystanders down Tennyson to Thirty-
sixth and Utica, to a back entrance to Elitch's. It was then that Hyatt
and Kevil saw what they had least expected—one of the park's oldest rides was alive with flames.[1] Before the fire was subdued and the
sun set on July 16, 1944, six people were dead and the Old Mill, a
ride that had brought laughter to thousands, was in ashes.

Unanswered questions still abound. Was the Old Mill ride safe?
Had four riders been sent to an avoidable yet certain death, after

Fire trucks arriving at the main entrance to Elitch Gardens at West Thirty-eighth Avenue and Tennyson Street on July 16, 1944, were directed by bystanders to a gate at West Thirty-sixth Avenue and Utica Street near the famed amusement park's Wildcat roller coaster. (Courtesy of The Denver Post.*)*

the fire had been discovered? Why did it take so long for the fire to be reported? And the most important question of all: What caused the blaze?

A coroner's inquest, held the Wednesday after the fire, called twenty-three witnesses and lasted six hours. Confronted with conflicting testimony about conditions in the Old Mill, the six-person jury could not reach a conclusion about the fire's origin. But a close reading of the words of witnesses in the 135-page coroner's report reveals the convergence of several factors: an aged facility, ignorance, neglect and carelessness.

It was, said one retired veteran of the fire department, the perfect combination for a devastating fire, just waiting for the right moment to erupt. Inadvertently, the tragedy ultimately had a positive side. Some twenty-five years later, one of those who fought the fire helped Denver institute one of the nation's strictest fire codes.

The Old Mill was a "dark ride," a tunnel of love, located just west of the carousel. Its patrons boarded small wooden flatboats and floated leisurely along a winding canal that carried them past lighted scenes of fairytale characters. Ironically, the Old Mill sat almost exactly on the site of a previous fire, an early-morning blaze in August 1914 that had destroyed a large pavilion housing a re-creation of the Civil War sea battle between the *Monitor* and the *Merrimac*.

Constructed in 1914, the Old Mill was rebuilt in 1928 and given an electrical facelift—new conduit to replace the antiquated and dangerous knob-and-tube wiring that had been strung through the original ride. By 1944, however, the Old Mill had again become dated, having received no other major renovation over the previous sixteen years. Some of the original wiring still existed even a dozen years after the 1928 remodeling.

An electrical contractor who had worked on the ride testified at the coroner's hearing that he made "a very good check and disconnected stuff that didn't look proper" two or three years before the fire and that some of the knob-and-tube still was in place then. But John Malpiede, Denver's chief electrician for thirty-five years, testified that he ordered conduit installed during the reconstruction in 1928, saying he "personally inspected to see that it had been done. Part of the old building remained ... and it had open wiring, and I insisted that [it] go into conduit."[2] Another witness testified that not only did old wiring remain, but that some of the small animated scenes were powered by wires spliced to extension cords, up to eight feet long, that snaked throughout the ride.

Fueled by wood construction and interior scenes made of painted canvas, muslin, papier mache and other flammable materials, the fire burned with a furious intensity within the two-hundred-foot-long building. "It was a terrible old, old building, a terrible hazard," recalled Frank Devine, a retired fire captain who was there that day. "I don't know why the city ever let them keep that thing open."[3]

The two couples who would die in the fire were thrown together by World War II. Army privates Robert McIlvain, 25, and Robert Jacobberger, 25, were new to town. Both were stationed at Buckley Field. McIlvain, who attended the University of Colorado in the late 1930s, enlisted in the army in June and was sent to Buckley, where he became buddies with Jacobberger. Mary McIlvain, 25, mother to a year-old son, arrived in Denver from the couple's home in Wichita, Kansas, on July 7. Maxine Jacobberger, 23, arrived from Omaha, Nebraska, on July 14, the Friday before the fire. She and Robert Jacobberger had been married in Los Angeles eighteen months earlier.

Part of a huge throng drawn to the park by a balmy summer Sunday, the foursome had decided to spend their day at Elitch's together. As the day of merriment waned into late afternoon, they stepped into a boat to begin the ride from which they would not return alive. A woman standing in line behind them noticed: "The back couple, when he got in, his wife didn't seem to want to step into the boat, and this man helped her, and then this young soldier, he reached up and helped her in the boat."[4]

Minutes later, barely halfway through the darkened ride all four were dead. Also killed were ride attendants Ed Lowery, 33, and George Keithline, 14, both of whom had rushed into the tunnel in a fruitless effort to rescue the four riders. All six deaths were attributed to carbon-monoxide poisoning.

One of the most tantalizing questions about the tragedy: Had the fire inside the narrow, twisting tunnel already been discovered when the soldiers and their wives began their ill-fated journey? Witnesses at the coroner's inquest were divided about what happened in the last few seconds before the Jacobbergers and McIlvains floated from sunlight into darkness.

Florence Cox, who had been waiting in line to board the ride, testified: "As I remember, after the boy (a 13-year-old attendant named Richard Cooper) told Mr. Lowery of the fire, [Lowery] pushed the boat into the tunnel and then he got into another boat and followed the death boat inside."[5] Cooper, however, who was thwarted by smoke and fire in his efforts to rescue those inside the ride, said at the hearing that no boats entered the tunnel after he told Lowery about the fire. "George Keithline and I ran to the entrance where our boss, Mr. Lowery, was standing," he testified. "He had just sent a boatload into the canal."[6]

A woman who may have been the first to notice the fire remembered it differently fifty years later at her home in Eaton, Colorado. Laurette Grimsley Collins was in a boat with her husband, two children and a friend when she saw the first flame. "We went, I would say, 25 feet [into the ride]. You went straight and then you went this way. When we came this way, I saw the fire. I heard a 'Shzzzz' sound. I looked up. It was burning. It was burning [horizontally] at the ceiling. In a matter of 30–40 seconds, it was burning fast. I said to 'Mom' (her former neighbor), 'There's a fire in here.' She said, 'I saw that. But with the kids there I didn't want to say anything.'"[7]

Collins also said it was she who alerted Cooper about the fire after she exited the ride. "I said to him — I didn't yell it, I didn't want anyone to panic—I said, 'Don't let that boat go in and you'd better stop that boat.' You could see the tail-end of a boat going around the corner. That kid ran and got to that boat and those people came running out of there. Two couples, white as ghosts. I never saw the boy again."[8]

Riders in two boats that preceded the Jacobbergers and McIlvains into the tunnel narrowly escaped the inferno, which quickly filled the Old Mill with acrid smoke. One group smelled smoke shortly after passing the first miniature scene. By luck, the foursome found a small rectangular opening on the side of the ride, just big enough to squeeze through. Army corporal William Kilbourne was in the boat just ahead of the Jacobbergers and McIlvains. "I heard a scream," he told the coroner's jury. "Someone hollered, 'Fire!' It was a woman. She said, 'Get us out of here, the place is on fire.' It became plain we had better get out as fast as possible or we'd all be lost. I knew we were not far from the exit of the tunnel, so we pushed out our boats as fast as we could."[9]

On June 15, 1994, one month before the fiftieth anniversary of the Old Mill fire, fireman Robert Hyatt died. The year prior to his death, while on a walking tour of the amusement park during its final summer at its North Denver location, he recalled vividly the events surrounding the fire. Hyatt worked on the fire rescue squad stationed at Twentieth and Curtis Streets, and his unit was one of the first to arrive. "When we got in there, there were people saying that there were a lot of people trapped in there. That's when we realized that it wasn't either of the places we thought; it was the Old Mill."[10]

As the fire burned at the front of the ride, firefighters worked to break open the building at the back to allow cool air in, to let smoke and superheated air out and to let crews put water on the flames. Unbeknown to any of them, the double doors they were working to break down would open on the exact spot where the riders and Keithline had perished.

The fire scene was chaotic, Hyatt recalled. "It's controlled madness when you first go into a deal like that because you know what you're supposed to do and the others are doing what they're supposed to do." The rescue crew immediately donned oxygen masks, he said. "I ran in with Tom Kevil and picked up a man and carried him out and laid him down and somebody helped him. Then I went back in and picked up a young lady and carried her out."[11] He would later carry another body out of the smoke and fire.

Firemen chopped open the back of the Old Mill to gain entrance to the dark ride. The bodies of two young couples were lying just inside two service doors that had been nailed shut to keep vandals out. The white-hot fire so totally consumed the building that a subsequent investigation could not determine a definite cause. (Courtesy of The Denver Post.*)*

Hyatt, who retired from the fire department as a captain in 1967, could not get over the fact that those who died "were never touched or burned by the fire. These people I picked up were sitting in a boat and they looked very normal. I was so amazed because this was the first time I'd ever seen somebody in the condition that she [one of the women] was in. She was not burned. She had a little pillbox hat on with lace and it wasn't burned at all. I can still see her dress. It was blue with white polka dots and she had a little hat to match. When I brought her out I laid her down on the tarp and put her head on her hand and turned her face toward her right side and started artificial respiration. We just assumed you could revive them. Then, after 20–30 minutes … " Hyatt wasn't sure how long he and others worked on the victims. "We tried everything to revive her and nothing worked. We gave up."[12]

But Hyatt's day wasn't done. When he, Kevil and others completed their search at the back of the building, some in the crowd gathered in front of the Old Mill wondered what had become of the man in charge of the ride. "They asked us to go all through the canals where the boats had been," said Hyatt. Despite the worsening blaze,

"Kevil and Terry and I walked through the canals and we didn't find anybody. We had all seen what appeared to be a tan or brown jacket floating on the water where the spare boats were kept, which was just off the side of the main canal. So we jumped down in there and I reached over to touch this jacket. It was flesh."[13]

An even greater shock awaited him. "I turned him over and it was Ed Lowery. I had known him so long, 10 years. It was a terrific shock. It was very sad for me." The two men had worked together at a mountain camp for disadvantaged city kids a decade before the fire. "He was a lovely fella. Very calm and very nice and all the kids liked him."[14]

SOME STATISTICS ABOUT
FIRE IN THE UNITED STATES:

* ABOUT 100 FIREFIGHTERS
  ARE KILLED EACH YEAR
  IN DUTY-RELATED
  INCIDENTS.
* FIRE IS THE THIRD
  LEADING CAUSE OF
  ACCIDENTAL DEATH IN
  THE HOME.
* DIRECT PROPERTY LOSS
  DUE TO FIRES IS
  ESTIMATED AT $8.5
  BILLION ANNUALLY.
* IN 1995, COLORADO HAD
  THE FIFTH LOWEST DEATH
  RATE PER CAPITA. HAWAII
  WAS THE LOWEST AND
  MISSISSIPPI THE HIGHEST.

—UNITED STATES FIRE
ADMINISTRATION

The first fire equipment arrived at Elitch's from Thirty-eighth Avenue and Osceola Street, a few blocks away, less than five minutes after the alarm had been called in at 4:58 P.M. It was already too late. "We had trouble getting in the gate at Thirty-eighth and Wolff," remembered Jack Franklin, a retired fireman who was with Company 12 in July 1944. "There was a key that was to open the gate but it didn't work real well."[15]

Once inside, firefighters found that there was only one hydrant in the park, meaning hoses had to be laid from outside the park and pulled toward the fire. "We had to get water clear from Thirty-eighth," recalled Jack Jaynes, who was at that time working out of Station 5 on Nineteenth Street between Larimer and Market in downtown Denver. "There was a big fountain just east of the theater entrance and the Trocadero dance hall. We couldn't lay beyond that; the buildings got in the way. Fortunately, we had the assistance of a lot of soldiers who were there.

"People were flocking up there to see it. We had to yell, 'Get out of the way!' The GIs were more mentally alert. They asked, 'Can we help?' We said, 'Grab ahold!'" Some of the water lines stretched eight hundred feet or more. "We had pulled everything we had on the wagon so we had enough to reach."[16]

Lillian Lally was a young working mother assigned to the Old Mill's ticket booth, located in front of the ride beside the large water wheel that drove the water through the canals. There was no warning of trouble, she remembered. "That was the funny part. There was no commotion, no nothing. It seemed like all of a sudden there was smoke and fire. It was an arch of flame."[17]

Witnesses said the fire was out of control in a matter of minutes. By the time fire crews arrived, smoke and flames were emerging from beneath the eaves of the building. Fifteen minutes later, the entire structure was engulfed. "It was pretty well going," remembered Franklin. "In fact, there wasn't a helluva lot you could do. All you could do was open up where you thought it was."[18]

"It looked like hell in there, everything boiling," said Jaynes, who arrived on a second alarm. "Just solid flame. It was coming out the entrance. We'd hit that with our line and push it back, then it would come out the exit. So we'd move over and hit that. The guy who was pumping [water] to us was really giving us pressure … and it pushed me back against a brick wall. It was so hot it blistered my back through my bunking coat, that heavy canvas, and a shirt and an undershirt. We were back 25 feet and the heat was enough to blister Frank [Devine's] face. It was hot!"[19]

In the confusion that followed, some spectators ran toward the fire while others, fearful that it would spread to adjoining buildings, ran away. The Blue Barron Orchestra, playing a matinee at the Trocadero Ballroom nearby, continued to play, hoping to calm the crowd.

Myrle Wise, a firefighter for forty-four years and chief for sixteen years before he retired in 1986, had been with the department barely a year when he was called to the Old Mill fire as a member of Company 6. Even half a century after the fire, he puzzled over apparent delays, between the time the fire was discovered and the first alarm, and between the first alarm and the second and third alarms. "The first-alarm companies were probably there within five minutes." But, he added, "I would say it … was 10 or 15 minutes before a second alarm was even pulled on the fire."[20]

Spectators on the Elitch Gardens midway crowded closer to get a better view of the flames from the Old Mill ride, impeding the progress of firefighters, some of whom had to drag hoses from Thirty-eighth Avenue, halfway across the park, to bring water to the blaze. (Courtesy of The Denver Post.*)*

The tinder-dry Old Mill ride, constructed in 1914, was engulfed by flames when firefighters arrived. The interior of the "dark ride" was crammed with flammable materials, including painted canvas, muslin and papier mache. Fire officials were criticized for their lax handling of the amusement park's annual inspections. (Courtesy of The Denver Post.*)*

According to contemporary newspaper accounts, Assistant Chief Guy Walker turned in a second alarm before his car entered the amusement park. He was quoted as saying, "In order for the fire to get that head start, there must have been some delay in turning in the alarm."[21] Devine, too, was sure there was a delay. "There was a great delay. The man in charge of the ride grabbed a fire extinguisher and got into a boat, the cashier grabbed the register and took off. Nobody thought to report the fire."[22]

Wise recalled, "When we got there, we were ordered to ventilate (cut open the building) so the hose crews could get in and get the lines on the fire. In the process of ventilating, we had opened up a place where it looked like there might have been a couple of doors at one time. Chopping them down and prying them open, we found that there were four bodies that we could see immediately."[23]

The grisly discovery had a lasting effect on Wise, so much so that one of the first actions he took when he became chief in 1970 was to order the formalizing of a stringent city fire code. "I don't think anybody could go through that without it changing their thinking. Up until that time we just took [inspections] for granted. We would look at the extinguisher and see if it had been recharged. Check the exit lights and see they're burning and if the exit doors were working. This type of thing is about all we did. Back in those days, we didn't have a fire code; we were the only major city of that size that didn't have one. We worked for years to come up with one of the best fire codes in the country, even by today's standards."[24]

Even if there had been a code at the time, it may not have helped. Inspections were often little more than courtesy calls. Assistant Chief Patrick J. Boyne, who joined the Denver Fire Department in 1897, was in charge of the five-person Fire Prevention Bureau in 1944 but admitted at the coroner's inquest that he hadn't been to Elitch's in twenty-five years. Confronted with the testimony of others at the hearing, he termed the building "a fire hazard" but said he had never taken steps to shut it down. Asked how regular inspection had failed to show the ride was a hazard, he replied, "I guess it was because the Old Mill had been approved so many years that no one thought about disapproving it."[25]

Even the city's chief building inspector could not recall at the hearing whether a certificate of occupancy was ever issued for the Old Mill. "From what I know now," L. G. Webber told jurors, "I would not have

The charred interior of the Old Mill surrounded the waterway (center), which carried riders in small boats past a series of nursery-rhyme scenes. Once inside, there was no way out until the boats exited on the opposite side. (Courtesy of The Denver Post.*)*

issued it. I don't believe the building was safe because of its type of construction, because of its arrangement, its exits."[26]

In fact, there were no marked emergency exits. Once patrons were inside the labyrinth, they were committed until their boat came out of the tunnel at the end of the ride. Raymond Cothran, a maintenance worker for Elitch's, said he was "quite familiar" with the ride and testified that the only doors out of the Old Mill were a pair of service doors at the back of the ride and that they were nailed shut to keep out vandals.[27]

What caused the fire? An electrical short? A discarded cigarette? Arson? Never determined. The destruction of the building was so complete that there was little left to inspect. The day of the fire, park officials told investigators that they believed the blaze had been started by a cigarette pitched into the darkness by someone on the ride. They maintained this position throughout the hearing. John Sack, Elitch's superintendent of operations, told the jury that the Old Mill had been inspected by the Fire Prevention Bureau just a week before the fire. "There were no problems other than oily rags, which were cleaned up."[28]

Elitch Gardens owner Arnold Gurtler said he was "positive [the cause] wasn't defective wiring" because the wiring had been inspected in the spring. There was, he added, very little wiring in the ride. "We didn't burn much electricity. Dim lighting was part of the entertainment."[29]

Nevertheless, several witnesses, some of whom escaped the fire only minutes before it erupted into a full-fledged inferno, claimed they had seen a small area of flame no bigger than a human hand near the ceiling. Laurette Grimsley Collins was certain what started it. "It was above all the decorations," she said in 1994. "Somebody would have had to have a sling shot to get a cigarette up there. I saw where the fire started. It could not have been a cigarette. The fitz and sizzle, that's what caused me to look up. It was the electricity that caused the fire."[30]

After deliberating for just twenty-five minutes, the jury reached its conclusion: Although the Old Mill was clearly a fire hazard, it was impossible to untangle the contradictory testimony of the witnesses and pinpoint the cause with any certainty.[31]

In the aftermath were the inevitable lawsuits. Lawyers for seven-year-old Robert Jacobberger (Jr.), the son of Private Robert Jacobberger by a previous marriage, sought $5,000, claiming negligence on the part of Elitch's. He was awarded $2,500 in Denver District Court.[32] Leona Keithline, whose fourteen-year-old son, George, died trying to rescue the four passengers killed on the ride, sought $75,000, claiming that the ride was "a fire trap" and that her son continued to work at the park after she had told Elitch officials she didn't want him working there because he was too young. The suit was settled before it reached court.[33] Based on the findings of the coroner's jury, the district attorney's office chose not to file any charges against Elitch's.[34]

Ed Lowery, the would-be hero who rushed into the burning ride with a fire extinguisher, was buried at Mount Olivet Cemetery near Golden. He left behind his wife, Margaret, who never remarried, and two children, ages three and one. According to Lowery's son, Ed (Jr.), "One of the things my mother said more than a few times was that shortly after she had gone down to ID my father's body, someone from Elitch's showed up with a form, some legal stuff. She signed something. It turned out to be a release on the part of Elitch's. Without thinking about what had happened, she talked to an attorney about getting some money for the funeral or for the children. He looked into it and said there was nothing that could be done."[35]

Chapter Ten

"Go Where the Smoke Is"

An electrical short and Valentine's Day dance decorations combine to create an inferno at the Denver Athletic Club. A man at the window, signaling for help, draws pleas from the crowd. A newspaper photographer, following the smoke, captures the defining moment on film. Three firemen, looking for survivors, barely escape death in a stalled elevator. In the aftermath, officials blame the devastation on an eight-minute delay in reporting the fire.

The man signaled frantically from a fourth-floor window. As yellowish gray clouds of smoke swirled around him, he tried without success to attract the attention of the crowd gathered below. Finally, in desperation, he waved his soft, gray hat, hoping firefighters would come to his rescue.

"Why the hell don't they do something?" one bystander asked. Trying to find firm footing on six inches of ice in the alley behind the building, firefighters strained to raise a heavy, fifty-foot wooden ladder to the window while carefully avoiding telephone and high-voltage electrical wires crisscrossing the alley like a spider's web. "Then, suddenly," *The Denver Post's* reporter wrote, "the man's hand relaxed. The hat dropped straight, brushed against the wires and tumbled to the alley. There was nothing but smoke at the window. 'He's gone,' someone said."[1]

Rocky Mountain News *photographer Bill Peery snapped the defining picture of the 1951 blaze at the Denver Athletic Club. Dr. Dan Monaghan (left) and J. Charles Wild tried to escape smoke pouring from the club. Faced with a difficult choice, firefighters rescued Monaghan first, and Wild died of smoke inhalation. (Bill Peery collection.)*

There would be no last-minute rescue. Exhausted and overcome by smoke, J. Charles Wild, a fifty-five-year-old retired businessman who lived at the club, sank out of sight to become one of four persons killed in the three-alarm, $1.5-million fire at the city's historic and exclusive Denver Athletic Club (DAC), 1325 Glenarm Place, on Saturday, February 17, 1951.

The DAC began in 1884 in an old church building with six members. On the club's first board of directors were William R. Rathvon, Harry C. Gray, John Elitch Jr., Charles Wheeler, Frank H. Wright and George F. Higgins, who pledged themselves to the advancement of "amusement, recreation and physical culture." The DAC immediately became a gathering place for the city's well-heeled and well-connected. Though it today covers a full block of Glenarm between Thirteenth and Fourteenth Streets, the club grew through a series of expansions, the first in 1890 when it moved to its present location. In 1926 the club opened a $425,000 addition, including the spacious gymnasium that would become the scene of one of the city's most spectacular and most potentially holocaustic fires.

Dozens of residents and employees were trapped in the smoke-filled club in the 1951 blaze. Dr. Menifee Howard, an oral surgeon who lived on the club's fourth floor, tried to flee out the door of his room but was almost bowled over by a blast of smoke and hot air. Instead, he went to a window and stuck his head outside for ten or fifteen minutes, awaiting rescue. "Finally," he told *The Post,* "a fireman knocked at the door. He had a mask and led me by the hand to the elevator. The elevator operator carried me to the main floor."[2]

Four maids were caught in a fifth-floor linen room. After her rescue, Delicia Baca told bystanders:

We were working on the fifth floor. I heard the fire—a crackling sound. We came out of the room into the little volleyball room. It was full of smoke. It hurt my eyes. We tried to go downstairs but there was too much smoke. The elevator wasn't running. We went back into the room. We put a table under the window. I crawled up on the table and tried to open it. Three times I fell off. I hit my head. Then the firemen came. They crawled down in. They took us out one at a time. They pushed us out of the window and carried us down the ladder.[3]

Though others were saved, Wild, the man at the window, was the unlucky victim of a "Hobson's Choice"—a choice that has a negative outcome no matter which decision is made. This particular choice was forced on the firefighters, who had to choose between Wild and another trapped man.

Ira Tanner Jr. and his brother-in-law, Dr. Dan Monaghan, were playing badminton in the club's fourth-floor gymnasium when the fire erupted in the ballroom two floors below them. Tanner (who still practices law in Denver today), recalled in 1998 that he and Monaghan were alerted to the fire by three club maids. "They kept saying, 'The place is on fire!' Dan opened the door by which we had come in and said, 'We're trapped! The smoke is so heavy we can't get out.' He said, 'Let's get down on our hands and knees and go to the window.' We said to the gals, 'You'd better follow us.' They were panicked and refused to move so Dan said to them, 'Take off your clothes and put them under this door.' At least one of those girls died. We never saw any flames but there was unbelievable smoke."[4]

Six inches of ice, a narrow alley and a spider web of live wires overhead made it difficult for firemen to raise unwieldy 300-pound, 50-foot wooden ladders. (Courtesy of The Denver Post.*)*

Tanner and Monaghan exited a fourth-story window, where Tanner slid down a drain pipe to safety, his brother-in-law behind, balancing precariously halfway outside, halfway inside the window. Attempting to raise three-hundred-pound, fifty-foot ladders in the narrow, ice-covered alley and hemmed in by wires, firemen realized that they only would be able to rescue Monaghan and Wild one after the other, not at the same time. They chose Monaghan first.

Jim Jordan, driver of Company 6's aerial truck, was the fireman who climbed the ladder to rescue Monaghan, despite the unsteady conditions in the alley. He recalled in a 1998 interview:

> *There was rutted ice and we were trying to get [the ladder] on a firm footing. Every time I went up one rung that sonofabitch was [moving sideways]. And [Monaghan] was telling me he was going to jump. I said, "If you do, you'll kill us both."*
>
> *As soon as we got [Monaghan] down we moved the ladder over and went up to get [Wild] and he had fallen inside. I leaned in as far as I could—you couldn't see anything—and felt around near the window. He wasn't there. We found out later he had been clear out of the building, forgot his billfold and went back into the building to get his money, and he died.[5]*

Two weeks after the blaze, city safety manager Harold MacArthur explained the incident publicly:

> *Due to the direction of the fire and smoke, it was necessary to make evacuations from the alley side. Life nets could not be used as this alley carries electrical wires on alley fixtures. Some of these wires carry as much as 4,000 volts and clearance between the DAC and the alley fixtures carrying these wires is about three feet. The order of evacuation was so made because it appeared that the one initially evacuated (Dr. Monaghan) was in the much more precarious situation. It was honestly felt that this individual might jump because the smoke and noxious fumes about his window were terrific.[6]*

The most enduring image of the fire was one that appeared the following day on the front page of the *Rocky Mountain News*. A full-page photo taken by photographer Bill Peery showed Wild and Monaghan at windows less than twenty feet apart, waves of smoke washing over them. Peery captured the plight of the two men in a single frame. In 1998 he said:

Harry Rhoades (another long-time News *photographer) always said, "Go where the smoke is," so that's what I did. I went around to the alley side of the building and there was this man, hanging out of the window. [Firemen] went to put up a ladder to him, but there was ice in the alley and they couldn't get a secure hold. Dr. Monaghan was trying to reach the drain. I changed the speed on my camera because I figured that pipe would break away and he would fall. The other guy was there in the smoke. For awhile, he was all right. Finally, he took his hat off and threw it down and I took the picture. I could see the smoke engulf him but the firemen couldn't get a ladder to him.[7]*

Though four people died of smoke inhalation, the miracle of the day was that less than five hours separated a sad event from being a catastrophe of holocaustic proportions. February 17, 1951, was unusually warm, with temperatures in the high forties—the kind of thaw that sometimes visits Denver in the dreary heart of winter. Inside the historic six-story structure, the oldest, central part of which was built in 1896 with its facade facing Glenarm Place, the ballroom was gaily decorated in red and white streamers in anticipation of the club's annual Valentine's Day dance that evening. More than four hundred guests were expected to attend and dance to the music of the Vern Byers Orchestra.

At 3 P.M., employees were finishing party preparations in the large, second-floor ballroom when a spark from an electrical short in the sound system ignited unfireproofed drapes, which burst into flame and ignited strands of red and white crepe paper. "The flames traveled like a deadly monkey in jungle vines," wrote *Post* reporter Bob Stapp. "Then the burning streamers fell on dining tables arranged on the floor below for the evening dinner party. Table cloths began to flame and it was only minutes before the blaze was out of control."[8]

Robert Davis and David Hall, waiters at the club, were first to spot the fire. "I was in the gym when this short developed in the wire leading to the loudspeaker," Hall told the *News*. "I ran for a fire extinguisher but by the time I got back, there was no chance of putting

The Denver Athletic Club ballroom was decorated for a Valentine's Day dance when an electrical short ignited paper streamers and, in a matter of minutes, sent flames racing up open stairwells to the attic. Four hundred revelers were expected at the dance, which was scheduled to begin five hours after the fire started. (Courtesy of The Denver Post.*)*

out the flames." Davis added, "I was in the gym with Dave and saw it start. He hurried but once those flames caught on there wasn't any stopping them. We did all we could and then we had to get out of the way of the fire."[9]

Herman Robinson, a third waiter, was unable to find an extinguisher because they were hidden behind draperies, which covered three walls of the gym. He was forced to search for one elsewhere. By the time he returned, the room was engulfed in flames.

Shortly after the first alarm was called in at 3:08 P.M., the first fire units, Pumper 1 and Truck 1, arrived from a station only a block away. Chief Allie Feldman called in a second alarm at 3:20 P.M., and then a third at 3:48 P.M. Other, single pieces of equipment were "specialed in" to fight the blaze. Ultimately, eighteen fire apparatuses and one hundred firemen would battle the fire for almost three hours.

Heavy smoke from the three-alarm fire at the Denver Athletic Club, 1325 Glenarm Place, drew curious onlookers from all over the metro area on Saturday, February 17, 1951. If one could find a space, parking was only 20 cents an hour at Bob's lot. (Courtesy of The Denver Post.*)*

Smoke choked the hallways and rooms of the historic club. Captain Murray Wolz of Engine 6 told reporters, "I was one of the first firemen in the building. ... Six of us went with hoses up the back stairs to the fourth floor. It was a flaming holocaust. We could keep the fire away from ourselves but we couldn't push it back. It was tougher than hell up there.

"By the time we got to the fourth floor, the fire already had gone out through the roof. This is the roughest one I've been on for a long, long time."[10]

The blaze was so intense that it trapped three firemen inside an elevator, nearly claiming their lives. After leading Monaghan to safety, Jordan went back to the front of the club on Glenarm Place, where he and two other firemen, Bud Antonio of Company 10 and Captain Hugh Duggan of Company 1, were ordered to take the elevator to the fifth floor and look for anyone who might still be alive. Recalled Jordan:

Duggan had a bunker coat on and no mask, Antonio had on an all-service mask and bunker coat and I had no mask or a coat.

We got up to the fifth floor and opened that door of the elevator and it was like looking into hell; the fire was right there. We shut the door and it didn't latch so we had to open it again and slam it shut. Duggan is working the controls of the elevator and we don't go no place; the controls were burnt out.

There was an elevator inspection card on the inside, a cardboard card, it was on fire and the paint was burning on the top of the elevator. Duggan is a very devout Catholic; he's been a fireman for, oh, hell, he had to have 22, 23 years on the job then and one of the best damned firemen I ever run into. He's down on his knees, praying. He said, 'We're dead. We ain't goin' nowhere. We're going to die.' Well, I told Antonio, I said, 'Throw Duggan's bunker coat over his head and we'll go out and see if we can make it to a window down the hall or someplace' because I wasn't going to die in that elevator.[11]

The three men prepared to make a dash through the flames.

"I just started to put Duggan's coat over him and I told Bud to open the door and [the elevator] starts down," continued Jordan. "A brand new kid on the job, he was still on probation, by the name of Jerry Sloan was working at [Station 1]. I don't think he had been on the job a month. He's walking through the basement and, force of habit, went by the elevators and punched the buttons. That was the only thing that brought us down."[12]

News photographer Morris Engle, who followed a firefighter into the burning building in hopes of capturing some of the drama on film, described his experience: "I thought I might get a picture of the many rescue operations going on inside the building. The building was filled with smoke and confusion. I … went into a room that must have been the ballroom. I opened the door and saw the entire ceiling of the room on fire. Then I guess a backdraft came. I heard a whoosh and the whole ceiling fell down. That's when I got out as fast as I could."[13] He recalled in a 1998 interview that the man he followed into the building was Chief Feldman. "Why the hell he would be in there, I don't know. When he saw me, he said, 'You sonofabitch, I told you not to come in here!'"[14]

Carl Bartz, who lived on the fourth floor near Wild, told a *News* reporter, "I was in shorts and had just finished taking a bath. I ran to the door and smoke began to pour through. The hall was filled with smoke. I saw flames shoot up through the ventilator in the room when I went back to get more clothes. I pulled on a pair of trousers and got out."[15]

At 4 P.M., a muffled explosion rattled the building. A section of the north wall blew out, showering bricks and mortar down on the Variety Club building at 1345 Glenarm Place. A huge bulge appeared in the DAC wall and it appeared that the DAC would crush its smaller neighbor, but the wall held fast. The Variety Club, however, was destroyed by an arson fire on November 21, 1953. In the 1920s, the Variety Club drew a measure of fame as the local headquarters of the Ku Klux Klan.

Chief Feldman, calling the blaze "one of the toughest I've ever had to fight," said his men poured an estimated six hundred thousand gallons of water on the fire.[16] "That Glenarm entrance looked like Niagara Falls," said Stan "Smokey" Sorenson, who spent twenty-five years in the fire department and was at the scene in 1951, having been called to duty on his day off. "There was a lot of water coming out. I don't think you could have walked through that front door. But when you've got a fire like that was there, when the whole damned six floors of the building was burning, you're going to use a lot of water and it's going to go somewhere. Water's going to find its way down."[17]

By 5:45 P.M., the DAC fire was whipped, but firefighters lingered, searching the smoldering ruins for additional victims and guarding against flare-ups. Sorenson said he was there until 2 A.M. Two decades later, he solved a mystery that had nagged him for years:

I don't know why I stuck around so long but several of us got to prowling the building, checking for hot spots, and we heard there was a lot of liquor down in the vault. Somebody said, "Go get a jump for us." It was all ruined anyway; it was all a write-off. Boy, the guys, they hauled it out, all right. I put a case in my car, which was parked in the triangle area where Colfax and Tremont and Thirteenth come together. I carried that up there and put it away and locked the car. It got stolen. And, years later, I was talking about that one night and one of my detective friends, Jack Hurlbut, said, "Was that your car, that old two-tone gray Chevrolet, four-door sedan?" I said, "Yeah." He said, "You forgot to lock one door on your sedan. I got your goddamned scotch."[18]

The eight-minute delay between the time Davis and Hall saw the fire and the time the first call was made to the fire department turned out to be monumental. Assistant Chief James Cain said the day after the fire, "There was something wrong. All fires start small except flash fires and those are caused by explosions. This was neither—yet it had roared out of control by the time we got there."[19]

The antiquated construction of the fifty-five-year-old central portion of the club provided the fire with fuel and ventilation. The DAC was near the end of a $200,000 renovation, part of which involved enclosing open staircases, but the work was incomplete. An open stairwell led up to the gym, where double doors left open provided the fire with plenty of oxygen. The building had no air-conditioning, but eight ventilators opened into the sixth-floor attic, acting like chimneys to carry smoke and noxious fumes up through the building to the roof. Fire doors prevented the blaze from spreading to an addition erected in 1926.

An estimated one hundred members, guests and employees were in the club when the fire broke out. When they poured out the front doors onto Glenarm, they were greeted by thousands of spectators. (*The Post*'s first, improbable estimate was one hundred thousand people, which would have been one-fourth of Denver's population at the time.) Even the *News*'s more conservative estimate of twenty-five thousand was too high, some witnesses said. There were plenty of amateur photographers, attracted by a pillar of smoke that soared two hundred feet into the air; eighteen fire apparatuses; and a dozen ambulances, summoned in anticipation of a high death and injury toll. Sixty police officers were dispatched to rope off streets around the club for two blocks in all directions.

Open stairwells in the fifty-five-year-old section of the Denver Athletic Club allowed smoke and flames to reach the six-story building's attic, and the fire broke through the roof in a matter of minutes. Despite heavy damage, the building's Glenarm Place facade is still there. (Courtesy of The Denver Post.*)*

Across Glenarm, the venerable Denver Press Club, hangout for the city's newspaper types, gave victims refuge and a vantage that allowed them to watch the fire and firefighters through the club's front windows. As the blaze wound down late in the afternoon, a group of five "distinguished-looking" gentlemen, residents of the DAC, sat at the bar, discussing where they would spend the evening. After a few cocktails, they decided to board an airplane for Las Vegas, Nevada, and quarter at the Flamingo Hotel. When last seen, they were in a cab, headed for Stapleton Airport.[20]

In addition to Wild, 55, those killed in the fire were members John McGinley King, 65, and Ernest D. Bowman, 55, and club maid Mrs. Jane "Jennie" Meade, 63. Fourteen others, including seven firemen, were taken to area hospitals, most suffering from smoke inhalation.

The toll might have been higher had it not been for the heroic efforts of elevator operators D. B. Sanchez, 74, and W. W. Woodling, 60, who made repeated trips up and down five stories through heavy smoke. "I must have made 30 to 40 trips to get people out," Sanchez said. "I stayed as long as I could until the firemen ordered me out."[21] Sanchez and Woodling stayed conscious by tying wet handkerchiefs around their faces while they ran the elevators. The club's two switchboard operators, Charlotte Swiers and Peggy Miller, stayed at their board and called the seventy-five rooms on the upper floors to alert tenants, about half of whom were permanent guests.

One of the hospitalized firemen was Leroy Newton of Station 11. He said in a 1998 interview:

> We had a crew on the third floor and you could see the basement and the sky. All there was was hallway through there; both sides were gone, so we were fortunate that we didn't lose some firemen there. The main detriment was that we didn't have the equipment they have now. We didn't have oxygen masks. We had masks that you couldn't breath in. You start puffing, you couldn't get enough air through them; they'd come right off. They were no good. I was roaming around, lost, full of monoxide. They were sticking pins in me for 10 hours because I had no feelings in my legs. I was in the hospital for ten days with monoxide poisoning, laryngitis, chronic bronchitis.[22]

Immediately after the fire, Mayor Quigg Newton asked for reports from Chief Feldman, Assistant Chief Cain, police captain Walter "Bud" Johnson, acting police chief Rugg Williams, police surgeon Dr. Harry Goldman and director of health and hospitals Dr. James Dixon. Newton's questions focused on whether the fire department's actions had been sufficient in fighting the blaze and whether any city ordinances had been violated in the building.

Safety manager Harold MacArthur concluded in his investigation that the eight-minute delay in calling the fire department and fast-burning draperies were the primary factors in the escalation of the DAC blaze. Firefighters who entered the building after the fire was out reported finding eight to ten empty extinguishers, apparently used in a vain attempt to beat back the flames. In his report to Mayor Newton, MacArthur recommended that city ordinances be changed to prohibit hanging of draperies and decorations in all places of public assembly, and that the public be urged to call the fire department immediately in the event of a fire. He also called for the city's police and fire departments to be equipped with walkie-talkie radios.[23] His report to the mayor concluded:

Within a matter of minutes, this fire spread completely around the gym and heat generated by the rapidly burning draperies and decorations traveled upward and through eight ceiling grills into the cockloft under the roof. It then mushroomed, spreading horizontally in all directions. ... An open stairway adjacent to the involved gymnasium contributed to the rapid spread of the heat and noxious fumes into the upper floors where the loss of life occurred.[24]

The club was not cited for any code violations (an inspection report in July 1950 pronounced the building to be in good condition, though it made no mention of either the draperies or the ventilating system), but George McCormack, city building inspector, reported that the DAC was rated a type 3 (non–fire resistant) structure. A building code instituted in 1949 required that all new downtown buildings be type 1 (solid masonry construction with nonflammable walls, floors and ceilings). Still, this problem was endemic to downtown Denver, where more than 160 of its older hotels still had a type 3 rating in 1951. "There's nothing we can do about the older structures except gradually enforce a program of eliminating such hazards as open stairwells and other factors that might contribute to fire."[25]

Later, MacArthur told the *News*, "We firmly believe that had there been no delay in conveying the alarm ... and [had] the ceiling ventilation grilles ... not transmitted the heat and fire into the cockloft area, the first alarm companies could have confined the fire to the gymnasium and extinguished it."[26]

VICTIMS IN THE DENVER ATHLETIC CLUB FIRE
February 17, 1951

Dead

Ernest D. Bowman, 55, club member, smoke inhalation

John McGinley King, 65, club member, smoke inhalation

Mrs. Jane "Jennie" Meade, 63, club maid, smoke inhalation

J. Charles Wild, 55, club member, smoke inhalation

Injured

Violet Asbury, 29, club maid, smoke inhalation, treated and
released

Delicia Baca, 44, club maid, smoke inhalation, treated and
released

John T. Black, 24, fireman, smoke inhalation, treated and
released

Dr. Henry French, 58, smoke inhalation, treated and
released

James Garner, 27, fireman, smoke inhalation, treated and
released

Howard W. Gifford, 39, fireman, cut hand, treated and
released

Wilhelmina Grimm, 67, club maid, smoke inhalation,
hospitalized

Frank Hoffman, 81, club member, smoke inhalation,
treated and released

Karl Loose, 51, fireman, heart attack, hospitalized

Walter Lydon, 65, club member, smoke inhalation, treated
and released

Leroy Newton, 36, fireman, severe smoke inhalation,
hospitalized

Leonard Shire, 35, fireman, first- and second-degree burns,
hospitalized

Ruth Walker, 38, club maid, smoke inhalation, treated and
released
Harry Worl, 31, fireman, first-degree burns, hospitalized

—The Denver Post
February 18, 1951

Chapter Eleven

"GOD WILL TAKE CARE OF HIS CHILDREN"

When the pilot of United Flight 859 reports difficulties with the plane's hydraulic system, the crippled airliner is put on "stand-by" rather than "panic" status. Attempting its landing at Denver's Stapleton Field, the plane skids out of control and bursts into flame. The airport fire station responds, but is understaffed and underequipped for jet-age aircraft. Sixteen passengers die in the fireball. The city immediately adds more equipment and firefighters to its airport station.

The first hint of trouble came from the pilot eighty-three minutes before United Air Lines Flight 859 touched down at Stapleton Field on July 11, 1961.

"We have a hydraulic problem and we'd like to hold in the vicinity of Strasburg [Colorado] until we check it out, and I'll keep you advised," radioed John Grosso, the flight's pilot and captain. "We'll maintain 14,000 [feet]. Once we check it out, we'd like to come right on in."

The airport tower queried Grosso, "What is the nature of your hydraulic trouble? Is it [landing] gear trouble?"

Grosso responded, "859 has lost [hydraulic] fluid, and I gotta check it out to see whether we're going to have a complete loss or whether it will be just partial."[1]

At 10:43 A.M., as the sixty-ton aircraft glided above the clouds over the plains of eastern Colorado, Grosso radioed again and asked to talk with the United dispatcher. "This is Grosso and we've lost our hydraulic fluid at the present time, and it looks like we'll be over Denver in about 35 minutes. So when we get over Denver, why, we'll see whether we have an abnormal situation or whether it's gonna be an emergency."[2]

At 11:27 A.M., approximately ten minutes from landing, Grosso got on the intercom to reassure the 122 passengers aboard his DC-8, which had originated in Philadelphia with stops in Chicago and Omaha. "We are experiencing hydraulic trouble and rescue equipment is standing by. We will make an emergency landing. Do not be alarmed. There is nothing to worry about." Some were not reassured. Morris Cutler, 81, of Sunland, California, warned his wife, Nettie, 78, "I know what that means. Hydraulic failure means we haven't got any brakes. Keep your head down."[3]

Grosso called the airport again. "Looks like we're gonna have an abnormal situation. At the present time seems that our fluid is holding, and pressure, and we'll have all the normal facilities. ... So we can have the equipment standing by and we'll come in for a landing. We're now over Byers [Colorado]; got it all checked out."

The dispatcher responded, "You say you have the pressure and you want the equipment standing by? You got it all checked out? You're over Byers and you're coming in for a landing?"

"Roger," replied Grosso.[4]

That brief conversation became a point of contention between airline and city officials the following September, when the Civil Aeronautics Board (CAB) conducted an investigation into whether firefighters were given adequate warning of an impending crash.

As Grosso began his final approach to Stapleton, the tower advised him to circle and come in from the west, but Grosso and his crew asked for and received permission to come straight in from the east. Satisfied that the plane's hydraulic difficulty was "abnormal"

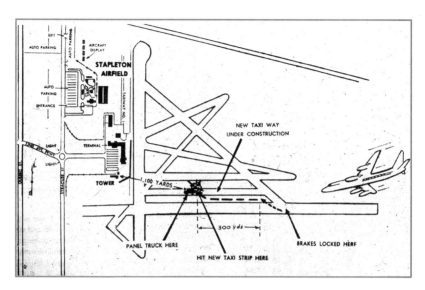

United Airlines Flight 859, a four-engine DC-8, struck the Stapleton Airport runway on July 11, 1961, slid to the right and plowed over a parked truck in full view of the terminal. The cause of the crash was laid to the loss of hydraulic fluid. (Courtesy of The Denver Post.*)*

but not serious, Grosso lowered the wheels and set the big airliner down on the east end of Stapleton's Runway 26 Left, the airport's longest, at 11:37 A.M.

The DC-8, its red-white-and-blue paint scheme gleaming in the summer sun, hit the runway at 120 miles an hour and bounced twice. The landing appeared to be reasonably normal. One passenger estimated the plane rolled one thousand feet without incident, but then two tires on the right side blew out, causing the plane to veer to the right. Grosso, in a last-ditch effort to slow the aircraft and regain control, applied hard braking and reversed thrust on the four engines.

It was no use. The plane veered off the right edge of the runway. In seconds, the outboard engine on the right side was ripped away as the wing tip clipped the ground. The plane shot across three hundred feet of bare ground, raising a huge cloud of dust. The left-side undercarriage and two engine pods under the left wing were torn away as the airliner slid sideways and slammed against a thirty-inch-high concrete slab on an adjacent taxiway under construction. It next struck a city worker's parked truck and dragged it fifty yards before sliding to a stop near the Stanley Aviation offices at the west end of the runway.

As the plane left the runway, an unidentified voice broke in on the radio and said, "Hey, tower, there he goes!" There followed several disjointed and unidentifiable comments, including, "All right, make a panic of it and call everybody down at City Hall. I mean, call police."[5]

High-octane fuel (eight thousand gallons of it were still on board) began leaking from a ruptured tank in the left wing and, when the fuel touched the hot engines, it burst into a hundred-foot-high orange fireball and ignited the plane's fuselage. A pall of dense black smoke drifted over the airfield. Passengers, those who could escape the fire, exited the plane and scattered in all directions.

During its slide down the runway, the plane rotated almost 180 degrees after it struck the new taxiway. Members of the Denver Fire Department's airport detail, designated Company 22, were waiting only a few hundred feet away. They rushed to the burning wreck and began spraying water and foam on the fire within thirty seconds.

Fireman Foy Wilkerson, one of five firefighters on duty—a woefully inadequate number—was riding on the running board of Company 22's low-pressure truck. "We were on top of that aircraft within seconds. We watched it leave the runway; the number-four engine came off as soon as he left the runway. I couldn't believe what was happening. When that thing left the runway, [Bob] McDermott (another fireman) said, 'Oh, shit! Oh, shit! Let's go! Here we go!'"[6]

At the same time, crews called for help from Lowry Air Force Base, but fire-department records showed that the first call for assistance from nearby city firehouses wasn't made until seventeen minutes after the plane touched down. No explanation for the delay was given.

Company 22's men rushed to the tail section of the DC-8 and sprayed the plane. Wilkerson and Joe Keelan, each dragging two hoses because of the firefighter shortage, unknowingly used a man's body, wedged against the new taxiway, as a stepstool when Wilkerson tried to boost Keelan inside the cabin. "I made a saddle with my hands but there was foam all over them and my hands slipped apart and I dropped him. About that time, the oxygen bottles inside let go. It was like a blowtorch came out of that door. That would have killed him."[7]

The crash was the first time such a catastrophe received extensive live coverage on Denver radio and television. Broadcast reports incited rubberneckers to speed to Stapleton, leading to traffic jams and hindering the arrival of city fire crews and emergency crews from nearby Buckley Air Field and Lowry Air Force Base. A truck company from Station 3 in Five Points outraced civilian vehicles along what became Martin Luther King Jr. Boulevard to reach the scene. Inaccurate reports from radio traffic spotters on the tardy arrival of fire equipment added to the confusion.

Before the plane slid to a stop, air force captain Clyde Autio, a passenger, threw open a door and the seven-member flight crew began helping passengers to the ground. Though the evacuation was hurried, panic seemed strangely absent; it all happened too quickly. Someone yelled, "Get out! Get out!" A woman screamed over and over, "God will take care of his children! God will take care of his children!"[8]

Grosso, second officer J. M. Beatie and Autio, the last seated in the plane's lounge area, led bewildered first-class passengers through the heavy black smoke and outside to safety. Grosso testified at the CAB hearings the following September:

The only way was to go in and lead them out. I made several trips. I would go back until I felt someone and I would lead them to the door and tell them to jump. I went back and felt the bare arm of a woman passenger. By this time the cabin was completely covered by flame but there was no other way. I pushed her out as far as I could and I jumped myself.[9]

Passengers in the first-class section at the front of the plane poured out the right-side doors, trying to escape the clouds of acrid smoke boiling through the cabin. Those seated toward the tail were hindered by aisles only fifteen and a half inches wide, which forced them into a single-file queue, as well as by a door that had become jammed by blankets, maps, brochures and other objects loosed from a storage closet. Further slowing their escape was the wreckage of the city truck, which had become pinned under the plane after it was struck. Coach passengers exited through a small buffet door used to load supplies.

Both groups, however, fared better than those in the forward area of the coach section, located over the airliner's wings. These unfortunates, trapped in their seats, quickly succumbed to the flames that raced through the cabin and choked oxygen from the air, leaving

The fire that swept the DC-8 immediately after the crash landing burned away most of the left side of the aircraft and reduced the left wing to a molten outline. (Courtesy of The Denver Post.*)*

deadly carbon monoxide in their wake. The DC-8 had nine rows of four seats in the first-class section, and fourteen rows of six seats in the tourist-class section. Firefighters later discovered that one of the escape doors over the right wing remained unopened.

All sixteen of those killed in the cabin were seated in rows 10–18 at the front of the coach section, nearest the ruptured wing fuel tank on the aircraft's left side. One of the first firefighters to enter the charred passenger cabin said the skin of the dead passengers was glazed, as if suddenly baked. Some were still strapped into their seats, indicating that they hadn't had time to escape, but most of the bodies were found lying in the aisles.

One victim was killed on the ground. Henry Blom, 53, a city engineer who had played flute in the Denver Symphony Orchestra as a youth, was sitting in a panel truck next to the airport's new taxiway, having lunch, when the out-of-control airliner barreled into the truck, rolling it into a ball and crushing Blom.

Survivors described vividly the first moments after the plane began to burn. "The smoke was terrible," said Lyle Oreck, a passenger from Phoenix who boarded Flight 859 in Omaha. "I don't know

Once the fire was extinguished, firemen began the grisly task of removing bodies from the smouldering wreckage. Sixteen passengers, all seated in rows 10–18, were killed. A city worker sitting in his truck beside the runway also died. (Courtesy of The Denver Post.*)*

how I got out. I really don't know what happened. All I know is that suddenly the plane belly-landed and caught on fire. We were trapped inside. We couldn't get out. It was horrible." He begged rescuers to "call my wife, please, call my wife; let her know that I am alive."[10]

Alerted to the crash by a garage owner, Father John Haley of Cure d'Ars Catholic Church just west of the airport was the first clergyman to reach the wreckage. He gave absolution to those who he could determine were Catholics and his blessing to those who weren't.

Edison Carter and his wife, Juanita, managed to escape the flames from their seats in the front of the coach section. Carter, an amateur photographer, turned to snap pictures of the plane as he ran to safety. He told reporters:

> *When we touched the runway, it sounded as though a tire popped, and then the plane seemed to roll on out of control at a high rate of speed. The plane lurched to the left, then began twirling, it seemed. When it came to a stop, the inside seemed aflame. My wife was sitting next to the emergency exit. Somehow, we got it opened and*

fell to the ground. I pulled my wife away from the flaming jet, then began shooting pictures. I stood in a sort of a daze, until I realized we were both burned about the arms.[11]

Most lamentable was the story of Omaha boxing promoter Lee Sloan, who was escorting his fighter, lightweight Louis Cappelano, to a bout in Los Angeles. When Sloan boarded the plane in Omaha, he agreed to accompany Jason Gale Jr., 10, the son of an attorney friend, during the flight. After the crash, Sloan repeatedly called out, "Where's Jason? Where's Jason? Is Jason all right?" He was told that the boy, seated six rows behind Sloan, Cappelano and a group of men in the lounge, was dead.

Enough was enough for survivor Sloan. The Stapleton crash was his second in three years. "This is it. I was in a private-plane crash three years ago on a Minnesota fishing trip and got out lucky that time also. No more planes for me. From now on I'm riding the rails."[12]

Morris Cutler and his wife, Nettie, whom Morris had warned of a possible crash in the minutes after the pilot informed passengers of problems in the hydraulic systems, survived. He recounted their escape to the *News*. "I put a handkerchief over my face because of the smoke. I told my wife to get down on the floor where she could breathe and we started for the door. She jumped just like a natural-born jumper. Then I went. I skinned my right hand and hurt my shoulder when I skidded on the runway, but then I don't weigh much."[13]

The intense heat melted the plane's left wing and consumed most of the fuselage from the cockpit to the tail section. Firefighters, wearing silvery fire suits and hoods for protection, approached the flames from the plane's tail section. "We put on those stinking old approach suits that we had," Wilkerson recalled. "You couldn't see out of them, you couldn't see out of those hoods. Joe [Keelan] and I took them off so we could see what we were doing."[14]

Wilkerson sustained serious damage to his right eye when bits of molten magnesium from the plane's burning engines splashed onto his face. He recalled the result of another injury sustained fighting the fire: "I was wading in boiling water up to here (just below his knees). They took me down to Denver General and pulled my socks off and pulled the skin right off with it. I don't grow any hair on my legs from there down."[15]

Silvery "approach suits" enabled firefighters to get close to the flames but fireman Foy Wilkerson recalled, "You couldn't see out of those hoods. Joe [Keelan] and I took them off so we could see what we were doing." (Courtesy of The Denver Post.*)*

Would-be rescuers searched the plane and the grounds for clues. They walked around a two-inch-thick outline of once-molten metal that had been the plane's left wing. They found a boy's left shoe, burned and smashed, lying near a pool of oil. They picked up the charred frame of an electric shaver and the cuff of a man's blue-striped shirt sitting amidst a pile of ashes.

Ambulances, pickup trucks, delivery vans and private automobiles were pressed into service to carry the injured to four hospitals in the city. The final toll: seventeen dead and eighty-four injured.

There was so little emergency equipment on site at Stapleton Field in 1961 that a potpourri of vehicles, including an upholstery-shop van and a station wagon, were pressed into service to transport eighty-four injured people to three area hospitals. (Courtesy of The Denver Post.*)*

Flight 859 remained the worst crash in the airport's history until Continental Airlines Flight 1713, a DC-9 bound for Boise, Idaho, somersaulted on the runway while taking off in a snowstorm on November 15, 1987, killing twenty-eight and injuring eighty-two.

Crews from Lowry Air Force Base wrapped the bodies of the sixteen victims who died in Flight 859's cabin in blankets and placed them in black plastic body bags. The bodies were transported to Smiley Junior High School in the Park Hill neighborhood, adjacent to the airport, forcing officials to displace the school's marching band, whose members were rehearsing in the gym. When the bags were neatly laid in two rows on the gymnasium's maple basketball floor, it was discovered that one of the "bodies" was actually a bag full of airplane parts scavenged from the wreckage. Among the dead were three sisters, ages 8, 4 and 1, from Fort Lyon, Colorado, who died with their mother as their father, Dr. Earl Guyer, watched the landing from the airport terminal.

The day after the crash, officials praised the city's fire crews for their efforts, but questions about the city's preparedness and equipment arose. Airline and city officials swapped accusations about why more fire-fighting help wasn't at the airport when the plane landed. Mayor Dick Batterton, reflecting the opinions of his fire chief, Allie Feldman, maintained that there was no warning of a "major emergency," which would have brought more firefighters and equipment to Stapleton.

The Denver Fire Department and the airlines using Stapleton Field had a peculiar arrangement that depended on the judgment of those on duty to determine how serious an emergency was. There were two levels of emergency status — "stand-by," which meant fire trucks stationed at the airport would roll out and be prepared for action (as happened 188 times in 1961 before the United crash) and "panic" (or red-alert), which meant the city would call in firefighters and equipment from nearby firehouses, including Stations 3, 10, 14 and 26, and military fire crews from nearby Lowry Air Force Base and Buckley Air Field.

By comparison, when the fifty-three-square-mile Denver International Airport (DIA), almost seven times larger than Stapleton, opened forty miles northeast of downtown Denver in 1994, it had one hundred fire-fighting employees, including a full-time fire inspector, and three fire stations. Twenty-four firefighters are on duty at all times.

Nor is there any shortage of equipment at the $4.9-billion airport, which in 1998 served thirty-seven million passengers. Among its fire apparatuses is a truck called the "Snozzle," which can puncture an aircraft and pump water or chemicals into its interior. Also on site are two rapid-intervention vehicles; nine water vehicles, five with a fifteen-hundred-gallon capacity and four with a three-thousand-gallon capacity; two trucks equipped with stairs allowing access to aircraft of any size; a class A aerial pumper; and a two-ton, four-wheel-drive "incident command" vehicle with a microwave transmitter/receiver and a television camera.

In addition, the city designed its own rigs, two low-profile pumpers each carrying 150 gallons of water and 5 gallons of foam. The low-level vehicles can access the airport's tunnels, baggage-handling area and parking structure. Total cost of fire-fighting vehicles: $2 million.

Even DIA's terminal, which covers 376,332 square feet, and its three concourses are protected with high-tech smoke-detection systems, the sensors for which are wired directly to computer screens in the city's airport firehouses and in a command center in the airport's administration building.

In the days following the 1961 crash, Chief Feldman defended his men. "I don't care what's said about what happened. My boys did a damn good job. I'm proud of them." He conceded, however, that the three trucks at the airport were antiquated. "The equipment we have there is at least 12 years old. It was the best we could get at the time. But the size and fuels of airplanes have changed. Our equipment has not."[16] One fireman later mused that fighting the Flight 859 blaze at Stapleton was like going bear hunting with a switch.

At the CAB hearings in September, an official of the board raised the question of whether Denver's firefighters were adequately trained, whether their training even included entering a burning aircraft. Chief Feldman replied testily, "I know they've all gone into fires. A fire's a fire. They are trained firemen and they go after an emergency, not away from it. They did that in this case, and they do that in every case."[17]

The debate over preparedness became heated. Why weren't more firefighters and equipment at the airport when the plane landed? Advised that the landing probably would be "abnormal" but given no indication that it was an emergency, the fire department made no request for extra fire crews. It was a critical decision.

The city blamed United. "There's going to be an attempt to blame the fire department," said John Schooley, city safety manager, in July before the CAB hearings. "If [United] had wanted extra emergency equipment standing by, they should have told us."[18]

W. A. Patterson, the president of United Air Lines, was questioned at the CAB hearings about the city's preparedness and the pilot's failure to request additional help:

> *QUESTION — Why didn't the pilot call for more equipment?*
> *ANSWER — The pilot never calls for equipment. He tells the tower his troubles and they decide whether to call for equipment.*

He grudgingly credited the fire department with doing "the best job they could with the facilities they had."[19] It was Patterson who negotiated a secret deal with federal officials, prior to the CAB investigation, to keep information on the crash out of the public eye until the investigation was concluded.

Stapleton Field opened in 1929 as Denver Municipal Airport, during the administration of Mayor Benjamin F. Stapleton. It was so far outside the city—on sandy plains seven miles to the northeast—that it was ridiculed as "Stapleton's Folly." It was used commercially only by Western Airlines until 1937, when United and Continental began service. It didn't officially became Stapleton International Airport until October 1964, but it was a busy place in 1961. It was the nation's third largest airport in total operations, and its passenger count exceeded two million.

BETWEEN 1988 AND 1997, DEATHS OF FIREFIGHTERS ON DUTY DROPPED FROM 136 TO 94 AND INJURIES DECLINED FROM 61,790 TO 40,920.

But the city and the airport were living on luck and borrowed time, mired in the propeller era while the jet age was taking off. No modernization of fire-fighting equipment, nor addition of firefighters at the airfield was made, not even after May 6, 1959, when a Continental Airlines 707 jetliner departed with ninety-three people on board, becoming the first commercial jetliner to use Stapleton.

The firefighters and equipment of Stapleton's Company 22 were quartered in Hangar 5, located near Syracuse Street on the west side of the terminal, meaning the firefighters had to drive a half mile to reach a point where the airport's two main runways intersected. The facilities were so small that one of the company's three fire-fighting rigs had to be parked at an angle to fit inside the building. The company's three trucks, the newest of which was built in 1948, included a high-pressure truck, a low-pressure truck and a water tanker, the last a converted gasoline truck that provided the company with its only source of extra water because there were no hydrants on the field.

Less than a dozen firefighters were assigned to the small station in Hangar 5, and only five of them, the usual roster, were on duty the day Flight 859 crashed. In addition to Lieutenant George Augusto, who was in charge of the crews but was away from the field at a training session when the DC-8 crashed, the five-person roster included Foy Wilkerson, Joe Keelan, Roland "Piggy" Mattson, Frank "Sandy" Glivar (who was in charge in Augusto's absence) and Bob McDermott.

Augusto conceded in a 1998 interview that the supply of firefighters and equipment was grossly inadequate. "But there hadn't been any crashes there since the airport was built. Jets were just starting to come in. When I first went out there, all we had was a little terminal building that didn't amount to anything. At the time they probably had only five or six gates. Probably in September or October of 1960, they started building the new terminal."[20]

Three days after the crash, the *Rocky Mountain News* revealed that the Federal Aviation Administration (FAA) told city officials on February 19, 1961, that fire protection at Stapleton was inadequate and recommended the city correct the deficiencies as soon as possible. Mayor Dick Batterton said he had never seen the report and even after the crash said, "We have adequate equipment available to meet emergency situations." Specifically, the FAA reported that the airport's water-fog unit "would be of little value on a major aircraft fire," the water-foam unit was deficient and the water unit had too little discharge capability.[21]

In December 1960, seven months before the crash, an airport safety specialist from the FAA inspected Stapleton's emergency equipment, specifically, water capacity, rate of discharge, fog and foam. He ruled that the airport was deficient in every category. The inspector concluded that it would take ten, not five, firefighters to operate the equipment at full efficiency. The FAA recommended that "Denver expedite the correction of these deficiencies as soon as possible."[22]

In 1960, the city paid an airport consultant $20,000 to recommend new fire equipment worth an estimated $176,000, to be delivered by May 29, 1961. It was never ordered. Asked three days after the United crash why the city ignored such expensive advice, Mayor Batterton replied tersely, "No comment. Draw your own conclusions; you will anyway."[23] He declined even to tell the press if he had ever flown in an airplane.

In another bit of irony, bids for building a $104,000 airport fire station, to be finished by January 1962, were opened the day before the crash.

"They were trying to blame the fire department for the fire," remembered Augusto, who testified at the CAB inquiry in 1961. "I said, 'Hell, we wasn't flying the plane! How could we be in charge?' We didn't have adequate equipment; I agree there. But we worked with what we had."[24]

Another point of contention: How long did it take fire crews to begin throwing water and foam on the blazing cabin? Some passen-

gers recalled that it took five minutes or more for the fire department
to arrive at the scene. In retrospect, that estimation is probably wrong.
Equipment called in from other city stations and from Lowry and
Buckley arrived late, largely because of traffic problems. But one of
the firefighters on the scene, Joe Keelan, who joined the department
as an auxiliary firefighter during World War II when he was only
sixteen years old, maintained, "We went out [after the pilot radioed
in] and positioned our truck so we figured about where they would
stop and then waited. We were close … to where they were landing.
We were there pretty quick. It was about half a minute [before the
fire truck reached the crash site]."[25]

As if by magic, nine days after the crash the city administration
became animated about obtaining more fire-fighting equipment for
the airport and announced that the U.S. Air Force would supply
two fire-fighting trucks with five times the capacity of equipment
on site the day of the crash. In August 1961 two large, red fire-
crash trucks, surplus equipment from the air force, arrived in Denver from Webb Air Force Base in Big Spring, Texas. Each was
capable of delivering four thousand gallons of a water/foam mix
and featured fog nozzles. However, both trucks, designated 0-10s
(Oh-tens) and inactive since the previous February, had to be recon-
ditioned at the fire department's shops at Nineteenth and Market
Streets. Both were decidedly "used" and no longer of value to the
air force. One of them never ran well and was constantly in need
of servicing. The trucks were assigned officially to the 9531st AF
Reserve Recovery Squadron, newly based at Stapleton, but were
operated by Denver Fire Department firefighters who helped train
air force personnel.

Also in August 1961, the city, using $176,000 in bond money,
solicited bids for two new high-tech fire-fighting trucks. Three companies, Walter Motor Truck Co., American LaFrance and Yankee
Motor Bodies, submitted bids. American LaFrance's bid was lowest
at $137,500, but city officials selected Walter Motor Truck, which
came in at $142,980, because, they said, the American LaFrance
bid failed to meet eighteen of the bid specifications. This led to a
bitter exchange between city officials and American LaFrance, which
objected to the fact that the so-called deficiencies (a claim refuted by
LaFrance) had been discussed in newspaper stories rather than in
private negotiations.

'IT'S A HELL OF A WAY TO RUN AN AIRPORT..!'

Criticism, including this Paul Conrad cartoon that appeared in The Denver Post *on July 16, 1961, was heaped on the Denver Fire Department for the antiquated equipment on hand at Stapleton Field. Chief Allie Feldman said at a subsequent inquiry, "I don't care what's said about what happened. My boys did a damn good job. I'm proud of them."* (*Courtesy of* The Denver Post.)

Though delivery of two Walter high-pressure trucks, designated Model CF 1500, was promised by May 1962 by the manufacturer, the city didn't take delivery of the first truck, capable of traveling sixty miles an hour over rough terrain and throwing eleven hundred gallons of foam per minute three hundred feet, until the following August. In a bizarre series of mix-ups, the second nineteen-ton truck wasn't delivered until November 1962. It suffered eight delays at the factory in Voorheesville, New York, and also was lost while being shipped by rail.

The delay moved *The Post* to editorialize, "We're glad Denver's new fire-fighting crash truck for Stapleton Field, which was scheduled to arrive May 1, wasn't on its way to a fire. A long and frustrating delay is over—almost. We'll be glad to see the two trucks, sleek and efficient, ready at their assigned stations."[26]

After the first truck was delivered, it failed preliminary pumping tests at City Park Lake, falling four pounds below the two hundred pounds of pressure required in the specifications. The shortfall was attributed to the city's high altitude and the company fixed the problem within the thirty days required by the contract. Once approved, the new truck was sent to Stapleton, where twenty firefighters were assigned to a new airport station completed the following January, and a new training program, headed by Lieutenant Art Neuman, a former pilot, was instituted.

The CAB investigators concluded in their final report, released almost a year after the crash, that the aircraft's sudden swerve off the runway was caused by failure of the two engines on the left side of the plane to engage into reverse thrust when the pilot tried to slow down. A contributing factor cited by the CAB panel was the failure of the co-pilot to monitor lights that indicate when the engine is producing normal reverse power. The panel also noted that several other DC-8s reported similar problems with hydraulics in the months before and after the crash.

However, the CAB failed to reach a conclusion on whether the response time of the fire department may have contributed to the death toll. The panel stated in their final report:

> *There was substantial variance in the estimated elapsed time between the accident and the fire-fighting personnel being in position to fight the fire.*
>
> *Eyewitness estimates of the elapsed time prior to the arrival of the first fire trucks varied from five to ten minutes, and up to fifteen minutes, before any effective equipment was in position.*
>
> *The members of the Stapleton Field fire-fighting crews state that their equipment was moving to the airplane before it had come to rest and that foam and fog were being applied to the fire within one to two minutes.*[27]

Keelan and Wilkerson, the first two firefighters to reach the scene, were never called to testify. "They didn't want any part of 'pilot error,'" said Wilkerson. "[The pilot] could have throttled back, he could have rolled the aircraft out without sliding off the runway. He was a long way from the end of the runway. He could have rolled that plane out off the end of [Runway 26] and run it against the fence and done less damage. That's why they (the investigators) didn't ask."[28]

In September 1962 the FAA released a study designed to reduce passenger fatalities. It made several recommendations: among them, that verbal instructions in emergency evacuation procedures be given to passengers; that aisle widths in the tourist or economy sections of cabins be reevaluated; that placards showing the location of emergency exits in other parts of the cabin be posted; and that further research designed to improve fire-fighting techniques at airports be conducted.[29]

CASUALTIES ON
UNITED FLIGHT 859
July 11, 1961

Killed
Henry Blom, 53, Denver (killed in a truck on the ground)
Jason Gale Jr., 10, Torrance, Calif.
Mrs. Nancy Guyer, Fort Lyon, Colo.
Cynthia Guyer, 8, Fort Lyon
Ann Guyer, 4, Fort Lyon
Jill Guyer, 1, Fort Lyon
George Hambrecht, 28, Willow Grove, Pa.
Earle R. Linne, Malvern, Pa.
Berneta Marple, address unknown
Leonard A. McDonald, Chugwater, Wyo.
Susan McDonald, Salt Lake City
CWO George Oake, Thule Air Force Base, Greenland
Ruth A. Pierce, 21, Farragut, Iowa
Mrs. Daisie D. Sheperd, Davenport, Iowa
Mrs. Kathryn Tobin, Santa Maria, Calif.
Mrs. Regina Vogel, Oakland, Calif.
Dr. E. A. Williams, Santa Barbara, Calif.

Injured

Barbara K. Able, Maywood, Calif.

Mrs. Ruth Ansen, 47, Sioux City, Iowa, treated and released

Roy Ansen, 14, Sioux City, treated and released

Clyde C. Applegate, 67, Moline, Ill., treated and released

Capt. Clyde Autio, Omaha, treated and released

William J. Baird, Omaha, condition unknown

Mr. and Mrs. J. J. Barmore, address/condition unknown

Rose Barrett, 54, Pomona, Calif., smoke inhalation

Merle T. Bittle, 46, Des Moines, Iowa, possible heart attack

Mrs. J. J. Cannella, Garden Grove, Calif., minor abrasions

Louis Cappelano, Omaha, treated and released

Edison Carter, 50, Des Moines, Iowa, broken rib

Mrs. Juanita Carter, 39, Des Moines, sprained ankle

Paul W. Cocklin, Omaha, condition unknown

Jody Cook, stewardess, Aurora, Colo., condition unknown

Mrs. Nettie Cutler, 78, Sunland, Calif., sprained right ankle, smoke inhalation

Robert DeGroate, Everett, Wash., condition unknown

Antoinette M. DeMoss, Omaha, condition unknown

L. DeMoss, Omaha, condition unknown

Pat Eberhardt, stewardess, Aurora, Colo., possible internal injuries

Joyce Fager, Denver, condition unknown

William Gamble, New York City, treated and released

Mrs. William Gamble, New York City, treated and released

Timothy Gamble, 15, New York City, treated and released

Thomas Gamble, 13, New York City, treated and released

Kathleen Gamble, 4, New York City, treated and released

Anna Belle Ginn, 22, stewardess, Aurora, Colo., treated and released

Mrs. Cena Glood, 87, Valborg, S.Dak., burns to legs and right wrist

Mrs. Nora I. Golden, 57, Omaha, broken right leg and
right wrist, burns to hand, shock
Ellen Goldstein, Omaha, treated and released
Dura Grace, 66, Iowa City, smoke inhalation, ankle injury
Eva Herschel, 64, Cedar Rapids, Iowa, arm, leg and back
burns
Fritz Hoebel, Los Angeles, broken foot
Mrs. George C. Holling, Omaha, treated and released
Walter Howarth, Omaha, condition unknown
Esther A. Howarth, Omaha, condition unknown
Mrs. N. S. Howe, Oyster Bay, Long Island, N.Y., treated
and released
Margaret Laura Howe, 12, Oyster Bay, treated and
released
Linda Hunter, 3, Casper, Wyo., treated and released
Mrs. Darlene Johnson, 22, Ontario, Calif., shock
Mrs. A. J. Kitzelman, 24, Denver, burns
Jennifer Kitzelman, 2 months, Denver, burns
Ruth Koth, 54, Los Angeles, broken right ankle, burns
R. Krulish, 52, Greensboro, N.C., treated and released
Mrs. Bernadine A. Lapple, Bergenfield, N.J., condition
unknown
Dr. Max S. Lentner, 73, Loveland, Colo., treated and
released
Mary S. Lentner, 66, Loveland, treated and released
Floyd Mable, 63, Greensboro, N.C., treated and released
Mrs. Jane Magnussen, Audubon, Iowa, condition unknown
Frank Maher, Long Beach, Calif., treated and released
Francis T. Martin, 56, Omaha, Nebr., elbow injury
Robert P. Martin, Glendale, Calif., condition unknown
Mrs. Dorothy McConaughey, 51, Burbank, Calif., treated
and released
Victor U. McDonald, Quincy, Mass., condition unknown
Dr. E. A. McMurray, 60, East Newton, Iowa, shock
Mrs. Elna McMurray, 53, East Newton, smoke inhalation
Sandra McMurray, 18, East Newton, smoke inhalation

Mrs. Ruth Moldenhauer, 67, Pomona, Calif., broken left
ankle

Richard Moline, Sioux City, Iowa, treated and released

Mrs. Lois Moline, 48, Sioux City, treated and released

Mrs. Maude Moon, 75, Knoxville, Iowa, burns

Capt. Bernard Neff, 26, Philadelphia, shock

Lyle Oreck, 56, Phoenix, possible internal injuries

Ethel Pirie, 62, Cedar Rapids, Iowa, burns

Howard Pollard, 40, Merced, Calif., smoke inhalation

Diane Pollard, 11, Merced, smoke inhalation

Mrs. Irene Randolph, 73, Los Angeles, cuts and bruises

Mrs. Hazel Reed, 58, Bakersfield, Calif., strained back

Morris J. Rubin, address/condition unknown

Lee Sloan, 42, Omaha, cuts and bruises, stress, shock;
treated and released

Quinn Smith, Casper, Wyo., treated and released

James H. Stansbury, 37, La Mirada, Calif., treated and
released

Charlene Sullivan, Leviton, N.J., condition unknown

Russell Sullivan, infant, Leviton, condition unknown

Elizabeth Tarney, Philadelphia, condition unknown

Willard Thiessen, Cedar Rapids, Iowa, knee injury

Jess Thurmond, Omaha, treated and released

Mrs. Eleanor Thurmond, 60, Omaha, treated and released

Charles W. Vaughan, United employee, Aurora, Colo., hurt
during rescue

William J. Vogel, Omaha, treated and released

Mrs. Dagmar Wilson, 52, Valborg, S. Dak., burns to arms
and hands

Lean M. Zessar, 52, Los Angeles, burns to upper and
lower extremities

Mrs. Lillian Zessar, 56, Los Angeles, burns to arms, legs,
face and back

— The Denver Post
July 12, 1961

Chapter Twelve

"In the Dark
of Night"

*An early-morning construction fire signals the
beginning of a fiery six-year reign of terror along the
Front Range. Suspicions, and the similarity of forty
fires, point to union organizers. In the ensuing events,
a lone undercover investigator gets the goods on one
of the conspirators, witnesses overcome fear and
intimidation to testify and the ringleaders go to prison.*

L ead prosecutor Richard T. Spriggs opened the first day of
accused arsonist Anthony Mulligan's 1975 trial with a thun-
dering accusation.

Mulligan, Spriggs told a Denver District Court jury, brought
"a new method of labor organizing to the state. That method was
arson."[1] Authorities had spent seven years getting the construction-
union leader to trial on charges of arson and conspiracy; Spriggs
wasn't about to let him wriggle off the hook at the last minute.

"On occasion after occasion, Mulligan would try to get contractors to enter into closed-shop agreements," Spriggs told the jury.
"Then he would hint retaliation if they didn't go along. Then shortly
after that—in the dark of night—their construction project would go
up in flames. Then Mulligan would come back and imply to them,
'See what can happen?' That went on fire after fire after fire."[2]

The National Fire Data Center estimates that one-quarter of all
fires in the United States are caused by arson, leading to more than
$3 billion in damage annually. In 1994, the most recent year for which

IN THE 1990S, MORE AND MORE ARSON FIRES WERE SET BY YOUTHS UNDER 18. THERE WERE 1,884 ARSON FIRES SET BY YOUTHS IN 1990, CAUSING $5,575,481 IN DAMAGES. BY 1996, THE NUMBERS ROSE TO 4,384 FIRES AND $9,826,218 IN DAMAGES. MORE THAN FIVE HUNDRED AMERICANS WERE KILLED BY ARSON FIRES IN 1996.

—NATIONAL FIRE PROTECTION ASSOCIATION

information is available, there were 548,500 arson fires and 560 deaths related to them.

Arson as a tool of destruction was extant almost from the day Denver was founded in 1858 at the confluence of Cherry Creek and the South Platte River. "Incendiaries" were legion, whether for moral or political reasons or just plain orneriness.

In the winter of 1862, a series of fires broke out in the town's houses of prostitution. "This incendiarism ... is looked upon by the majority of our citizens as part of the sanitary arrangements of the city," the *Commonwealth* and *Republican* noted with pride, while at the same time issuing a warning that although these "habitations of vice and misery located in our midst are a grievous nuisance," such solutions could lead to disaster, to "such a conflagration ... that Denver never yet has witnessed the like."[3]

The following April, the newspaper's premonition came true. A fire that began near 2:30 A.M. at the back of the Cherokee House, a saloon at F (Fifteenth) and Blake Streets, swept through almost half of Denver's downtown district, destroying the isolated frontier town's precious stores of staples and hardware. Reports were circulated but never proven that the fire was ignited by drunken revelers.

In 1882 a series of unexplained fires hit churches located in what is today the Platte Valley redevelopment area. And in the 1890s, a difficult period economically for Denver because of the "Panic of 1893," the arson tradition was revived yet again. As in any period when economic hard times arrive, the firebug's hand is sure to follow. Hundreds of businesses failed, banks collapsed, thousands were put out of work. Thieves set fires in downtown buildings that served as sleeping quarters, some of them little more than flophouses for unemployed miners and others, merely to steal the inhabitants' meager possessions.

Arson increased dramatically during the Great Depression of the 1930s. Some estimated that as many as three-quarters of the fires during this period were set deliberately. Among the arsonists were businesspeople who, having been bankrupted by the economic crash, chose to incinerate their properties to collect insurance money.

One of the most spectacular arson fires in the city's history occurred at the Crescent Flour Mill, at Jason Street and West Twenty-ninth Avenue, on September 22, 1949. Fourteen Denver fire companies fought the four-alarm blaze for two days. Explosions of wheat dust punctuated the roar of flames as bins on upper floors broke and thousands of bushels of wheat cascaded through the building, mixed with air and ignited. The mill, erected in 1895, suffered $1 million in damage.

Despite its long and tragic history of arson fires, the Denver Fire Department had no formal arson bureau until 1957. Thus in 1949, officials declared that the Crescent Mill fire was caused by "spontaneous combustion," a frequently blamed culprit when no other reason could be found. The owners of the flour mill weren't satisfied with that explanation and hired members of the Chicago Fire Department's arson squad to come to Denver to investigate. Within three days, the Chicago team had determined that the Crescent Mill fire, as well as fires in two other grain elevators, were deliberate. Shortly after that, a suspect, described as one who derived "sexual satisfaction" from fires, was arrested.

In January of 1957, the Denver Fire Department sent a number of firefighters and two police officers to arson schools, and the city's first arson squad followed. Jim Jordan, a Denver fireman who had been injured at a fire, was the first person moved into the Fire Prevention Bureau, assigned specifically to investigate suspicious fires. Prior to Jordan's arrival as a one-person arson squad, investigations were left to division chiefs, and were hit-or-miss propositions. Jordan recalled:

What they did prior to me going up in the bureau, there was a lot of fairly large arson fires, and they were investigated by a captain in the [prevention] bureau, some of them. A lot of this you pick up just at ordinary fires. You go to enough fires and you see where it's obvious. If you smell gasoline, you've got something. There was a guy in the bureau named Art Book that went around to every fire over $50 damage, looked to see if it was obvious what caused it and *leave them a card to send out with the insurance information for statistics. There was no organized arson bureau at all. Several of the people in the detective bureau would get involved if the fire department determined it was arson, and the police department handled it as far as any prosecution or further investigation. Basically, it was only the big ones they worked.*[4]

Thirteen years after Jordan's assignment, the fire department added two more investigators to its arson detail; today the department has eleven assigned to fire investigation.

Anyone can light a fire—jilted lovers, delinquents, pyromaniacs, rival gang members and drug pushers. "On top is the professional arsonist who does it for money—who uses better systems, better cover and devices designed to disintegrate in the heat of the fire to make it more difficult to catch him," said Captain Ronald Brown, head of the Denver Fire Department's arson bureau, in a 1971 interview with the *Rocky Mountain News*.[5]

It was professionals who spread a fiery reign of terror over Denver and Colorado from 1968 to 1974. The campaign began just after dawn on April 12, 1968, when a partially completed, five-story apartment house at 1075 Washington Street in Denver's Capitol Hill neighborhood literally exploded in flames, scorching nearby homes and destroying several automobiles parked on Washington Street. What appeared to be an unfortunate accident at a construction site turned out to be the first of forty deliberate fires (see Appendix C) that would cost $10 million before the combined efforts of the Denver Fire Department, the CBI, the FBI and local investigators throughout Colorado brought an end to the arson campaign. Only the CBI, which continued its investigation for a year after other law enforcement agencies dropped out, pursued the case to its conclusion.

The late 1960s and early 1970s marked one of Denver's economic growth periods, like the ones that buoyed the city in the 1860s, 1880s and the post–World War II era. The oil boom, which would come unwound in the 1980s, was just beginning its liftoff. Skyscrapers rose downtown and housing developments, accelerated by the networking of interstate highways, crawled over the landscape to the city's south and east. Thousands of young workers chased the economic opportunities Denver provided. But where would they all live? In apartments and condominiums, partly, which sprung up like wildflowers in

A fire at a condominium under construction at 8525 East Hampden Avenue on February 5, 1972, caused $400,000 in damage. The arson was one of forty by trade-union organizers between April 1968 and June 1974. (Courtesy of The Denver Post.*)*

the suburbs, particularly in Aurora and Glendale to the east and southeast. Subdivisions with bucolic names like Pheasant Run, Heather Ridge and Village East sprouted almost overnight. Aurora's population, for example, grew 111 percent during the 1970s.

The building frenzy meant plenty of construction jobs, but to some they weren't the right kind of jobs — union jobs. Shortages of skilled craftsmen in the building trades meant that practically any carpenter, for example, could walk onto a job site and find employment, and he didn't need a union card to do it. In 1972, seventy-five unions representing seventeen trades pulled together twenty-five thousand members to form the Colorado Building and Construction Trades Council, an attempt to organize non-union workers in construction and, it was said, to help draft legislation that would aid these workers. But some union enthusiasts were way ahead of the council.

The early-morning fire at 1075 Washington Street was only the beginning. Fires at non-union or open shops occurred every three or four months until May 20, 1974. By the end of 1969, ten fires were linked by the fact that all were at unfinished construction sites, nearly all were set after the wood framing had gone up but before fire-resistant dry wall had been installed and all but three could be connected to union conflicts.

Among the fires was one set on September 3, 1969, at a forty-unit luxury apartment complex at East Warren Avenue and Grape Street, which was destroyed despite the efforts of seventy-five Denver firefighters and twelve men from the Skyline Volunteer Fire Department. At another, on June 24, 1970, three apartment buildings under construction in the 3400 block of South Monaco, part of a twenty-three-apartment complex, were leveled in a blaze estimated to have cost builders $300,000. Fires followed in Englewood, Colorado Springs, Grand Junction, Boulder and Durango. Fires that fit the arson pattern also struck projects in Missouri, New Mexico, Washington, California, Arizona and Kansas, leading investigators to believe that national union leaders were directing the attacks. Law-enforcement officials' findings were reported to the Justice Department in Washington, D.C., but were never followed up.

The widespread nature and negative nationwide publicity of the fires led Governor John Love to call for the CBI to step in two years after the arson began. Carl Whiteside, who became director of the CBI and served in that post until his retirement in 1999, was lead investigator on the arson fires that occurred between April 1968 and December 1974. "I think the CBI received an executive order," he said in 1998. "Somebody made this a concern of Governor Love and the CBI was ordered to investigate."[6]

Those responsible for the fires eluded authorities for more than six years, but the plot eventually came unraveled, beginning in May 1972 when Colorado's first statewide grand jury was called to investigate eighteen fires in the metropolitan area. Members of the grand jury, whose foreman was Roger W. Rice of Denver, were from Denver County (two), Arapahoe County (three), Jefferson County (three), Adams County (two) and Boulder County (two).

A long series of legal arguments, including the legality of telephone wiretaps, delayed the grand jury's work for more than two years, but on Friday, December 13, 1974, William Swanson, business agent for the Cement Masons Union, Local 577, and Anthony Mulligan, business agent for the Colorado Building and Construction Trades Council, were indicted for "aiding, counseling and procuring the burning of condominium-type buildings" in connection with fires at two large construction projects in Denver, each of which caused about $500,000 in damages. The fires occurred at the Hampden Place Apartments, 8525 East Hampden Avenue, on February 5, 1972, and the Spring Water Apartments, 3131 West Mexico Avenue, on July 24, 1972.

Mulligan, 50, was charged with first-degree arson, second-degree arson and conspiracy to commit criminal mischief, and Swanson, 37, with first-degree arson, second-degree arson, two counts of criminal mischief and conspiracy. Swanson also was indicted by the grand jury for his part in vandalizing non-union concrete projects with acid, but the charges were dropped because they were unrelated to the condominium fires.

Also named in the indictments were Wayne Suggs, 39, assistant business agent for the cement union local who was named with Swanson on two charges of felony criminal mischief, and a woman, Cecil Dobbs, 28, who lived with Swanson. She and Swanson were charged with illegal sales of marijuana and amphetamines.

The CBI investigation was hampered by a number of problems, not the least of which was that union officials were prime suspects. The Denver Fire Department's arson bureau saw a pattern to the fires—that they probably were the result of union organizing efforts—as early as 1969, but proving it was another matter. In 1970, the FBI launched an investigation, interviewing local leaders of the building unions. Though the FBI lost interest in the case late in 1971, its questioning alerted the unionists to the fact that they were being investigated. As a result, union officials became doubly cautious, and wiretaps set up later by the CBI were far less productive than they might have been.

"There were a lot of people involved in this investigation, a lot of suspects because it would go from one to the other," Whiteside said. "We had a lot of early information about Mulligan and this guy [Paul] Welch (business manager for the Lathers Local 63 in Denver). It wasn't like you were going to go out and interview them and they were going to confess. They were interviewed by the FBI. They knew they were under the scrutiny of a criminal investigation for these fires early on and that made them more apprehensive ... more cautious in the conversations they did have over the telephone because an FBI agent went out there and interviewed them."[7]

The FBI, convinced that threats of violence directed at potential witnesses would result in an unsolvable case, withdrew its investigation, but the CBI labored on for another year, virtually alone because local fire departments had neither the personnel nor inclination to chase firebugs all over the state. Its first break in the case was no fluke. The pursuit that eventually brought an end to the fires and put two union officials behind bars could have been taken straight out of a Raymond Chandler private-eye paperback.

Undercover agent Kenneth Brown, described by his CBI co-workers as a "genius" at the dangerous task of befriending suspects and prying information out of them, was the man of the hour. Based on information from sources whom Whiteside and others involved with the case decline to reveal, Brown, assigned to the CBI's Organized Crime Strike Force, was reassigned to befriend suspected arsonist William Swanson, a union associate of Anthony Mulligan. He began his grand deception in a flamboyant way. On September 27, 1974, Brown strolled into the Berkeley Inn at 3834 Tennyson Street, across the street from Elitch Gardens amusement park, armed with two key weapons—plenty of cash and a hidden tape recorder, not to mention a riverboat gambler's intestinal fortitude.

At his trial for arson and conspiracy in 1975, Swanson—described by investigators as "a tough guy" who feared other union officials ("I'm more afraid of them than I am of you and your penitentiary," Swanson said when he turned down repeated offers of immunity)[8] —told the jury that he first met Brown when the latter offered to buy everyone at the Berkeley Inn a drink. "I kind of liked that," Swanson said, smiling.[9]

Before long, Brown was sitting with Swanson and his friends in the North Denver bar and flashing large sums of money, which caught everyone's attention, especially Swanson's. Brown spun an elaborate tale of wanting to get revenge on a man who had cheated him of $40,000. In short, he wanted the man's bar blown up. Swanson had a better idea: "Burn it up."[10]

Prior to Brown's contact with Swanson, wiretaps were set up by the CBI at Mulligan's home and at the offices of the Colorado Building and Construction Trades Council. Investigators listened to hours of conversations. Jim Jordan, head of the Denver Fire Department's arson bureau before working the CBI investigation, was among those tuned in. He and other eavesdroppers found that union officials and their friends had become shy conversationally.

"There was all kinds of talk by implication, but nothing concrete," Jordan said some twenty-five years later. "I never got so tired of listening to tapes in all my life. Mulligan had a kid about 12 years old and apparently [the boy's] mother worked. They'd go to work and

An arson fire at 3131 West Mexico Avenue at 10:43 P.M. on July 24, 1972, became a key piece of evidence in the investigation of the series of blazes that struck unfinished condominium and apartment fires in the metro Denver area and other cities in Colorado. This one caused $500,000 in damage. (Courtesy of The Denver Post.*)*

this kid would call the time of day at least every three minutes until it was time to go to school."[11]

Though they later became the focus of legal maneuvering, the wiretaps made during a sixty-day period in January and February 1972 proved almost worthless compared to the wealth of information Brown gathered in his conversations with Swanson. At Swanson's June 1975 trial before Judge George McNamara in Denver District Court, tape recordings revealed that during a series of meetings with Brown, Swanson bragged that he could "get hold of the man" who could set fires. He went on to relate that this particular gentleman, from Fort Collins, he said, was involved in a series of fires at non-union construction sites. Swanson even drove Brown around town and pointed out burned-out projects to show the undercover agent that his contact was good at his work.[12]

Swanson was an ardent unionist, an enthusiastic participant in meetings where members of the trades council passed the hat, collecting cash and even postage stamps for organizing activities. But by the end of his testimony during his own trial, Swanson was telling a different story about his relationship with Mulligan and the arsonists. He contended he never intended to put Brown together with an arsonist, allowing only that he wanted the cash Brown was waving around in the bar. "I was trying to get my hands on that $20,000 [Brown had offered him]. He had his scheme and I had mine." Swanson also claimed that the only knowledge he had about the series of apartment and condominium fires was what he read in the papers or heard through union gossip.[13]

Attorney Richard T. Spriggs, who prosecuted both Mulligan and Swanson, grilled Swanson with a stinging cross-examination:

> SPRIGGS — *You're willing to make illegal campaign contributions or to break up cement slabs?*
> SWANSON — *Yes.*
> SPRIGGS — *You're not willing to burn down buildings. That's where you draw the line, Mr. Swanson?*
> SWANSON — *No, I'm not.*
> SPRIGGS — *When you told Brown the location at 3131 West Mexico Avenue was one where a fire had occurred, was that just a lucky guess, Mr. Swanson?*
> SWANSON — *I think he pointed it out to me.*
> SPRIGGS — *When you told Brown about how many labor leaders had been called before the grand jury, was that just another lucky guess?*
> SWANSON — *Yes, it was.*
> SPRIGGS — *When you told Brown how the fires were started [that] was just another coincidence.*
> SWANSON — *Yes.*[14]

Not only did Swanson's contentions have no effect on the jury (he was sentenced to five years in the state penitentiary at Canon City for conspiracy), but his free-ranging conversations with the undercover agent would turn up again in co-defendant Anthony Mulligan's trial, which began in Denver District Court on October 29, 1975. It was Mulligan, Swanson told Brown, "who got it together in Denver. He brought in new organizing methods. He's the man who handled the torch man who burned down between $5 million and $10 million worth of buildings."[15]

Once again, Swanson repeated at Mulligan's trial in October that the taped conversations with Brown were all horsefeathers. He was merely bragging, he said, to impress Brown with names of important people he knew. Once again, Spriggs would have none of it. He ques-

Thermite, a chemical compound that burned with high heat, was used to torch condominiums and apartments under construction. The fires usually were set in the early-morning hours and timed to erupt after wood framing was done and before drywall went up. All but three fires were traced to union conflicts. (Terry Brennan collection.)

tioned which of Swanson's stories was true. "I think Swanson was a liar of one kind or another," Spriggs taunted.[16]

In the course of both men's trials, the arsonists' method of operation was outlined in detail by Spriggs and assistant district attorney Robert Swanson (no relation to defendant William Swanson). First, Mulligan or some other union organizer would show up at a construction site and chat with the builder. Sometimes a pleasant conversation would sway the builder to acquiesce; other times an obvious demonstration of implied threats would ensue, as when picketers walked sites with their placards tacked to baseball bats.

Though officials were never able to pinpoint the "torch," all but three of the fires followed a similar pattern. The arson would happen after the framing was completed but before dry wall went up, maximizing the chances of destruction. Witnesses would report that a bright glow appeared inside the structures shortly before fire broke out. And investigators would find that gasoline or other accelerants had been sprayed around the premises.

Jordan, who investigated many of the fires for the CBI, explained, "As far as I'm concerned it was Thermite," a simple chemical compound used for incendiary bombs during World War II. "Basically, all it is is aluminum powder and ferric oxide. Once it's ignited, it burns at around 4,000, 5,000 degrees. You could make it. Hell, I've made it many times for demonstrations at [arson] seminars."[17]

Intimidation, whether overt coercion or implied retribution, was a major obstacle to the investigation. "Everybody was afraid," said Jordan.[18] Recalled Whiteside, "[Swanson] was terrified of Mulligan. We would talk to union officials, and I'm going to tell you, they were terrified. You know, 'the oath of silence.' I remember an old man, and this guy was just deadly afraid what would happen to him. You weren't going to go out and interview people who were members of the union who possessed certain types of information, and they weren't going to communicate that."[19]

Instead, the CBI decided to pursue what Whiteside called "nontraditional investigative techniques"—wiretaps, informants and secret tape recordings. One informant, the one who fingered Mulligan, has not been identified publicly to this day. Mulligan's attorneys, including John L. Kane, who later became a colorful and controversial federal judge, argued during Mulligan's trial that the informant should be named or the case dismissed. Judge George McNamara agreed initially, but after what Kane later would claim was "a backdoor meeting" with prosecutors and a weekend to think it over, McNamara sided with prosecutors, ruling that the informant's safety would be compromised.

A key witness who testified against Swanson and, by implication, Mulligan, despite reservations, was Paul Welch, a vice president of the Lathers International Union and business manager for Lathers Local 63 in Denver. Welch hesitantly told a jury about fund-raising activities, including weekly meetings at which Mulligan would pass the hat. Many members of the trades council, he said, "assumed Mulligan was involved in the fires." Officially, he said, the money was "for the purpose of organizing. But, it was confusing what happened to the money. It was just given to Mulligan." Not everyone went along; members opposed to the use of violence walked out of the meetings. One member said, according to Welch, "all we have to do is get a fireman killed."[20]

At the same time, a power struggle was raging inside the statewide trades council between Mulligan and a faction led by George Westerberg, of the Northern Colorado Building and Construction Trades Council, and Lou Stone, business manager for the International Brotherhood of Electricians Local 68. The battle ended in

November 1972 when the northern and southern branches of the trades councils merged and Mulligan was transferred to Fort Collins from his job in Denver.

Obviously struggling with his testimony, for which he was given immunity, Welch said he couldn't remember what transpired in conversations with Mulligan shortly after the first fire in December 1968. Later, under prodding by prosecutor Spriggs, he told of a trip he made with Mulligan to a Northglenn construction site on February 27, 1970. He and Mulligan, Welch testified, had been drinking in Northglenn bars for several hours when the conversation turned to fires. His testimony continued:

> *He said something about a fire. I was frightened and suggested we go back to the car. And then I was driving but this is where it all gets very dim. We went to where his car was parked. He got two packages. He directed me to drive to an area where there was new construction. Then he said something about stopping, letting him out and driving around the block.*
>
> *He got out and took the parcels with him. I drove around three or four blocks. I stopped, and he got back in the car. I was petrified. I was stumbling and mumbling. He asked me, "What the hell's wrong with you? This is nothing new."* [21]

A neighbor in the area testified that a home under construction was burned that night. Philip Drake, projects coordinator for Perlmutter Associates, which built the home as part of a larger development, said that Mulligan visited him several times prior to the fire to encourage the hiring of only union labor. The last meeting, he said, "turned in to a shouting match. I told Mulligan to get out of my office. His parting shot was, 'You'll be hearing from us.'" [22]

Twelve owners and managers of construction projects also were called to the stand during Mulligan's trial to describe the sequence of events in fires at their job sites. Thomas Waters, a construction company president, recalled that he and Mulligan had "harsh words" when the union leader paid him a visit. "He told me that problems had been known to happen when people refused to have a closed shop." There was a fire a few days later at Waters's project. "After the fire, Mulligan came back and said it was a terrible thing that had happened to the project." [23]

Colorado Bureau of Investigation arson investigator Jim Jordan (left) arrested union organizer Anthony "Tony" Mulligan at his attorney's office, bringing to an end a six-year reign of terror. Mulligan served almost three years in the state penitentiary for his role in the conspiracy. Others were given lesser sentences. (Jim Jordan collection.)

An executive for Redman Construction Co., two of whose projects had been struck by fires, told the business newspaper *Cervi's Journal* that his company had obtained injunctions against the Northern Colorado Building and Construction Trades Council and the Carpenters' District Council of Southern Colorado because of repeated visits. After sustaining $400,000 in damages, Redman added fences, dogs, guards and motion detectors to its sites.[24]

In the course of their investigation of Swanson and Mulligan, CBI agents landed an unexpected bonus — Edward Urioste, a New Mexico labor leader connected to union organizing in Colorado who, in tape-recorded conversations with agents, claimed credit for fires in the Four Corners area and in California. Urioste also boasted, though his claims were never substantiated, that he had powerful contacts inside the office of New Mexico governor Jerry Apodaca.

In April 1975, CBI agents investigating the arson fires posed as crooks and convinced Urioste, executive secretary of the New Mexico Building and Construction Trades Council in Albuquerque, that they needed his help to blow up part of the Southglenn Shopping Mall in Denver. The agents obligingly flew Urioste — and a hundred pounds of dynamite — to Denver in a CBI plane. After being wined and dined, Urioste unknowingly accompanied the agents to CBI headquarters, where he was arrested.

Urioste, 38, was charged with felony counts of possession, unlawful shipping and transporting of explosives and conspiracy to commit first-degree arson. In January 1976, he was convicted on the charge of illegally transporting explosives (the other charges were dropped in plea bargaining) and was sentenced to two years in prison, thus becoming the third union organizer jailed.

As Mulligan's trial headed into November of 1975, his attorney, John L. Kane, a quick-witted man with an enormous knowledge of the classics and a wicked sense of humor, mounted a stirring defense of his client. "Mulligan never hired any hotshot to come in and start fires. He knew no more than anyone else about the fires. He merely knew they were happening." The charges against his client, he said, "are nothing more than an empty ... easy explanation for the problems we've had in this state. It's pretty easy to pick a scapegoat, and the one person is here."[25]

THE CITY'S LAST FIRE-ALARM BOX WAS RETIRED FROM HAPPY CANYON ROAD AND SOUTH EUDORA STREET ON JULY 12, 1979, REPLACED BY THE 911 EMERGENCY CALL SYSTEM STILL IN PLACE TODAY.

Kane suggested other causes for the series of fires — security guards, unhappy contractors passed over for jobs or, perhaps, even the owners themselves. Several union members vouched for Mulligan's character, and his wife, Gertrude, testified that he was at home during the time the two 1972 fires occurred.

In rebuttal, prosecutor Spriggs continued his assault on the Irish-born Mulligan, whose face, reminiscent of a boxer who had stopped quite a few blows with his nose, reflected his rough-and-tumble days growing up in New York City. Mulligan, Spriggs argued, was a dedicated, violence-prone labor official. The prosecutor reiterated his opening statement, insisting that it was Mulligan who introduced condominium fires to Colorado as a union organizing tool.

Shortly after noon on Monday, November 10, after two weeks of trial and six days of testimony, the jury began deliberations on the fate of Anthony Mulligan. Three or four votes were taken that afternoon, but no verdict was reached; Judge McNamara recessed the jury for the weekend. Shortly before noon on Monday, after three more hours of deliberations, the jury returned its verdict: guilty on two counts of second-degree arson and one count of conspiracy. Mulligan, who didn't testify at his trial, showed no emotion. He was facing up to ten years in the Colorado State Penitentiary and a $30,000 fine for each count of arson, and up to five years and $15,000 for the count of conspiracy.

Kane appealed, but the motion was rejected. On January 29, 1976, Mulligan was sentenced to ten years for his involvement in the series of destructive fires that swept the state. One of Mulligan's three convictions was later struck down by the Colorado Supreme Court, based on a "dearth of evidence" in the Spring Water Apartments fire at 3131 West Mexico Avenue, and his sentence was reduced to five years. Mulligan, sentenced on November 10, 1975, walked into prison in Canon City, Colorado, on November 15, 1977. The reign of terror was over. He was paroled on August 10, 1979, having served just under twenty-one months.

Who was responsible for the actual lighting of the forty arson fires? The question remains unanswered. Some twenty years after Swanson and Mulligan were dispatched to the Colorado State Penitentiary, Carl Whiteside pondered the question, thought a moment and said, "I'm not sure we got everybody who was involved in this case, but I think we got the lion's share of the people, the ringleaders."[26] Jim Jordan, who retired from the CBI in 1987, was even more philosophical. "At least," he laughed, "I had one bit of satisfaction out of this whole damned thing. I got a chance to arrest Mulligan in his attorney's office."[27]

SECONDS FROM DEATH

An almost-forgotten event that came within seconds of being a major tragedy occurred as investigators were closing in on the men responsible for the series of union-related arson fires that took place between 1968 and 1974.

In the fall of 1971, investigators were certain that an arson fire would be set at 3131 West Mexico Avenue, where the Spring Water Apartments were under construction. It fit perfectly the events leading up to other fires: Union officials visited a contractor, attempted to organize the job, then hinted that an "accident" could strike the job if the contractor didn't sign up. A fire usually followed.

The helicopter carrying photographer Terry Brennan (left), assistant chief Bob Hart and pilot Charles Nidey was 50 feet in the air when it lost power and crashed en route to study a possible arson site in September 1971. (Terry Brennan collection.)

The department decided to keep an eye on the project. To do this, they would use the city's police/fire helicopter to photograph the scene from the air to locate likely points of entrance and fire hydrants.

At about 3 P.M. on Thursday, September 2, 1971, the helicopter rose gently from its pad on the Speer Boulevard side of Currigan Hall as an admiring Chief Myrle Wise and others watched from near the department's headquarters across the street. Aboard the copter were Assistant Chief Bob Hart, 49; one of the department's two official photographers, Terry Brennan, 43; and the pilot, Police Technician Charles Nidey, 35. Two of the men waved and smiled at those watching from the ground.

As the helicopter rose to fifty feet, it lost power and began to sink back to earth. Witnesses said it struck a telephone pole near Speer Boulevard and fell to the ground directly behind the Fire Department Headquarters Building, 914 Twelfth Street, narrowly missing one corner of the

Brennan and Hart were sharing a seat belt when the copter crash landed on its side. They were unable to free themselves from the flaming wreck and only quick work by bystanders prevented the copter's passengers from burning to death. (Terry Brennan collection.)

building. It came so near the building it chipped some of the bricks on its downward plunge.

The copter flipped on its side, leaving Brennan and Hart, who were sharing a seatbelt, unable to free themselves. Wise, fireman Tom Manerbino and others rushed down an alley to the crash site. Heavily loaded with fuel that sprayed the crash scene, the craft and its occupants, the copter already was in flames. Brennan's hair was on fire.

Working quickly, rescuers, particularly Manerbino, who loosened the safety straps, freed the three men seconds before flames engulfed the helicopter. "If they had come down anywhere else they would have burned to death before we could get to them," Wise recalled in 1999. "They were within ten seconds" of dying.

Ironically, the Spring Water Apartments were torched, on July 24, 1972.

One further irony: There were no extinguishers in the fire department's headquarters.

—*The Denver Post*
September 3, 1971

CONSTRUCTION IN A DESIGNATED "FIRE DISTRICT"

The following ordinance was passed by the Denver City Council on April 20, 1863.

Be it ordained by the City Council of the City of Denver, that chapter six of the City Ordinances entitled "An ordinance concerning the fire department," be and the same is hereby amended by the addition of the following sections, to be known as Article Three of said ordinance, as follows, to-wit:

ARTICLE III
Fire Limits

SEC. 1. All that portion of the City of Denver embraced within the following described limits, shall hereafter be known as the fire limits of said city: Beginning in the centre of the alley between Wazee and Wynkoop streets, where the same intersects Cherry Creek; thence along the center of said alley in a northeasterly direction to the centre of G street; thence southeasterly along the centre of said street to the centre of the alley between Larimer and Lawrence streets; thence along the centre of said alley southwesterly to its intersection with Cherry Creek; thence down to Fifth Street; thence westerly along the centre of said street to the centre of the alley between Ferry and St. Louis streets; thence northerly along the centre of said alley to the centre of Second street; thence along the centre of said street in an easterly direction and up Cherry Creek to the place of beginning.

SEC. 2. No building shall be erected hereafter within the fire limits, unless the same shall be constructed in conformity with the following provisions:

First. All outside and party walls shall be made of stone, brick or other fire-proof material.

Second. Outside and party walls not exceeding twenty-four feet in height, from the top of the sidewalk to the under side of the roof joists or rafters, shall not be less than eight inches in thickness if of brick, or less than sixteen inches in thickness if of stone; but all outside walls exceeding twenty-four feet in height shall be not less than twelve inches in thickness for the first twenty-four feet if of brick, nor less than eighteen inches in thickness if of stone.

Third. All joists, beams, and other timbers in outside and party walls shall be separated at least four inches from each other with stone or brick laid in mortar.

Fourth. All end and party walls, except end walls fronting on streets, shall extend above the sheeting of the roof at least seven inches or three courses of brick, and in no case shall the planking or sheeting of the roof extend across any party or end wall, except end walls fronting on street: Provided, That wooden buildings, sheds or other structures may be constructed or erected in said fire limits, or removed from one place to another within the same by the special permission in writing from the Mayor—which permission shall be granted upon a written application or petition, and shall be issued upon the express condition that the said building, shed or other structure shall be removed without said fire limits on or before the 21st of October A.D. 1863—and it shall be the duty of the person or persons obtaining such permit to file the same together with the petition, with the city clerk within one day from the issuing of the same, upon which filing, such permit shall be evidence of his or her right to construct, erect or remove such building as aforesaid, and of his or her acceptance of the condition contained therein, and the same shall be notice to all subsequent purchasers, lessees or persons having any interest in such building.

SEC. 3. That any wooden building erected or removed within said fire limits as provided in the foregoing section shall not exceed eighteen feet in height to the comb of the roof, nor extend more than fifty feet in depth from the front or street, and no other building of wood shall be erected in the rear thereof except for wood or coal, of no greater dimensions than twelve feet square and eight feet in length.

SEC. 4. No wooden building or part of a building within the fire limits shall be raised, enlarged or removed to any other place within the same, nor shall any such building be removed into the fire limits, except as hererinbefore provided. That privies not exceeding ten foot square and twelve feet in height at the peak may be constructed of wood, and shall not be subject to the provision of this article; but all depositories for ashes within or without the fire limits shall be of brick or other fire-proof materials, without wood in any part thereof.

SEC. 5. Any owner, builder or other person who shall own, build or aid in the erection of any building or part of building within said limits, contrary to, or in any other manner than authorized by the provisions of this article, or who shall own, remove or assist in removing any wooden building with said limits from one place to another therein, or who shall own, remove or assist in removing any such building, from without said limits into the same, shall be subject to a fine of not less than twenty-five dollars and not exceeding one hundred dollars in the discretion of the court, for the first offense, and to the like fine for every forty-eight hours such person shall fail to comply with the provisions of this article, or continue in violation thereof. If any person shall violate any other provisions of this article, he shall be subject to the like fine.

SEC. 6. Any wooden building which may be erected, enlarged or removed, or in process of erection, enlargement or removal, contrary to this article, shall be deemed a nuisance; and any building erected under any permit granted in pursuance of the proviso contained in section two hereof, which shall be permitted to remain in said fire limits after the time specified in such permit, shall be deemed a nuisance; and upon information, it shall be the duty of the mayor, after due notice to the owner or builder thereof, to abate the same, by an order in writing to require the city marshal to raze the building to the ground. The expenses of such removal shall be reported by the marshal for assessment, and may be collected of the owner of such building by suit.

SEC. 7. That this ordinance shall take effect upon publication, by posting the same in three of the most public places in the city.

Passed April 20th, 1863
AMOS STECK, Mayor
Attest: Chauncey Barbour, City Clerk

LOSSES IN THE "GREAT FIRE"

April 19, 1863

The following list begins with losses sustained at the western edge of the fire. Buildings referred to as having sustained "damage" are brick "fire-proofs," the contents of which are untouched; brick buildings, the walls of which are standing and can be repaired; or else buildings on the outskirts of the burnt district that were scorched, damaged by water or partially torn down. When the word "damage" is not used, either building or contents are totally destroyed.

BLAKE STREET, NORTH SIDE

Douglas, damage to house and stock	$300
Baldwin, Pegram & Co., building	1,200
Campbell & Jones, groceries	4,000
Campbell & Jones, commission goods	3,000
Cole (late Cotton), house	300
Geo. Tritch, stoves and hardware	3,000
Hawken, building and merchandise	4,000
Moore, building	700
Poznanski & Co., building	500
Blake & Williams, Elephant Stables	1,500
Fleming & Co. (lessees), contents	1,000
Wilson, contents	800
Commission, contents	4,200
Hodge, building and shoemaker's stock	400
Palmer, building and liquors	2,000

Chase & Heatley, building	$600
Lancaster & Co., saloon stock	900
Roath, building and jeweler's stock	400
C. A. Cook & Co., damage to building	2,000
J. A. Jackson & Co., flour, etc.	9,000
Brendlinger, building	2,000
Brendlinger, tobacco, etc.	1,000

F (FIFTEENTH) STREET, WEST SIDE, BELOW BLAKE STREET

Brendlinger, building	$500
Belden & Co., groceries	2,000
McGee & Co., building	800
Brannan & Mittnacht, groceries	2,000
Putnam, building	250
Saunders, stoves and hardware	800
Ben. Wood, building	1,200
Nye & Co., stoves and hardware	2,500
Nye & Co., money	1,000
Geo. Tritch, two buildings	1,500
Geo. Tritch, stoves and hardware	2,000

F (FIFTEENTH) STREET, EAST SIDE

Malony, blacksmith shop	$100
Gillett & Richardson, tools, etc.	200
Moody, shop building	300
Gillett, tools, etc.	200
C. A. Cook & Co., building	200
Pfouts & Russell, damage to house and stock	400
Broadwell & Cook, house and contents	1,500
Crawford, house	500
Hiney, house and saloon stock	500
Dan Dougherty, house and saloon stock	900
Ullman, building and meat market	800

DOWN BLAKE STREET, NORTH SIDE

Madison, building and saloon stock	$800
J. M. Fisher, building and groceries	600
Piles, building and groceries	1,500

Stebbins & Porter, damage to building	$2,000
Stebbins & Porter, merchandise	2,000
Kiskadden & Co., merchandise	6,000
B. L. Ford, damage to building	2,000
Daniels & Brown, merchandise	15,000
Smith, damage to building	500

UP BLAKE STREET, SOUTH SIDE

Mickley, building and saloon stock	$1,000
Mayfield, building and cigar store	500
Reithmann, building and bakery stock	2,000
B. L. Ford, building and restaurant stock	5,500
Chase & Heatley, building and saloon stock	7,000
C. H. Keith, building	400
D. D. Towle, damage to building	2,500
Cheesman & Co., drugs, etc.	10,000

UP F (FIFTEENTH) STREET, EAST SIDE

Bartlett, building	$150
Mrs. Smith, building	400
Cahn, hides	50
Leonard, jeweler's tools	100
Walker, building	2,000
Sherwood & Bro., merchandise	20,000
S. A. Rice, building	500
Arbour, Clark & Fitchie, groceries	1,000

McGAA (MARKET) STREET, BELOW F (FIFTEENTH) STREET

Ford & Bro., stable	$200
French, stable	500

F (FIFTEENTH) STREET, WEST SIDE, BELOW McGAA (MARKET) STREET

Steck & Cook, two stables	$500
Ebrung, building and bakery stock	600
Ohlfing & Co., building and merchandise	1,000
Feuerstein, building	900
Ruffner, restaurant stock	900

Fillmore, building (insured)	$2,000
John [last name unlisted], saloon stock	600
S. A. Rice, groceries	3,000
Porter & Co., buckskin, clothing, etc.	1,300
Voorhees & Hawkins, groceries, etc.	4,800
Lavin, groceries, etc.	5,000
Lavin, money	1,000
Stickney, stationery, etc.	100
Graham, drugstore	1,500

UP BLAKE STREET, SOUTH SIDE, ABOVE F (FIFTEENTH) STREET

Gardner, Crocker & Fillmore, Cherokee House	$2,000
Fairchild & Co. (lessees), contents	2,000
Rieshaw, building	800
Picket & Lincoln, merchandise	1,200
McMechatt, merchandise	2,500
Commission, merchandise	2,500
Rieshaw, building	500
Shiner, bakery and flour	2,000
Roath, building	100
Goldberg, cigar-store stock	300
Harlan, building	1,200
Wilhelm, cigar-store stock	600
Newman, building	800
Bay, groceries	600
Newman, building	500
Arbour & Smith, barbershop	1,500
Rieshaw & Harlan, building	500
Thatcher & Co., bowling alley	300
Turck, damage to building	300
Inslee, damage to merchandise	100
Bayaud & Mason, building (insured)	6,000
Dixon & Durant, auction goods	500
Brown, clothing	200
Probate court and lodgers house	200
Honore, building and hardware	700
Gottleib, building	500
Fink, bootmaker's stock	400

Ed Jacobs, building	$600
Morris & Bro., tailor shop	150
Tiltons, damage to building, etc.	100
Total	$200,000

SOURCE: *Weekly Rocky Mountain News*, April 23, 1863.

Appendix C

COLORADO FIRES
SET BY UNION
ARSONISTS
1968–1974

The following is a list of the forty fires attributed to union arsonists between April 12, 1968, and June 14, 1974. It was compiled to enable the Colorado Bureau of Investigation (CBI) to determine a pattern to the fires, and is provided here courtesy of former CBI agent James Jordan. Law-enforcement pursuit of the arsonists is detailed in Chapter Twelve.

The list shows the name of the builder, whether it was a union, non-union or open shop, time and date of the fire, address of the building and the estimated damage.

1. Stopa Construction. Open shop. 5:33 A.M. on Friday, April 12, 1968. 1075 Washington Street, Denver. $170,000.
2. George A. Bettger. Open shop. 5:05 A.M. on Tuesday, June 25, 1968. 5620 West Twenty-seventh Avenue, Denver. $68,000.
3. Sullivan Builders. Non-union. 5:35 A.M. on Wednesday, September 16, 1968. Twentieth and Quail Streets, Lakewood. $11,600.
4. Wolff Development. Open shop. 7:13 P.M. on Tuesday, November 26, 1968. 3280 South Oneida Way, Denver. Damage unknown.
5. Irwin J. Horowitz. Open shop. 11:41 P.M. on Wednesday, November 27, 1968. East Quincy Avenue and Happy Canyon Road, Denver. $10,000.
6. Midwest Construction. Open shop. 7:15 P.M. on Monday, February 17, 1969. 11051 West Sixty-third Avenue, Arvada. $135,000.

7. Lynch Construction. Open shop. 9:25 P.M. on Wednesday, August 6, 1969. 12044 Archer Place, Aurora. $135,000.

8. Redman Construction. Open shop. 9:18 P.M. on Monday, August 25, 1969. 7400 Deacon Street, Adams County. $125,000.

9. Newport Construction. Open shop. 8:46 P.M. on Wednesday, September 3, 1969. 5401 East Warren Avenue, Denver. $87,500.

10. Perlmutter Associates. Open shop. 7 P.M. on Friday, February 27, 1970. 921 Kennedy Drive, Northglenn. No damage.

11. Hettinger Construction. Open shop. 8:18 P.M. on Saturday, March 21, 1970. 1925–29 South Depew Street, Denver. $50,000.

12. F-D Development Co. Open shop. 9:14 P.M. on Tuesday, May 5, 1970. 4100 South Bannock Street, Englewood. $5,000.

13. Modular Basic Construction. Union. 7:29 P.M. on Wednesday, June 24, 1970. 3422–24 South Monaco Street, Denver. $300,000.

14. H & K Investments. Non-union. 9:30 P.M. on Wednesday, September 16, 1970. 3161 Madison Avenue, Denver. $75,000.

15. Redman Construction. Open shop. 6:44 P.M. on Wednesday, October 7, 1970. 7495 East Quincy Avenue, Denver. $125,000.

16. D & B Construction. Open shop. 6 P.M. on Sunday, November 8, 1970. 4461–77 South Lowell Boulevard, Denver. $300,000.

17. GMC Properties Inc. Open shop. 8:30 A.M. on Saturday, February 5, 1972. 8525 East Hampden Avenue, Denver. $400,000.

18. Hallcraft Homes. Union. 6 P.M. on Friday, February 4, 1972. 8800 West Custer Place, Lakewood. $50,000.

19. Cimarron Development. Non-union. 4:45 P.M. on Thursday, June 1, 1972. 700 Hathaway Drive, Colorado Springs. $450,000.

20. Bolden Construction. Open shop. 8:47 P.M. on Monday, July 24, 1972. 2890 East Aurora Street, Boulder. $350,000.

21. Hubchik & Davis Inc. Union. 10:43 P.M. on Monday, July 24, 1972. Spring Water Apartments, 3131 West Mexico Avenue, Denver. $500,000.

22. Shelton Construction. Open shop. 3:54 P.M. on Tuesday, October 17, 1972. 591 West Prentice Avenue, Littleton. $1,000.

23. H. S. Meinberger & Son. Open shop. 7:24 P.M. on Wednesday, October 25, 1972. Four Seasons, 100 Ridge, Breckenridge. $150,000.

24. Paul Walden Construction. Open shop. 4:45 P.M. on Wednesday, November 29, 1972. 1855 South Lee Street, Lakewood. No damage.

25. Statewide Builders. Non-union. 2:07 A.M. on Saturday, December 23, 1972. Rock-N-Pines, nine miles west of Glenwood Springs. $200,000.

26. Witkin Homes. Open shop. 8:05 P.M. on Wednesday, February 28, 1973. 7995 Chase Circle, Arvada. $80,000.

27. Darrel Farr Development. Non-union. 5 P.M. on Thursday, March 8, 1973. 4155 East Jewell Avenue, Aurora. No damage.

28. Witkin Homes. Open shop. 2:40 A.M. on Thursday, April 5, 1973. 4588 South Hannibal Street, Aurora. $85,000.

29. Witkin Homes. Open shop. 12:05 P.M. on Monday, May 21, 1973. 4588 South Hannibal Street, Aurora. $190,000.

30. Mesa Homes. Open shop. 5:15 P.M. on Thursday, May 31, 1973. 1005 Winters Avenue, Grand Junction. $600,000.

31. Mission Viejo. Open shop. 3:45 A.M. on Thursday, June 21, 1973. 3600 South Kalispell Street, Aurora. No damage.

32. Baker-Crow Construction. Open shop. 1:23 A.M. on Thursday, July 5, 1973. 7196 South Vine Circle, Arapahoe County. $200,000.

33. Wood Brothers. Open shop. 4:25 P.M. on Thursday, July 12, 1973. 1508 South Owens Street, Jefferson County. $800,000.

34. Russell Construction. Open shop. 2:40 P.M. on Saturday, August 11, 1973. 1700 block of Main Street, Grand Junction. $100,000.

35. Evenshaw Construction. Open shop. 4:46 A.M. on Sunday, August 12, 1973. 2859 Elm Avenue, Grand Junction. $30,000.

36. Amcon Construction. Open shop. 2:45 A.M. on Thursday, August 16, 1973. Florida Village, Durango. $600,000.

37. Jeffco Manufacturing. Open shop. 11:10 A.M. on Wednesday, September 5, 1973. 3150 Youngfield Avenue, Wheat Ridge. $35,000.

38. Ridgewood Realty. Open shop. 10:05 P.M. on Friday, January 4, 1974. 14618 West Sixth Avenue, Jefferson County. $300,000.

39. Paul Walden Construction. Open shop. 8:14 P.M. on Thursday, May 30, 1974. 10452 West Florida Avenue, Lakewood. $150,000.

40. Shelton Construction. Open shop. Between 5:30 P.M. and 9:30 A.M. on Friday, June 14, 1974. 1744 Garfield Avenue, Louisville. No damage.

DENVER FIRE CHIEFS
1872–Present

CHIEFS, VOLUNTEERS (1872–1881)
1872–1873: Phillip Trounstine
1873–1875: Joseph A. Bailey
1875–1877: Julius Pearse
1877–1879: Thomas S. Clayton
1879–1881: George Duggan

FIRE AND POLICE BOARD (1891–1901)
1891–1892: Egbert Johnson, Robert S. Roe, Robert W. Speer
1893: C. B. Stone, D. J. Martin, G. H. Phelps
1894: Jackson Orr, D. J. Martin, Dennis Mullins, S. D. Barnes, A. J. Rogers
1895: Frank Church, A. W. Hogle, C. F. Wilson
1896: DeWitt C. Webber, A. W. Hogle, C. F. Wilson
1897: Frank Church, Robert W. Speer, Earl B. Coe
1898: Ralph Talbot, Robert W. Speer, Earl B. Coe
1899–1900: Robert W. Speer, Daniel Sayer, C. L. Burpee
1901: Frank Adams, J. T. Bottom, W. H. Griffith

FIRE COMMISSIONERS (1894–1912)
1894: Dennis Mullins
1895: Frank Church
1896: DeWitt C. Webber
1897–1899: Ralph Talbot
1899–1901: Robert W. Speer
1901–1904: Frank Adams
1904–1912: D. A. Barton

CHIEFS, DENVER FIRE DEPARTMENT (1881–PRESENT)

1881: George Duggan

1881–1883: Thomas F. Clayton

1883–1894: Julius Pearse

1894–1895: William E. Roberts

1895–1897: Julius Pearse

1897–1903: William E. Roberts

1903–1912: Terry Owens

1912–1945: John F. Healy

1946–1964: Allie Feldman

1964–1970: Cassio Frazzini

1968–1970: Daniel Cronin (acting chief)

1970–1986: Myrle Wise

1987: Stan Sponsel (acting chief)

1987–Present: Richard Gonzales

THE CHIEFS

JULIUS PEARSE

One of the city's longest-serving public servants, Julius Pearse had the misfortune to be swept up in the Fire and Police Commission showdown between Governor Davis Waite and the City of Denver between 1891 and 1901.

Fed up with corruption in Denver's fire and police departments, Waite appointed members of the Fire and Police Commission to oversee both departments.

Julius Pearse. (Photo from Representative Men of Colorado, 1858–1902.*)*

Pearse, associated with the department as early as 1872 when it was still all-volunteer, was removed as fire chief in 1894 because he refused to pledge allegiance to Waite's newly appointed board. The following year, when another board was appointed, he was reinstated as chief and 20 of those who had remained on the department were asked to resign. Pearse and William E. Roberts then swapped the chief's job every year until Pearse retired in 1897.

After his retirement, Pearse formed the Julius Pearse Fire Department Supply Co., specializing in fire-fighting equipment. Not surprisingly, the Denver Fire Department was his best customer.

Pearse, a native of Germany, died at his home at 2528 Stout Street at age 70 on April 27, 1917.

TERRY OWENS

Chief of the department from 1903 to 1912, Terrance Owens was a heroic and much-loved leader.

He was only 17 when he joined the volunteers in 1871. On his retirement, he proudly proclaimed, "I was never carpeted for neglect of duty or reprimanded for any cause whatever."

Born in Canada, Owens remained humble, even after his career ended. In 1932, he told *The Denver Times,* which lauded him as "the idol of his men," "I have carried a few people out of burning buildings and done some other stunts but that's nothing. I get paid for it, and it's just what all the other boys will do when the opportunity comes."

CHIEF WILLIAM E. (BILLY) ROBERTS

Handsome "Billy" Roberts arrived in Denver from Wales in 1873 and two years later joined the city's volunteer fire brigades. He was chief of the paid department in 1894–1895 and again from 1897 to 1903, when he retired to become a security guard for Colorado National Bank.

As a youth, Roberts was considered one of the fastest and most athletic men in frequent and spirited competitions held among volunteer departments.

William E. (Billy) Roberts. (Photo from Representative Men of Colorado, 1858–1902.*)*

As chief, Roberts was in charge at many major fires, including the Gumry Hotel, the old City Hall and the St. James Hotel. He also was a staunch supporter of the abilities of the city's black firefighters in the 1890s.

At age 79, he shot and killed a man on January 15,

1937, in a downtown restaurant after the man called Roberts "a liar" for claiming he was a working cowboy in his younger days. Roberts said he shot in self-defense after the man "lunged at him" several times. The court agreed and a directed verdict found him not guilty.

He died on January 1, 1944, at age 86 at the home of his daughter.

JOHN DULMAGE

John Dulmage may have had the most exciting career of any of Denver's fire chiefs. His tenure, beginning as a volunteer in 1881, was fraught with mishaps, accidents and close brushes with death.

In 1894, he nearly fell through the floor of the fire at Union Depot. He escaped death in 1895 when a wall collapsed during a fire at Nineteenth and Blake streets. In 1908, he and a policeman, trying to rescue a patron of the

John Dulmage. (Courtesy of the Denver Public Library/Western History Department.)

Belmont Hotel, crashed through the floor. Twice he was injured in collisions while racing to fire scenes in his buggy.

While helping quell a nitric-acid spill at *The Denver Post* in 1904, Dulmage was overcome by fumes and suffered from asthma and respiratory problems the remainder of his life. At one point, he was declared by the city's newspapers to be as good as dead from breathing acid fumes.

For all that, Dulmage was revered by his fellow firefighters as a heroic figure. After his retirement in 1910, the department held annual gatherings in his honor. Dulmage died at his home, 860 Emerson Street, at age 68 on April 6, 1923.

JOHN F. HEALY

Chief John F. Healy ruled the department as a virtual king from July 1912 until his death in 1945.

During thirty-three years at the head of the department, much of it served before civil service was in effect, Healy could, and did, decide who was hired, who was given promotions and whose careers would founder. "I don't want any of those college guys," he told one applicant. "What I'm interested in knowing is whether a fellow knows building construction and has he got guts. Guts, hear me!"

John F. Healy. (Courtesy of the Denver Public Library/Western History Department.)

He was a man who could drink and swear with equal alacrity. But he was also a crusader for the department. He fought to get more hydrants built near schools and more fire alarms and he knew which buildings in downtown were well-constructed and safer for his men to enter during a blaze. He also stood up for his men with the city administration.

He was so fired-through with the department that after the death of his wife, he took up residence in one of the city's fire houses.

Healy joined the department in 1894 and worked his way up the ladder, ultimately serving fifty-one years. When he died at age 72 on April 24, 1945, his obituary in *The Denver Post* read dramatically, "There are plenty of citizens who recall the big, brawny, blue-eyed Irishman sitting the driver's seat, shouting to the dashing horses and using the reins like pushers to make them go faster."

MYRLE WISE

Born in Oklahoma on March 14, 1918, Myrle Wise joined the department on May 7, 1943, as a young recruit. He worked his way up through the ranks and on July 10, 1970, became chief.

In 1956, he became the youngest assistant chief in department history at the age of 38.

As head of the department's Fire Prevention Bureau, Wise spearheaded formulation of a fire code,

Myrle Wise. (Courtesy of the Denver Fire Department.)

adopted, after he became chief, in 1979. It became a national model as the Uniform Building Code. It dictated such innovations as interior sprinklers, alarms, adequate exits and stand pipes in large buildings.

The department hired its first women employees (secretary Ida Stines was the first) the day he became chief in 1970. He also advanced minority hiring, instituted a 911 emergency calling system, oversaw the building of twenty-one fire stations and switched the department's apparatus from gasoline to the more efficient and reliable diesel.

Wise was regarded as a master politician in city government and his tenure was, at times, tumultuous. When he retired on February 1, 1987, his 16-year tenure as chief was the department's third-longest, ranking behind only John F. Healy (33 years) and Allie Feldman (18 years).

In 2000, Wise was living in Denver.

NOTABLE

DENVER FIRES

1860–1999

1860

March 18: Summers & Dorsett Stables, Twelfth and Walnut (Market) Streets.

1863

April 19: Downtown business district, Wazee to McGaa (Market) Streets, Cherry Creek to Sixteenth (G) Street.

1872

January 31: Estabrook Stables, Fifteenth and Holladay (Market) Streets.

1875

February 23: Planters' House, Sixteenth and Blake Streets.

1877

March 19: Old Denver Theatre, Sixteenth and Lawrence Streets.

March 20: Overland Hotel, Grand Central and Union House and Iowa House, Twenty-first and Blake Streets.

1878

January 5: Colorado Central Railroad depot, Sixteenth and Delgany Streets.

1879

May 24: St. Charles Hotel, Eighteenth and Holladay (Market) Streets.

1880

October 21: Estabrook Stables, Fifteenth and Holladay (Market) Streets.

October 25: Balcom House, Eighteenth and Larimer Streets.

1882

January 10: Hallack & Howard Block, Eighteenth and Holladay (Market) Streets.

1883

April 12: Continental Oil and Transportation Co., Nineteenth and New Haven Streets.

1884

January 29: Academy of Music Theater, Sixteenth and Holladay (Market) Streets.

February 24: National and Nashville Hotels, Nineteenth and Wazee Streets.

March 25: Street Car Stables, Sixteenth and Curtis Streets.

1885

January 4: Melburn's Carriage Works, 238 Twenty-second Street.

October 8: Ernest & Wilbur Stables, Sixteenth and Wazee Streets.

1886

July 6: Academy of Music Theater, Good and News Blocks, Sixteenth and Holladay (Market) Streets.

1887

January 15: Clifford Block, Sixteenth and Lawrence Streets.

March 27: Tabor, Baur and Currier & Knox Blocks, Sixteenth and Larimer Streets.

May 3: Collier & Cleveland Printers, 1541 Holladay (Market) Street.

May 15: Kerstens, Peters & Co., 1621 Blake Street.

August 25: J. S. Brown and Bro., 1524 Wazee Street.

October 3: Cooper & Hagus Furniture Co., Sixteenth and Lawrence Streets.

1888

August 25: J. S. Brown & Bro., 1524 Wazee Street.

1889

February 2: F. P. Scott Hardware, Musee Building, Seventeenth and Lawrence Streets.

March 13: King Block, Seventeenth and Lawrence Streets.

April 4: Golden Eagle Dry Goods Co., Sixteenth and Lawrence Streets.

1891

April 22: Davis-Creswell Brass Foundry, 1624 Blake Street.

November 9: Mansion Stables, 1816 Lawrence Street.

December 28: Appel & Co., Sixteenth and Lawrence Streets.

1892

June 11: People's Theater, Fifteenth Street and Cleveland Place.

1893

January 5: Hallack Paint and Glass Co., Eighteenth and Market Streets.

March 24: Summit Fuel and Feed Co., Third and Larimer Streets.

March 24: R. B. Chatfield Paint Store, 908 Fifteenth Street.

August 14: Crescent Milling and Elevator Co., West Twenty-ninth Avenue and Twentieth Street.

1894

March 18: Union depot, Seventeenth and Wynkoop Streets.

March 22: Champa Block, Fifteenth and Champa Streets.

1895

March 23: St. James Hotel, 1528 Curtis Street.

August 19: Gumry Hotel, 1725 Lawrence Street.

August 22: McPhee & McGinnity Co., Eighteenth and Wazee Streets.

October 6: Cooper & Hagus Furniture Co., 1636 Lawrence Street.
December 20: Riche-Jacobson Block, 1615 Curtis Street.

1896

July 12: Denver Consolidated Electric Co., Twenty-first and Wynkoop Streets.

1897

June 4: Quincy Building, 1008 Seventeenth Street.
June 10: Studebaker Carriage Co., 1612 Fifteenth Street.

1899

March 7: Colorado Milling and Elevator Co., Seventh and Wazee Streets.
June 18: Western Chemical Co., South Seventh (Osage) Street and West Bayaud Avenue.
July 1: Western Chemical Co., South Seventh (Osage) Street and West Bayaud Avenue.

1900

January 10: Davis Iron Works, Eighth and Larimer Streets.
February 17: Kansas Moline Plow Co., 1533 Wazee Street.

1901

May 22: American Can Co., 1717 Fifteenth Street.
November 30: City Hall, Fourteenth and Larimer Streets.
December 2: Croke & Thome Furniture Co., 1613 Welton Street.

1902

December 7: McPhee & McGinnity Co., Eighteenth and Wazee Streets.

1903

March 11: Hurlbut Grocery Co., 1138 Fifteenth Street.
May 14: St. John's Church of the Wilderness, Twentieth Avenue and Broadway.
July 17: McPhee & McGinnity Co., Eighteenth and Wazee Streets.

1904

March 30: Cooper Building, Seventeenth and Curtis Streets.
May 7: Curtis Theater, 1744 Curtis Street.
May 7: Hurlbut Grocery Co., 1439 Lawrence Street.
September 20: The Denver Post, 1623 Curtis Street.
December 2: Crystal Theater, 1717 Curtis Street.

1905

February 19: Symes Building, Sixteenth and Champa Streets.
February 25: Gettysburg Block (vacant), 1720 Champa Street.
June 2: Tivoli Brewery, 1336 Tenth Street.
July 5: Hurlbut Grocery Co., 1439 Lawrence Street.
November 6: McPhee & McGinnity Co., Twenty-sixth and Blake
    Streets.

1906

January 6: LaCombe Electric Co., West Thirteenth Avenue and
    South First (Zuni) Street.
February 13: Colorado & Southern RR shops, Seventh and Chest-
    nut Streets.
March 22: Western & Hewitt Candy Co., 1819 Market Street.
April 29: Twenty-eight fires, between Ogden and Vine Streets and
    Nineteenth and Twenty-fifth Avenues.
May 4: Western Glass Co., South Eighth (Navajo) Street and West
    Bayaud Avenue.
May 5: Denver Transit warehouse, 1421 Wynkoop Street.
December 25: Ernest & Cranmer Building, Seventeenth and Curtis
    Streets.
December 26: Colorado Casket Co., 1231 Wazee Street.
December 26: Ernest & Cranmer Building, Seventeenth and Curtis
    Streets.

1907

March 20: Jefferay Hat and Furnishing Co., 1635 Curtis Street.

1908

April 8: J. P. Paulson Manufacturing Co., Fifteenth and Wynkoop
    Streets.
September 3: A. T. Lewis & Sons, Sixteenth and Stout Streets.

September 8: Belmont Hotel, 1723 Stout Street.

September 24: Coliseum Hall, Eighteenth and Champa Streets.

October 21: Hungarian Mill & Elevator, 1447 West Seventh Avenue.

1909

March 9: Cottrell Clothing Co., Sixteenth and Welton Streets.

April 6: Hallack & Howard Lumber Co., Seventh and Larimer Streets.

May 24: Benight-Latchman Carpet Co., 1540 Welton Street.

October 4: Spengel Furniture Co. warehouse, Twenty-sixth and Walnut Streets.

1910

May 16: Hollis & Platt barns, 4686 Lafayette Street.

May 30: Spratlen & Anderson Co., Fifteenth and Wazee Streets.

June 8: Western Chemical Co., West Bayaud Avenue and South Osage Street.

November 2: Weiner Wine Co., Sixteenth Street and Glenarm Place.

1911

January 17: Davis & Shaw Furniture Co., Fifteenth and Larimer Streets.

March 11: American Furniture Co. warehouse, Sixteenth and Platte Streets.

August 25: Barteldes Seed and Moore Hardware, Fifteenth and Wazee Streets.

November 30: Famous Cafe and Charleston Rooming House, 1501 Curtis Street.

1912

January 14: The Derby and skating rink, Lakeside Amusement Park, 4601 Sheridan Boulevard.

February 10: Great Western Oil Co., 489 Lawrence Street.

March 20: McCue Lumber Co., Third and Lawrence Streets.

May 20: Larimer House and Golden Eagle Co., 1548 Larimer Street.

August 1: Murphy Paint Co. and Belvedere Hotel, Fifteenth Street and Glenarm Place.

September 29: Colorado Zinc Co., West Virginia Avenue and Platte River.

October 4: Western Chemical Co., West Bayaud Avenue and South Osage Street.

1913

March 11: Paloma Rooming House and Livery Stable, 1818 Arapahoe Street.

April 25: Dewar Trunk Co., 731 Broadway.

November 9: Nave & McCord Mercantile Co., 1117 Wazee Street.

1914

March 29: Tivoli Brewery, 1310 Tenth Street.

May 30: Herbert Catering & Watrous Cafe, 1517 Curtis Street.

1915

March 4: Perkins Epeneter Pickle Co., 900 Lawrence Street.

April 11: Western Chemical Co., West Bayaud Avenue and South Osage Street.

August 21: White Clover Butter Co. and Keys Manufacturing Co., 1518–20 Wazee Street.

October 21: Hardesty Manufacturing Co., 1809 Market Street.

November 24: Mountain Motor Fuel Co., West Thirty-sixth Avenue and Fox Street.

December 15: L. A. Watkins Co., 1515 Wazee Street.

1916

January 26: Saint Joseph Hospital, East Eighteenth Avenue and Humboldt Street.

July 8: Rittenberger's Stables, 2012 Lawrence Street.

December 28: Proudfit-Ormsby Commission Co., 1547 Market Street.

1917

January 9: Hollis & Platt barns, 4686 Lafayette Street.

October 28: Orahood Garage, 2424 East Colfax Avenue.

1918

June 6: Bogue-Wensley Lead Co., 1529 Eighteenth Street.

1919

July 10: Maddox Ice Co., West Seventh Avenue and Alcott Street.
November 18: A. T. Lewis & Co. Stables, 2100 Humboldt Street.
December 5: O. P. Baur, 1512 Curtis Street.

1920

January 20: Longmont Farmers Milling & Elevator Co., 2100 Twentieth Street.
June 21: Broadway Ball Park, West Sixth Avenue and Bannock Street.
July 9: Methodist Episcopal Church (abandoned), 1846 Arapahoe Street.
July 9: Mutual Oil Co. warehouse, 2061 Blake Street.
July 9: Scott Auto Body (East Turner Hall), 2150 Arapahoe Street.
November 23: Barnard Block, West Eighth Avenue and Kalamath Street.

1921

March 22: F. W. Woolworth, Sixteenth and Champa Streets.
July 10: Denver Union Stockyards, East Forty-sixth Avenue and Humboldt Street.
November 2: Schieren Leather Co., 1750 Arapahoe Street.

1922

April 18: Lindquist Mercantile Building, Arapahoe School and Club Building, 1721–1731 Arapahoe Street.
May 12: American Fixture Co., Twelfth and Arapahoe Streets.
June 12: Denver & Rio Grande shops, West Tenth Avenue and Quivas Street.
July 12: American Wholesale Drug Co., Eighteenth and Lawrence Streets.
October 28: Plains Iron Works, Eighth and Larimer Streets.
November 16: Greber Garage, 2835 Tremont Place.

1923

January 8: United States Army Store, 1433 Larimer Street.
March 10: Kissel Auto Agency, 1333 Broadway.
March 16: Moffit Zook Garage, East Sixteenth Avenue and Williams Street.

April 9: Ayres Mercantile Co. warehouse, West Sixth Avenue and Blake Street.

December 31: Apartment house, 1305 Acoma Street.

December 31: Ariel Apartments, 2108 Tremont Place.

1924

January 5: Summit Grain Co., Nineteenth and Navajo Streets.

February 16: Grimes & Friedman warehouse, Eleventh and Wynkoop Streets.

March 13: El Jebel Temple, East Eighteenth Avenue and Sherman Street.

April 24: Apartment house, West Forty-ninth Avenue and Tennyson Street.

July 1: City Warehouse, 901 Wazee Street.

July 22: Merchants Transfer Co., West Twenty-ninth Avenue and Inca Street.

December 10: Warriner-McReynolds Auto Co., 1248 Broadway.

December 24: Tabor Grand Theater, Sixteenth and Curtis Streets.

1925

April 19: Shorter A.M.E. Church, East Twentieth Avenue and Washington Street.

April 29: Western Dry Goods Co., 1723 Lawrence Street.

1926

November 17: Blenheim Apartments, 1137 Sherman Street.

1927

February 10: Universal Stove Co., 1231 Wazee Street.

March 31: Denver Tramway Corp., Fourteenth and Water Streets.

May 8: Grimes Paper Co. warehouse, 1333 Eleventh Street.

July 4: National Jewish Hospital, 1432 Jackson Street.

August 8: Don Hogan Motor Co., 1227 Broadway.

November 13: Deline Paper Box Manufacturing Co., 1070 Santa Fe Drive.

December 15: Cribben & Sexton and Universal Stove Co., 1235 Wazee Street.

1928
July 2: Western Development Metal Co., 451 South Elati Street.

August 13: A. D. Radinsky, 2000 West Colfax Avenue.

September 6: Loop Public Market, 1124 Fifteenth Street.

December 9: Grimes Paper Co. warehouse, 1326 Eleventh Street.

1929
February 2: Quincy Building, 1010 Seventeenth Street.

May 20: J. Zerobnick, 1929 West Fourteenth Avenue.

June 20: Grimes & Friedman, 2251 Walnut Street.

August 18: National Shoe Co., 822 Fifteenth Street.

October 26: Queen Theater, 110 Broadway.

December 17: Linder Packing Co., 1521 Market Street.

1930
January 15: Swift & Co., 1410 Blake Street.

February 18: Gross Manufacturing Co., 1340 Lawrence Street.

May 10: Fred Davis Furniture Co., 2300 Eighth Street.

September 2: Allison Candy Co., 1009 Fifteenth Street.

November 1: Ralston Purina Mills, East Forty-sixth Avenue and York Street.

November 10: Texas Oil Co., 805 West Thirty-eighth Avenue.

November 21: Hungarian Mills, 1447 Seventh Street.

1931
January 10: Furniture City Upholstering Co., 1125 Wazee Street.

August 13: F. C. Ayers Mercantile Co., 533 Market Street.

September 22: Robinson-Chase Tire Co., 777 Broadway.

November 26: Cut Rate Shoe Store, 9 Broadway.

1932
February 17: Barnett Building, Sixteenth and Larimer Streets.

April 2: Longmont Milling & Elevator Co., 2100 Twentieth Street.

April 21: McPhee & McGinnity Co., Twenty-sixth and Blake Streets.

May 5: Wright & McGill Co., Seventeenth and Lawrence Streets.

June 24: A. D. Radinsky, 2000 West Colfax Avenue.

July 13: J. A. Battin Stove Co., 1741 Lawrence Street.

September 13: Western Elaterite Roofing Co. warehouse, 1425 West Thirteenth Avenue.

December 16: Union Refining Co., 2900 Walnut Street.

1933

February 5: Heinz Roofing Co., West Third Avenue and Tejon Street.
February 25: Joe Alpert Clothing Co., Fifteenth and Larimer Streets.
March 6: Plaza Theater, 1721 Curtis Street.
March 25: Tober Shoe Store, 1519 Lawrence Street.
June 20: Slack Horner Brass Co., 1626 Blake Street.
June 27: Colorado & Southern RR vegetable dock, 2200 Nineteenth Street.
October 21: Denver United Breweries (Zang's), Seventh and Water Streets.

1934

January 3: Bekins warehouse, 1401 Arapahoe Street.
July 24: Jacobson Building, 1604 Arapahoe Street.
July 25: Blackmer Furniture warehouse, 1650 Eleventh Street.
November 30: Midwest Trunk Factory, 1524 Fifteenth Street.

1935

January 25: Equitable Building, Seventeenth and Stout Streets.
March 12: The Denver Post, 1544 Champa Street.
April 4: Denver & Rio Grande Western RR shops, West Tenth Avenue and Quivas Street.
April 6: Grimes & Friedman warehouse, 2253 Market Street.
May 23: S. Friedman warehouse, 1522 Twenty-third Street.
May 28: Brown Palace Hotel, Seventeenth Street and Tremont Place.
July 9: C.M.A. Stores, 10 Broadway.
September 21: Mandarin Cafe, 1646 California Street.
November 6: Kraft-Phenix Cheese Co., 2636 Walnut Street.

1936

January 10: Eggert Ice Co., Third and Walnut Streets.
January 11: Ady & Crowe Mercantile Co., 1900 Fifteenth Street.
March 1: South Denver Bowling Alley, 171 South Broadway.
May 28: Rialto Theater, 1540 Curtis Street.
June 19: Thrifty Mart, 99 Broadway.
September 27: Gordon Construction Co., Thirty-first and Platte Streets.

1937

February 4: J. E. Isenhart Furniture Co., 1523 Eighth Street.

June 22: Barnett Fuel Co., Thirty-eighth and Wynkoop Streets.

July 4: Moore Hardware and Iron and Bristol Hotel, 1529 Fifteenth Street.

July 5: Hell's Kitchen, 1856 Larimer Street.

August 9: Logan Moving & Storage Co., East Thirty-seventh Avenue and Marion Street.

1938

January 25: Maddox Ice Co., 684 Alcott Street.

March 14: Brownleigh Apartments, 1410 Grant Street.

July 17: Elitch Gardens, 4620 West Thirty-eighth Avenue.

December 1: Paxton Hotel, 1862 Curtis Street.

1939

February 16: Mining Exchange Building, 1030 Fifteenth Street.

May 5: Home Public Market, Fourteenth and California Streets.

July 27: H. P. Cohan Inc., 1920 West Colfax Avenue.

August 18: Dawes Products Co., 2356 Fifteenth Street.

August 25: Ady & Crowe, 1900 Fifteenth Street.

October 24: Denver Union Stockyards, East Forty-sixth Avenue and Lafayette Street.

November 19: Carney Lumber Co., 1295 South Broadway.

1940

June 12: Summit Grain Co., 3144 Navajo Street.

June 16: Gates Rubber Co., 999 South Broadway.

July 23: McMurtry Manufacturing Co., 2600 Blake Street.

November 2: Robinson Brick Co., East Third Avenue and Grape Street.

December 2: Rocky Mountain Fuel Co., 2230 Fifteenth Street.

1941

January 23: Colorado Wood Box Co., 1220 Curtis Street.

February 3: Humanitarian Heart Mission (vacant), 2403 Sixteenth Street.

February 4: Denver & Rio Grande Western locomotive explosion, West Thirtieth Avenue and Osage Street.

April 4: Colorado Animal Byproducts, 4400 Brighton Boulevard.

April 19: Hoeckel Building, 1524 Arapahoe Street.

June 5: Auto Body Shop, 445 Broadway.

August 2: Marble Hall, 1508 California Street.

November 30: Whittier School, East Twenty-fourth Avenue and Marion Street.

1942

February 8: A. Carbone & Co., 1833 Wazee Street.

October 5: Aladdin Theater, 2010 East Colfax Avenue.

December 19: Cobusco Steel Products, 2145 South Mariposa Street.

1943

January 28: E & E Glass Products Co., 3557 Wazee Street.

January 30: McMurtry Manufacturing Co., 2524 Twenty-second Street.

February 12: Montaldo's, 1632 California Street.

March 1: Mack Building, 629 Sixteenth Street.

March 31: R & H Motor Truck Service, 3440 Brighton Boulevard.

April 27: Hungarian Flour Mills, 1441 Seventh Street.

April 27: Colorado Sanitary Cloth Co., 2637 West Colfax Avenue.

September 12: Colorado State Highway shops, 8090 East Colfax Avenue.

September 21: Tunnel 10, Denver & Salt Lake Railway, Clear Creek Canyon.

September 26: Army B-24 bomber crash, 2500 block South Marion Street.

October 17: Edelweiss Restaurant, 1644 Glenarm Place.

November 7: Western Battery & Supply Co., 4201 Galapago Street.

1944

February 10: E & E Glass Products, 3557 Wazee Street.

March 2: Rossonian Hotel, 2640 Welton Street.

May 5: Excel Products Co., 2859 Walnut Street.

May 25: Model Tire Store, 781 Broadway.

June 14: Sigman Meat Co., 1617 Market Street.

June 24: Denver Dry Goods warehouse, 1201 Wazee Street.

June 26: Goldberg Bros., 3500 Walnut Street.

July 16: Elitch Gardens, 4620 West Thirty-eighth Avenue.

August 8: Model Tire Store, 781 Broadway.

November 1: Denver Pump & Manufacturing Co., 1531 Wazee Street.

November 30: Canary Pulverizing Co., 3501 Wazee Street.

December 29: Peerless Alloy Co. and Wesley Metal Products Co., 1445 Osage Street.

1945

April 2: Colorado Mill & Elevator, 1441 Seventh Street.

April 18: Club Algerian, 413 Seventeenth Street.

July 19: Hallack & Howard Lumber Co., Seventh and Larimer Streets.

December 8: S & S Manufacturing Co., 3235 Larimer Street.

1946

March 31: Railroad Building, 1515 Larimer Street.

June 3: Lowry Field Technical School, East Sixth Avenue and Quince Street.

August 29: Jacobson Building, 1604 Arapahoe Street.

1947

January 3: Amick Transfer & Storage, 1025 Santa Fe Drive.

May 25: Rocky Mountain Blueprint, 437 Seventeenth Street.

July 9: J. E. Good Auto Body, 511 Broadway.

October 25: Colorado Ice & Cold Storage, Fifth Street and West Colfax Avenue at Curtis Street.

December 3: Interstate Trust Building, 1130 Sixteenth Street.

December 11: Modern Appliance Co. and NuAd Process Studio, 731 Broadway.

1948

January 12: Colorado Mattress Co., Twenty-fourth and Walnut Streets.

January 16: Buckingham Lumber Co., 665 Mariposa Street.

March 11: Kenmark Hotel, Seventeenth and Welton Streets.

March 28: Barnes School of Commerce, 1410 Glenarm Place.

August 1: Ace Box Co., 2950 Platte River Drive.

August 2: Davis & Shaw Furniture Co., 1545 Fourteenth Street.

August 14: Davis & Shaw Furniture Co., 1545 Fourteenth Street.

September 22: Park Lane Hotel, 450 South Marion Street.

November 4: Rio Grande Fuel Co., 123 Santa Fe Drive.

1949

January 1: Navajo Truck Lines, 10 Galapago Street.

January 6: Hotel (condemned), 1332 Fifteenth Street.

February 15: Republic Drug, 1040 East Colfax Avenue.

April 23: Scott A.M.E. Church, East Twenty-second Avenue and Ogden Street.

June 1: Denver Bowling Co., 1523 Champa Street.

July 29: King Soopers, West Thirty-eighth Avenue and Irving Street.

September 22: Crescent Flour Mill, West Twenty-ninth Avenue and Jason Street.

November 26: Burlington and Colorado & Southern RR trestle, West Thirty-first Avenue and Fox Street.

November 30: Denver Stove Co., 400 Fifteenth Street.

December 6: Lawson & Maxwell Building, Twenty-sixth and Welton Streets.

December 19: Crescent Flour Mill, West Twenty-ninth and Jason Streets.

December 21: Hungarian Flour Mill, 1441 Seventh Street.

1950

February 7: Arbuckle Building, Speer and Federal Boulevards.

August 26: Denver Hotel, Seventeenth and Market Streets.

December 23: Beth Hamedrosh Hagodol Synagogue, East Sixteenth Avenue and Gaylord Street.

1951

January 20: Platte Valley Truck Co., 1420 West Thirty-eighth Avenue.

January 28: Penn-Hill Apartments, 739 Pennsylvania Street.

February 15: Kenney Construction Co., 1635 Clay Street.

February 17: Denver Athletic Club, 1325 Glenarm Place.

February 18: Wolhurst Country Club, Littleton.

September 5: Thompson Pipe & Steel, Thirty-second and Walnut Streets.

September 8: Lamont School of Music, 909 Grant Street.

September 14: Kenmark Hotel, Seventeenth and Welton Streets.

November 18: Castle of Commerce & Culture, Sixteenth Street and the Platte River.

December 3: B-29 crash, East Ellsworth Avenue and South Eudora Street.

December 31: Shaner's Tavern, Jones Coffee Shop, Vayas Shoe Shining and Hat Cleaning Shop, Jacobson's Store for Men and Jerry's Newsstand, Seventeenth and Welton Streets.

1952

January 19: Research Center, University of Denver, 2199 South University Boulevard.

February 10: Contractors Heating & Supply Inc., 65 Inca Street.

March 29: Miller Furniture Co., 1640 Larimer Street.

July 6: Gump Glass Co., 1519 Cheyenne Place.

October 9: Colorado Lumber Co., 3701 Wazee Street.

October 26: Hungarian Flour Mill, 1441 Seventh Street.

November 15: Majestic Wax Co., 2139 Blake Street.

December 6: Carpenter Paper Co., 2231 Blake Street.

December 17: Denargo Market, Twenty-ninth Street and Broadway.

December 23: Plotkin Brothers, 1408 Larimer Street.

1953

January 8: All Saints Catholic Church, 2559 South Federal Boulevard.

March 20: The Tropics, 4842 Morrison Road.

March 26: Mount Calvary Lutheran Church, 3560 York Street.

May 22: Millar Coffee Co., 1822 Blake Street.

June 24: Western Elaterite Roofing Co. warehouse, 1425 West Thirteenth Avenue.

July 24: Manual High School, East Twenty-seventh Avenue and Franklin Street.

October 10: Garfield School, West Eleventh Avenue and Yuma Street.

1954

January 1: L & R Cabinet Works, 608 Umatilla Street.

September 2: Western Foundry, 3938 Wynkoop Street.

September 18: Sears & Roebuck, East First Avenue and University Boulevard.

September 28: Colorado Milling and Elevator Co., Twenty-second and Wewatta Streets.

October 9: Safeway, 1460 Leyden Street.

1955

March 12: Safeway, 3920 Federal Boulevard.

May 2: Bryant-Webster School, West Thirty-sixth Avenue and Quivas Street.

June 24: Economy Plumbing Co., 757 Santa Fe Drive.

September 24: Claridge Hotel, 1926 Curtis Street.

November 20: Cathedral School, East Eighteenth Avenue and Logan Street.

1956

March 23: Tritch Building, 1650 Arapahoe Street.

June 13: Graystone Medical Building, 1801 Williams Street.

June 24: Public Storage & Fixture Co., 1560 Platte Street.

September 9: Continental Paper Co., 1000 West Louisiana Avenue.

1957

January 3: Mountain States Wholesale Co., 414 East Alameda Avenue.

January 10: Niederhut Carriage Co., 3560 Walnut Street.

February 11: Lowry NCO Club, Lowry Field.

May 23: Colorado By-Products Co., 4400 Brighton Boulevard.

July 7: King Cole Show Bar, 1082 Broadway.

October 30: Reliable Linen Service, 3030 Downing Street.

December 4: Loop Cafe & Bar, 1125 Fifteenth Street.

December 20: Windsor Hotel, Eighteenth and Larimer Streets.

December 24: L. O. Wells Produce Co., 1617 Market Street.

1958

January 1: Luxurest Furniture Manufacturing Co. warehouse, 1532 Market Street.

May 8: Dempster Mill Manufacturing Co., 50 Rio Grande Boulevard.

September 9: Rio Grande RR warehouse, West Eighth Avenue and Pecos Street.

September 12: Health Food Sales, 1523 Nineteenth Street.

November 12: Capitol Laundry, 2046 West Colfax Avenue.

1959

January 4: Denver-Chicago Trucking, 3888 East Forty-fifth Avenue.

January 14: Railroad Building, 1515 Larimer Street.

May 21: Western Mineral Corp., 111 South Navajo Street.

December 17: Farmers Union Marketing Association, 3500 East Forty-sixth Avenue.

1960

January 28: Timpte Bros., 2300 East Fortieth Avenue.

February 9: Phillipson Rod & Tackle Co., 2705 High Street.

August 19: Katchen's Bonus Corner, 1405 West Thirty-eighth Avenue.

August 23: Colorado Milling and Elevator Co., Twenty-second and Wewatta Streets.

October 18: Mayfair Hotel and Lyer Drug Store, 700 Fifteenth Street.

October 31: Protecto Wrap Co., 2255 South Delaware Street.

December 13: Veterans Foundation Store, 2029 Larimer Street.

1961

April 30: Stanley Plaza Hotel, 1560 Sherman Street.

May 19: New York Furniture Co., 2308 Welton Street.

May 20: Burlington Hotel, 2205 Larimer Street.

May 22: PSC Arapahoe Plant, 2601 South Platte River Drive.

June 10: Cinder Concrete Products, 1155 West Fifth Avenue.

July 6: Furr Food Store, 755 South Colorado Boulevard.

July 11: United Air Lines DC-8 crash, Stapleton Field.

August 2: Apex Die & Box Co., 1245 South Inca Street.

August 29: Capitol Insulating Co., 2037 West Fourteenth Avenue.

September 26: Ellis Canning Co. warehouse, West Sixteenth Avenue and Clay Street.

September 27: Morrison-Merrill & Co., 505 Raritan Way.

November 2: Phipps Auditorium, City Park.

December 13: North Denver Seventh-Day Adventist Church, 3925 Shoshone Street.

1962

January 18: Capitol Box & Bag Co., 2122 Lawrence Street.

May 8: Wellshire Country Club, 3333 South Colorado Boulevard.

May 19: Union Pal Discount Store, 2796 South Federal Boulevard.

May 20: Interstate Moving and Storage, 10 Galapago Street.

August 5: Perkins Pickle Co., Ninth and Lawrence Streets.

August 28: Public Distributing Co., 1520 Wazee Street.
September 2: Albany Hotel, Seventeenth and Stout Streets.
October 17: Frigidaire Sales Corp., 215 Wazee Street.

1963
January 21: Walker Piano Co., 1345 Broadway.
May 9: Fibre Products Inc., 2002 Delgany Street.
May 30: North Denver Transfer & Storage Co., 1529 Fifteenth Street.
June 9: Consolidated Freightways Building, Twenty-fourth and Arapahoe Streets.
June 12: George O'Day Feed Mills, 5300 Race Court.
August 1: Economy Lumber Co., 350 South Colorado Boulevard.
October 12: Ace Box Co., 2950 Arkins Court.
December 11: Model Furniture Co., 2145 Blake Street.
December 24: Sunland Mills, 1900 Fifteenth Street.

1964
February 5: Crockett and Renalde Bit & Spur Co., 1525 Eighteenth Street.
February 25: Thermo Tech Inc., 1400 South Lipan Street.
April 27: Ace Box Co., 2950 Arkins Court.
June 24: Millar Coffee Co. warehouse, 1834 Blake Street.
September 2: Luby's Cafeteria, Cherry Creek Shopping Center.

1965
January 5: J. A. Sharoff & Co., 1644 Market Street.
January 6: Protex Industries, 1331 West Evans Avenue.
March 17: Warehouse (vacant), Twenty-third and Welton Streets.
August 6: Denver Riding Stables, 4300 East Kentucky Avenue.
September 17: King Soopers offices, 1400 West Third Avenue.

1966
April 22: Trinity Church, 1820 Broadway.
May 5: Panel Corp. of America, 745 South Cherokee Street.
September 6: City Elite Laundry, 2701 Lawrence Street.
September 21: Plateau Supply Co., Seventh and Larimer Streets.
October 20: Central Wood Products, 1418 Wazee Street.
November 22: A. B. Hirschfeld warehouse, 501 Broadway.

1967

March 9: Acme Auto Body, 1550 Clarkson Street.

March 11: Gordon Neon Sign Co., 2930 West Ninth Avenue.

September 14: Polo Club Apartments, 3131 East Alameda Avenue.

December 7: Denver Hotel, 1647 Welton Street.

December 25: St. Vincent de Paul warehouse, Speer and Federal Boulevards.

1968

January 16: American Linen Supply Co., 1220 Arapahoe Street.

February 23: Apartment house (vacant), 810 East Colfax Avenue.

April 12: Apartments under construction, 1075 Washington Street.

June 18: Motor Vehicle Building, Merchants Park Shopping Center, 600 South Broadway.

July 2: Public Service Building, Fifteenth and Champa Streets.

July 8: Elitch Bowling Lanes, West Thirty-eighth Avenue and Tennyson Street.

August 7: Lincoln Bar, 1603 East Thirty-fourth Avenue.

September 6: Fort Logan Chapel, Fort Logan.

September 14: Hole in the Wall, 220 Broadway.

September 17: Clark Products Inc., 1625 Clay Street.

November 22: Denver Ice Co., 2612 Blake Street.

November 26: Three Fountains Condominium, 3346 South Oneida Way.

December 24: Bennett Distributing Co., 1400 Blake Street.

1969

January 17: Home of the Good Shepherd, 1401 South Colorado Boulevard.

February 8: Miller Hotel, 1126 Seventeenth Street.

February 8: Carney Lumber Co., 1295 South Broadway.

February 8: Empire Roofing Co., 2332 Fifteenth Street.

March 19: Dreher Pickle Co. warehouse, 860 Navajo Street.

May 31: Western Photo Co., 816 Federal Boulevard.

July 6: Lehrer's Flowers greenhouse, 4751 York Street.

August 18: Private residence (vacant) and storage garage, 980 South Sheridan Boulevard.

September 3: Condominiums under construction, East Warren Avenue and South Grape Street.

September 3: Mastercraft Inc., 3107 East Fifty-second Street.

October 8: Bull Ring restaurant, Merchants Park Shopping Center, 600 South Broadway.

December 26: Mine & Smelter Building, 1427 Seventeenth Street.

1970

February 5: Denver Public Schools buses, 2800 West Seventh Avenue.

February 17: Harry Hansen Inc., 1652 Downing Street.

February 17: Presbyterian Hospital, 1719 East Nineteenth Avenue.

February 18: Joy Manufacturing Co., 1422 Seventeenth Street.

February 20: American Divers Supply & Manufacturing Co., 4030 West Colfax Avenue.

March 21: Apartments under construction, 1909 South Depew Street.

March 30: Cardinal Plastics Inc., 5757 East Forty-second Avenue.

April 5: Denver Wood Products, 1945 West Third Avenue.

June 24: Condominiums under construction, 3351 South Monaco Parkway.

July 4: Law & Sons Casket Co., Nineteenth and Platte Streets.

August 2: Empire Hotel (vacant), 530 Eighteenth Street.

August 22: Meat Processing Co., 733 Santa Fe Drive.

October 3: Lumberyard Supply Co., 112 South Santa Fe Drive.

October 7: Condominiums under construction, East Quincy Avenue and South Quebec Street.

October 16: Murphy Mahoney Building (vacant), Speer and Federal Boulevards.

November 8: Apartments under construction, East Radcliffe and South Lowell Boulevard.

November 30: Harding Glass Co. warehouse, 650 South Lipan Street.

1971

January 7: Karpet King, 2501 West Alameda Avenue.

January 10: Scottish Rite Masonic Temple, 1730 Grant Street.

February 9: Western Seed Co., 3407 Fox Street.

March 19: 20th Century Bowling and The Bowl night club, 1229 Broadway, and Soderstrom Dance Hall, 1247 Broadway.

June 20: Contractors Heating & Supply Co., 70 Santa Fe Drive.

July 7: Denargo Box Co., Denargo Market.

August 10: Ideal Furniture Manufacturing Co., 1025 Thirty-third Street.

November 2: Warehouse (old Zang Brewery), 2200 Zuni Street.

November 6: Condominiums under construction, Parker Road and Rosemary Way.

December 11: Glenarm Apartments, 2330 Glenarm Place.

December 31: Trans-World Moving and Construction Co., 3700 Chestnut Street.

1972

February 5: Apartments under construction, East Hampden Avenue and South Willow Street.

February 29: Goldberg Bros., 3500 Larimer Street.

July 24: Spring Water Apartments (under construction), 3131 West Mexico Avenue.

August 12: Wilscam Enterprises Inc., 585 South Jason Street.

October 13: National Metal & Iron, 100 South Santa Fe Drive.

November 10: Weir Building, West Thirty-second Avenue and Zuni Street.

1973

July 7: Private residence, 2840 Clermont Street.

July 18: Western Food, Forty-seventh Avenue and Packing House Road (National Western Drive).

August 11: Salvation Army Store, 1200 Larimer Street.

December 18: Pillow Manufacturing Co., 1520 Twentieth Street.

1974

March 15: Denver & Rio Grande Western RR shops, West Ninth Avenue and Quivas Street.

May 12: Denver Laundry and Cleaning plant, 810 West Eighth Avenue.

June 13: Western States Wholesale Co., 3891 Forest Street.

June 23: Western Rubber Inc., 4262 Madison Street.

September 10: Friedman & Son Paper Co., 2345 Walnut Street.

1975

January 23: First National Bank of Denver, 1742 Champa Street.

March 14: Scaffco Inc., 3738 Morrison Road.

March 23: Lake Apartments, 13859 Albrook Drive.

April 13: Bon Air Apartments (vacant), 1055 Lincoln Street.

May 3: Warehouse (vacant), Fifteenth and Delgany Streets.

October 2: Protex Industries, 1331 West Evans Avenue.

October 11: Stony Brook Apartments, 4601 South Yosemite Avenue.

October 20: Whale Scientific Supply Co., 4949 Ironton Street.

1976

January 29: Margery Reed Hall, University of Denver, 2200 East Evans Avenue.

February 28: Boarding house, 2405 Federal Boulevard.

March 25: Alcott School (condemned), 4131 Tennyson Street.

June 2: Aaron Gove Junior High School, 1325 Colorado Boulevard.

June 9: Fistell's Electronics Supply Co., 1085 Lincoln Street.

June 24: Mountain Shadows Apartments, 2 Adams Street.

July 3: Mountain Bell Building, 1425 Champa Street.

August 27: Warehouse (vacant), 2500 Fifteenth Street.

October 11: Chez Paree Show Bar, 1649 Court Place.

November 30: Pioneer Hall, University of Denver, 2130 South Race Street.

December 27: Federal Square Apartments, 3150 West Floyd Avenue.

1977

January 6: Bryant House Apartments, 2601 West Thirty-second Avenue.

February 28: Rocky Mountain Marine, 5411 Leetsdale Drive.

April 18: Foster Auto Supply Co. warehouse, 540 Acoma Street.

April 24: The Stores Equipment Corp. (Constitution Hall), 1501 Blake Street.

June 4: Apartment house, 569 Cherokee Street.

July 5: Reprocessing Paper Co., 2 Santa Fe Drive.

July 18: Ballpark Health Club, 107 South Broadway.

August 7: Unity Church of Christ and unfinished apartment building, 2428 Ogden Street.

August 31: Sterling Lumber & Investment Co. warehouse (vacant), 875 Wazee Street.

October 8: Private residence, 1143 Milwaukee Street.

October 23: Mother's Home Bakery, 2733 West Eighth Avenue.

December 25: Apartment house, 1478 Detroit Street.

1978

February 17: Newman Lighting Co., 2016 Blake Street.

February 23: Private residence, 3158 Champa Street.

March 15: Denver Urban Renewal building (vacant), 2145 Court Place.

June 19: DeSmet Hall, Regis College, Regis (West Fiftieth Avenue) and Lowell Boulevards.

July 31: Alcove's Carpets, 4200 East Colfax Avenue.

September 18: F. J. LeGrue Co., 476 South Broadway.

October 9: Kacey Furniture Co., 1652 Wazee Street.

October 14: Sigma Chi fraternity house, University of Denver, 1978 South Josephine Street.

October 20: Paramount Theatre, 521 Sixteenth Street.

December 4: Crest Motors, 7100 East Colfax Avenue.

December 8: CCS Supply Co., 351 West Forty-fifth Avenue.

1979

January 12: Apartment house, 621 East Seventeenth Avenue.

January 28: Fort Logan Mental Health Center building (vacant), 3520 West Oxford Avenue.

February 2: Denver Housing Authority development office, 291 East Fifty-first Avenue.

March 7: Nellis Inc., 1408 West Colfax Avenue.

March 10: Sportsman's Inn, 623 Fifteenth Street.

March 12: Allied Linen and Uniform Rental Co., 1317 Federal Boulevard.

August 7: Immaculate Conception School, 1636 Logan Street.

November 21: All Nations Church of God in Christ, 1000 Kalamath Street.

1980

May 1: Office building (vacant), 912 Broadway.

August 12: Jefferson Hotel, 1529 Champa Street.

September 10: Radio stations KBNO and KUVO, 1601 Jewell Avenue.

November 12: University Club, 1637 Sherman Street.

November 25: The Queens lofts, 2563 Champa Street.

1981

February 2: Cherry Condominiums, 880 Cherry Street.

February 8: Griswold Apartments, 15 Logan Street.

March 17: Auditorium Hotel, 1406 Stout Street.

April 11: Warehouse (vacant), 950 Yuma Street.

April 25: Friedman & Sons, 2425 Walnut Street.

April 30: Mariposa Apartments, 2128 California Street.

August 26: Mayflower Hotel (abandoned), 1700 Grant Street.

1982

April 8: Farmers Marketing Association Grain & Feed Mill (abandoned), 4545 Madison Street.

August 11: The Ross Co., 1641 Blake Street.

November 17: Hamilton Rental Services, 2315 West Twenty-ninth Avenue.

1983

April 21: Apartment building, 3806 Gilpin Street.

May 21: Sunglow Corp. warehouse, 1495 Delgany Street.

July 11: Continental Theater, Interstate 25 and Hampden Avenue.

July 20: Buchtel Memorial Chapel, University of Denver, 2160 East Evans Avenue.

November 2: Santa Rita Apartments, 1170 Logan Street.

November 23: University Hills Mall, 2700 South Colorado Boulevard.

December 18: Zuni Apartments, 2942 Zuni Street.

1984

January 1: Wells Fargo office building, Denver Tech Center, 7801 West Belleview Avenue.

January 20: Kessler's Egg Market and Johnny Downs Fresh Vegetable Package Co., Denargo Market.

February 28: Pine Creek Apartments, 600 South Dayton Street.

March 3: Masonic Hall, Sixteenth and Welton Streets.

April 1: Katzke Paper Co., 2495 South Delaware Street.

June 18: Squire Lounge, Always Better Bargains Thrift Shop, New Art Tailors, John's Liquor Store and Boots & Bo's Self-Service Laundry, 1800 block East Colfax Avenue.

June 26: LPK Construction Co. and Sunburst Electric warehouse, 2967 Inca Street.

July 14: Radio station KBNO, 4785 Tejon Street.

July 17: Marquis Building (vacant), 2501 Fifteenth Street.

September 8: Townhomes under construction, 1300 Garfield Street.

November 27: Denver Animal Shelter, 666 South Jason Street.

1985

January 31: Public Service Company substation, 5901 Leetsdale Drive.

June 30: Socrates Inn, Waxman's Camera, Laikon Restaurant, Georgie's Shine Parlor, and John's Market, 901 Fifteenth Street.

October 20: Jackson Laundry Co., 3411 York Street.

December 8: First Unitarian Church, 1400 Lafayette Street.

December 9: Casablanca Apartments, 1950 Trenton Street.

1986

January 5: Stuart Buchanan Antiques and Design Gallery, 1235 South Broadway.

March 3: Armour meatpacking plant (vacant), 5075 Packing House Road (National Western Drive).

April 12: Denver Barrel & Drum Co. warehouse (vacant), 2201 Blake Street.

November 21: Private residence, 2457 South Cook Street.

1987

March 8: Thomas M. Field House, East Iliff Avenue and South Clarkson Street.

July 6: Capital Paint Co., 1000 West Mississippi Avenue.

July 7: Armour meatpacking plant (vacant), 5050 Packing House Road (National Western Drive).

October 6: Denver Fiberglass Co., 5000 National Western Drive.

November 15: Continental Airlines DC-9 crash, Stapleton International Airport.

1988

January 31: Apartment house, 2700 Federal Boulevard.

February 14: Private residence, 78 West Cedar Avenue.

May 19: Apartment house (vacant), 2040 California Street.

June 13: Crusade for Justice Building (condemned), 1567 Downing Street.

September 6: Apartment house (vacant), 2030 Champa Street.

November 1: American Roofing Supply Co. (vacant), 900 Wewatta Street.

1989

February 17: Behavior Intervention Center of Colorado, 2015 South Pontiac Way.

February 22: Hungarian Flour Mill (abandoned), 2100 Twentieth Street.

March 2: Griswold Apartments, 15 Logan Street.

June 15: Spring Water Apartments, 3131 West Mexico Avenue.

June 21: Public Fixture Co., 1550 Platte Street.

August 14: Blessed Sacrament Church, 4900 Montview Boulevard.

November 7: Todd's Pedigree Shop, 719 South University Boulevard.

November 26: Newberry Greenhouses, 201 Garfield Street.

December 10: Warehouse (abandoned), 2100 Twenty-ninth Street.

December 17: Empire Building, 430 Sixteenth Street.

December 27: Atlas Metals, 1145 Fifth Street.

1990

February 17: Shorthorn Building (vacant), 2239 Larimer Street.

March 3: Larimer Street Hotel (vacant), 2058 Larimer Street.

October 30: Apartment house, 2419 California Street.

November 25: Fuel depot, Stapleton Airport.

December 2: Apartment house, 1642 Pearl Street.

1991

April 30: Holy Trinity Church of God in Christ, 2201 Court Place.

October 5: Longhorn Saloon and Hotel (condemned), Park Avenue West (Twenty-third Street) and Market Street.

October 31: Polo Club Condominiums, 3131 East Alameda Avenue.

1992

January 11: Private residence, 3025 West Iowa Avenue.

February 7: Valas TV and Appliance, 475 South Broadway.

March 2: Capitol Hill Apartments, 701 East Fourteenth Avenue.

July 1: Rocky Mountain Moulding, Progressive Peripherals Software and Magnum Recovery Co., 440–464 Kalamath Street.

September 28: Silver State Printers and Chinese Printing Co., 1625 South Broadway.

November 29: Park Preserves, 10025 East Girard Avenue.

December 19: Burlington Hotel (vacant), Twenty-second and Larimer Streets.

1993

January 31: Private residence, 2836 Humboldt Street.

March 3: Shadow Wood Condominiums, 7395 East Eastman Avenue.

December 25: Private residence, 3173 West Exposition Avenue.

December 30: Monarch Mills, 1495 Delgany Street.

1994

January 1: Tamarac Square Shopping Center, South Yosemite Street and East Hampden Avenue.

January 27: Alexander Manor Apartments, 1125 Washington Street.

May 21: Valley Park Apartments, 675 Wolff Street.

August 6: Denver Rescue Mission warehouse, 3501 East Forty-sixth Street.

October 5: Apartment house, Twenty-third Street and Tremont Place.

October 13: Fox Hole, 2900 Fox Street.

November 29: Private residence, 3620 Williams Street.

December 23: Windsor Gardens, 9360 East Center Avenue.

1995

January 7: Private residence, 1809 South Pennsylvania Street.

January 14: Bella's Beauty Salon and B & D Sportswear, 2709 West Thirty-eighth Avenue.

October 18: Moffat Railroad depot (abandoned), 2101 Fifteenth Street.

October 20: B & M Hotel and Kaminsky Barrel Co. (vacant), Twenty-ninth and Fox Streets.

November 3: Elitch Gardens (abandoned), 4620 West Thirty-eighth Avenue.

December 23: Private residence, 5523 Tucson Street.

1996

January 18: Garage, private residence, 3729 Navajo Street.

April 1: Private residence, 46 Xavier Street.

August 30: Sunset Park Apartments, 1865 Larimer Street.

November 11: Warehouse (vacant), 2201 Market Street.

1997

January 10: Sweet Dee's Saloon, 913 Fifteenth Street.

July 18: Pine Creek Apartments, 600 South Dayton Street.

1998

February 18: St. Francis de Sales Catholic Church, 301 South Sherman Street.

April 29: Giambrocco Food Service Co., 3755 Wazee Street.

1999

May 19: E & R Pallet Repair and Service Co., 5101 York Street.

October 31: St. Andrew's Episcopal Church, 2013 Glenarm Place.

DENVER VOLUNTEER
FIRE COMPANIES
1866–1884

Denver Hook and Ladder Company No. 1, March 25, 1866–September 1, 1881.

James Archer Hose Company No. 2, April 9, 1872–May 10, 1881.

James E. Bates Hose Company No. 3, May 24, 1872–March 18, 1882.

Woodie Fisher Hose Company No. 1, July 31, 1872–September 1, 1881.

Denver Hook and Ladder Company No. 2, January 1, 1873–January 1, 1883.

Hose Company No. 4, January 1, 1873–January 1, 1883.

H.A.W. Tabor Hose Company No. 5, February 6, 1880–January 12, 1885.

Broadway Hose Company No. 6, February 27, 1880–July 1, 1883.

J. W. Richards Hose Company No. 7, Fall 1881–May 1, 1884.

James Archer Hose Company No. 4, May 1881–Spring 1884.

HONORED DENVER FIREFIGHTERS

A Firefighter's Prayer

When I am called to duty God
  Wherever flames may rage,
  Give me strength to save some life,
  Whatever be its age.
Help me embrace a little child
  Before it is too late,
  Or save an older person from
  The horror of that fate.
Enable me to be alert and
  Hear the weakest shout,
  And quickly and efficiently
  Put the fire out.
I want to fill my calling and
  To give the best in me,
  To guard my every neighbor and
  Protect their property.
And if according to my fate
  I am to lose my life,
  Please bless with your protective hand
  My family one and all.

—Anonymous

KEY
V— VOLUNTEER
X— INTERRED AT FIREMEN'S MEMORIAL, FAIRMOUNT CEMETERY,
  DENVER
M— NAMED ON THE MEMORIAL PLAQUE, DENVER FIRE DEPART-
  MENT HEADQUARTERS, WEST COLFAX AVENUE AND SPEER
  BOULEVARD

There are two major memorials to dead firefighters in Denver. One, the Firemen's Memorial in Fairmount Cemetery, was erected in 1891 and bears the inscription: "In memory of the firemen that died in the performance of their duty."

Though there are fifteen men buried there, not all died "in the performance of their duty." Charles Tufts, for example, was killed when he fell under an electric train during Cheyenne Frontier Days in Wyoming in 1912; John Atkinson died during the flu epidemic of 1918; and Fred Williamson, an early-day volunteer firefighter, was buried there when he died at age 74 in 1926.

Another, more recent, memorial stands at the Denver Fire Department headquarters, West Colfax Avenue and Speer Boulevard. It bears a simple inscription—"Denver's Fallen Fighters Since 1881"—and lists the names of fifty-one firemen killed since the paid department was founded.

Some men are named on both memorials. Volunteer firemen Aaron P. Shallcross, Alfred Gardiner and Benjamin Barret, all of whom died in service, are not mentioned at either site. Here's how the sixty-two men included here died:

Aaron P. Shallcross—In failing health, volunteer Shallcross nevertheless helped fight a fire at the Planters' Hotel, Sixteenth and Blake Streets. He collapsed and died shortly afterward, becoming the first man to die in Denver's fire service. February 23, 1875. (V)

Alfred Gardiner—A volunteer member of Hook & Ladder 2, Gardiner was caught under a falling wall when fire swept the blocks between Wazee and Blake and Twenty-second and Twenty-third Streets. March 19, 1877. (V)

Benjamin Barret — Barret, a member of the volunteer James Archer Hose 2, appears on some early lists as having been killed in a fire at the Estabrook Stables on March 18, 1878. No fire for that date was found. However, during a fire at Estabrook on October 21, 1880, Barret fell victim to a wall that collapsed upon him. He survived, but in *Fire Service of Denver*, published by the Firemen's Mutual Benefit Association in 1890, he is reported to have died of his injuries in July 1881 at his family home in Warrensburg, Missouri. No other information. (V)

James Lloyd — While taking fire horse "Jumbo" out for exercising at Hose 4, the horse became unmanageable and fell on Lloyd, who died within hours. Lloyd was the first member of the paid department, founded in 1881, to die on duty. September 24, 1886. (M)

Horace Knight — The driver of Steamer 5, Knight was killed instantly at 4:30 A.M. while crossing railroad tracks at Nineteenth and Bassett Streets. He was thrown from the vehicle and died of a broken neck. Knight was the first man buried at the Firemen's Memorial in Fairmount Cemetery. October 11, 1891. (X,M)

Emanuel Emerick — Emerick, 24, a member of Steamer 2, was described by other firefighters as "one of the best fellows in the department." He was killed accidentally by a shotgun blast while returning from a hunting trip with three Denver policemen near Barr, Colorado. The gun was sitting between his legs when the wagon struck a rough spot in the road and both barrels discharged, hitting Emerick in the left arm and chest. October 27, 1892. (X)

Frederick C. Pierrepont and **Frank P. Mahoney** — Pierrepont, 33, of Hook & Ladder 1, and Mahoney, 28, of Hose 4, were crushed beneath a falling wall at the Summit Fuel and Feed Co. warehouse, 222 Larimer Street. Pierrepont was killed outright. Mahoney was found unconscious in the rubble and taken to the city physician's office at City Hall, where he died of a fractured skull and internal injuries at 8 P.M. Each of the men's heirs received $950 from the city. March 24, 1893. (M)

Stephen Ambrose — Ambrose was a fire-department operator, stationed at City Hall, Fourteenth and Larimer Streets. He previously worked for the city as a health inspector and as a police officer. His funeral was held in the council chamber of City Hall, with six firemen as pallbearers and led by Pinney's Band. No other information. January 18, 1894. (X)

Harold W. Hartwell, Frederick S. Brawley, Richard D. Dandridge and **Stephen Martin**—All members of Engine 3, Hartwell, 36, Brawley, 33, Dandridge, 24, and Martin, 28, were killed when they fell through the lobby floor during a smoky fire at the St. James Hotel in the 1500 block of Curtis Street. Captain Hartwell was white; the other three men were African American. March 23, 1895. Hartwell (M); Brawley (V); Dandridge and Martin (X,M)

Lee E. Bottom—The driver of Steamer 7, Bottom was pitched forward when the horse-drawn rig he was driving struck a hole. He was en route from the station at West Thirty-second Avenue and Erie Street to a railyard fire at Seventeenth and Platte Streets. His chest was crushed when he fell under the wagon's wheels. Bottom, brother of well-known attorney John T. Bottom, died thirty minutes later at St. Luke's Hospital, the day after his 21st birthday. In December 1899 the city council awarded $1,500 to his parents, who previously had sued unsuccessfully for $5,000 in two trials. October 14, 1897. (M)

Harry Robinson—Driver for Assistant Chief John Dulmage, Robinson, 43, of Company 2, rushed into a small fire at the Western Chemical Co. on June 18, 1899, and, while carrying carboys of muriatic acid from the burning building, breathed the noxious fumes. He developed pneumonia and was near death several times before he died at his home, 1329 Clark Street (Fifty-second Avenue). A second, larger fire occurred on July 1 at the chemical works. July 20, 1899. (X,M)

Charles Dolloff, John McGlade, Frank Lunt and **Charles Eymann**—All four men died after entering the engraving room of The Denver Post, 1623 Curtis Street, on September 20, 1904, to fight a nitric-acid spill. Dolloff, 28, of Engine 4, died on September 21; McGlade, 35, of Truck 2, on September 21; Lunt, of Hook & Ladder 2, on October 12; and Eymann, of Truck 1, on October 21. Fourteen other firemen were overcome and suffered various stages of bronchial and lung infections for months. Dolloff (M); McGlade and Lunt (X,M); Eymann (M)

August Borgemenke—A pipeman for Hose 1, "Gus" Borgemenke resided at 1328 Lincoln Avenue (Glenarm Place). December 8, 1904. No other information. (X)

Robert Geddes—Lieutenant Geddes, 42, father of five, suffered a broken pelvis and rupturing to his bowels and bladder when Hook

& Ladder 1 was struck by a Denver Tramway streetcar at Fifteenth and Market Streets on March 1, 1908, pinning him under the fire rig's wheel springs. March 2, 1908. (M)

Vincent ("Vinson") Davidson — Captain Davidson died when Hose 13 skidded on wet pavement at Fifteenth and Market Streets and one of the vehicle's wheels caught in the rut of streetcar tracks, overturning Hose 13 and hurling three firemen to the street near noon on September 18, 1910. Assistant Chief Robert Davidson, racing to the same fire in another vehicle, was among the first to reach his brother's side. Captain Davidson, 35, sustained what was thought to be a bad gash on the back of his head, but died the next day of a brain hemorrhage at St. Joseph Hospital. September 19, 1910. (M)

Charles W. Tufts — Waiting for an electric train carrying passengers from downtown Cheyenne, Wyoming, to the Frontier Days rodeo grounds on the outskirts of town on August 15, 1912, Tufts was forced under the train by crowds surging to board. Tufts, a member of Station 5 at 1817 Blake Street, suffered a crushed right leg and chest and head injuries. August 16, 1912. (X)

Joseph M. Sullivan — Sullivan was buried from his home, 1619 Gilpin Street, on February 18, 1914. He was an engineer with Engine 8. No other information. February 15, 1914. (X)

Harry Cox — Hose 4, backing out of the station onto Broadway at Sixteenth Street on July 31, 1916, was hit by a Denver Omnibus & Cab Co. "Seeing Denver" open-air bus, crushing Cox's left leg and severing an artery. He died from shock six hours after doctors removed his leg two days later. Cox, 47, was the first city employee to receive benefits under provisions of the new compensation act. His widow was awarded $2,500 by the industrial commission. August 2, 1916. (M)

John C. Atkinson — Having been promoted to lieutenant in June 1918 after ten years on the department, Atkinson, 48, died at home of the flu during the worldwide epidemic. November 28, 1918. (X)

Joshua Hefkins — A former member of the famous early-day Chemical Company No. 1, a team of strapping six-footers that included Terry Owens, Tim Davidson, Mike Ryan, John Dalwin and Sydney Eastwood, Hefkins, 70, died of dropsy at Denver General Hospital. He was, for a number of years, captain of Engine 10, Thirty-third and Arapahoe Streets, and narrowly escaped death in January 1894 when a horse-drawn rig he was riding crashed while racing to a false alarm. He retired from the department in 1897 and took up mining in Colorado. His name appears as "Hopkins" on his head-stone at the Firemen's Memorial at Fairmount Cemetery and in the cemetery's files. April 27, 1924. (X)

Fred Williamson—One of Denver's first volunteer firefighters and a member of the Veteran Volunteer Firemen, Williamson, 74, died at Denver General Hospital the day after suffering a heart attack at his home at 422 Twenty-first Street. March 16, 1926. (V,X)

Thomas H. Hyder—Responding to an alarm at a grocery store at 301 South Logan Street, Pumper 21 collided with a loaded South Pearl Coal & Fuel Co. truck at East Virginia Avenue and South Clarkson Street and overturned, crushing driver Hyder, 29. Three other firemen were injured seriously. Hyder was the son of Thomas M. Hyder, a prominent man in Denver politics. The fire caused $200 in damage to the store. August 23, 1928. (M)

William Barber, Richard Schwairy and **Silas Briggs**—Racing to a fire, Truck 12 and Pumper 7 collided at West Forty-fourth Avenue and Federal Boulevard. Barber died en route to the hospital; Schwairy and Briggs succumbed a few hours later. Briggs's son, William, was killed on November 30, 1944, in a similar traffic mishap. October 12, 1928. (M)

Elmer C. Palmer—Palmer, 34, was found dead, slumped over the wheel of his car in the garage behind his home at 4785 Quitman Street, after a quarrel with his wife. His death was ruled a suicide. September 17, 1931. (M)

James J. Moses—Deputy Chief Moses died at his home following a heart attack, less than three hours after answering a call to a burning car at Eighth Avenue and Broadway. He was acting chief at the time in the absence of Chief John F. Healy and Assistant Chief Patrick J. Boyne. He was appointed to the department on May 1, 1903, and served twenty years as a deputy chief. June 14, 1932. (M)

Curtis A. Dendinger—Dendinger, a member of Engine 16, was taken ill on duty June 14, 1934, and was diagnosed with pneumonia the following day. He died a week later. Dendinger, 46, a father of five, was promoted to lieutenant on August 1, 1925. June 21, 1934. (M)

Colin C. Taylor—Overcome by smoke, Taylor collapsed at a house fire at 421 Williams Street on June 20, 1934. He was revived but died in bed later in the day after being taken home from the station house. Taylor, 39, of Engine 16, joined the department in 1923. June 28, 1934. (M)

Andrew J. Mahon — Twelve firemen were buried under bricks and debris when a wall fell on them during a fire on November 30, 1934, at the Midwest Trunk & Bag Manufacturing Co., 1524 Fifteenth Street. Assistant Chief Mahon, 47, sustained a fractured left leg and left arm and spinal and internal injuries and was taken to Denver General Hospital, where he died at 4:30 A.M. the next day. December 1, 1934. (M)

John H. Reisbeck — Engine 10, en route to a false alarm at East Fifty-fifth Avenue and Washington Street, collided with a meat truck at East Forty-sixth Avenue and Washington. Reisbeck, 42, riding on the left side of the fire rig, was crushed between the truck and the fire rig. He suffered a crushed chest and internal injuries and was taken to Denver General Hospital, where he died a few hours later. Engine 10 had responded to another false alarm in the same area less than two hours earlier. March 20, 1936.(M)

William Feely — A Denver native, Feely, 40, died of pneumonia in Denver General Hospital three days after he was taken ill while on duty at Engine 12, West Twenty-sixth Avenue and Federal Boulevard. March 21, 1936. (M)

Edward Carlson — Denver had a record September snowfall, twenty-six inches, between September 26 and 28, 1936, which downed thousands of trees and crippled streetcar service. Carlson, 54, who posted a stop sign in front of Station 9, 1672 East Forty-seventh Avenue, so children could cross the street safely, was shoveling snow in the street to make a path for the children when he was hit by a sliding automobile trailer and thrown into the side of a streetcar. September 28, 1936. (M)

George W. Brooks and **James E. Simpson** — The department's all–African American crew of Pumper 3, "covering in" for another company, ran a red light at high speed at Twentieth and Larimer Streets and hit Hook & Ladder 4 broadside, causing the pumper to overturn and spilling the firemen across the intersection. Captain Brooks, 49, was killed instantly, and Simpson, 42, died soon after at Denver General Hospital. Two other firemen, James Harrison and Sidney Frelow, were so seriously injured that they were forced to retire. July 17, 1938. (M)

Ralph Johnston — Captain Johnston, a member of Truck 8, suffered a heart attack while on duty on October 9, 1938. He died six days later, following a second heart attack. No other information. October 15, 1938. (M)

Henry Miller — A member of the department since August 10, 1910, Miller, 55, died of a heart attack at his home, 1817 Vine Street. Doctors theorized that he was left in a weakened condition after being struck by an automobile on July 11, 1938, while crossing the street at Fifty-second Avenue and Brighton Boulevard. At the time, he was carrying a chemical tank to a weed fire as a member of Engine 9. Miller was hospitalized for several weeks following the accident. November 25, 1938. (M)

Elmer J. Hair — Hair, 58, who worked at various engine companies after joining the department in 1905, suffered a heart attack while on duty at the Engine 19 house, 1401 West Alameda Avenue. He died at home, 649 Delaware Street. December 28, 1940. (M)

Stephen P. Keating — Assistant Chief Keating, a forty-two-year veteran of the department, died of pneumonia after being taken ill on duty three days earlier. Doctors said an injury suffered in 1930 and a beating by muggers in April 1932 may have contributed to his death. Keating, 71, was the father of fireman Stephen P. Keating Jr. September 3, 1941. (M)

Douglas V. Parrish, James Williams and **John H. Kennedy** — All three men volunteered to help extinguish a persistent fire in Tunnel 10 on the line of the Denver & Salt Lake Railway in Clear Creek Canyon, twenty-seven miles west of Denver, in September 1943. Parrish, 48; Williams, 39; and Kennedy, 37, were overcome by carbon monoxide while working in the tunnel. Portions of the tunnel later collapsed, burying Kennedy's and Williams's bodies for more than a month; they were recovered on November 21 and 24, respectively. September 20, 1943. (M)

William W. Briggs — Captain Briggs, riding in the front seat of Hook & Ladder 6, was thrown from the vehicle when it was struck by a truck at Twelfth and Larimer Streets and hit a curb. Briggs, 45, was the son of Denver fireman Silas Briggs, who was killed in a similar crash on October 12, 1928. November 30, 1944. (M)

Robert V. Parker — Parker, 48, was struck and killed by a hit-and-run driver as he stepped off the curb to cross Federal Boulevard at West Eighth Avenue. He died of head injuries suffered in the accident. March 17, 1945. (M)

Leonard Shire and **Fred Erb** — Shire, 36, and Erb, 26, were crushed in the basement of the Miller Furniture Co., 1640 Larimer Street, when the building's second and third floors collapsed, sending twenty tons of debris down upon them. A third fireman, Herman

Orblom, also was buried in the rubble but survived. Ten other firemen were injured at the fire. March 29, 1952. (M)

Chester T. Block — Captain Block, 47, head of the rescue squad, collapsed shortly after lunch at Engine Company 2 headquarters, 930 Ninth Street, and died of a heart attack. January 17, 1955. (M)

Charles McCaddon — McCaddon, 32, died unexpectedly at home. He became a fireman in 1950 and was assigned to Station 6, 1515 Thirteenth Street. No other information. March 16, 1958. (M)

Robert W. Parrahm — Captain Parrahm, 40, was killed when Engine 5, responding to a false alarm at Twenty-ninth Street and Brighton Boulevard, collided with an automobile at Twenty-third and Market Streets and overturned, crushing him. March 20, 1960. (M)

Joseph H. Hotchkiss — Captain Hotchkiss, 47, of Engine 2, collapsed and died of a heart attack at the scene of a fire at Alton Wright Welding Co., 2077 South Cherokee Street. July 29, 1960. (M)

Victor H. Sullivan — Sullivan, 35, was hurled from the rear step of Pumper 6 when it collided with a car at Speer Boulevard and Lawrence Street en route to a false alarm at Thirteenth and Stout Streets. Sullivan sustained severe head and internal injuries and died within hours without regaining consciousness. June 28, 1967. (M)

John Keller — Assigned to Station 15, Keller, 32, suffered an apparent heart attack at his home, 1284 South Beach Court, and was dead on arrival at the hospital. Keller was exposed to cyanide gas at a greenhouse fire a few days before his death. January 13, 1968. (M)

Wayne D. Manaugh — Manaugh, 53, was found dead on the floor of the bathroom at Station 21, East Virginia Avenue and South Franklin Street, after returning from a call. Death was attributed to a heart attack. September 17, 1971. (M)

Mark Langvardt — Langvardt, 39, of Station 16, was pulled unconscious from the second story of a three-alarm arson fire at 1625 South Broadway. He was on a search-and-rescue mission when he became trapped in small room on the building's second floor. He died of smoke inhalation. September 28, 1992. (M)

Douglas K. Konecny — Assisting police on a domestic-disturbance call, Konecny, 48, of Station 10, was shot in the neck and killed as he tried to enter the second-story window of a duplex at 2836 Humboldt Street. After a four-hour standoff, the shooter, Lamar Edwards, set fire to the house and committed suicide. Chief Richard Gonzales called the shooting an "ambush." January 31, 1993. (X,M)

Notes

Chapter One

1. *Colorado Springs Gazette*, April 30, 1896.
2. Ibid.
3. Julie Luckraft letters, Colorado Springs Pioneers Museum, May 1, 1896.
4. Ibid., April 28, 1896.
5. Edward J. Goodspeed, *History of the Great Fires in Chicago & the West*, p. 552.
6. Ralph W. Andrews, *Historic Fires of the West*, p. 105.
7. Christian J. Buys, "Of Frozen Hydrants and 'Drunken Sons of Bitches,'" *Colorado Heritage* magazine, Summer 1997, p. 7.
8. Arnold Genthe, *As I Remember*, p. 89.
9. *Helena Daily Herald*, August 24, 1872.
10. *Daily Central City Register*, May 22, 1874.
11. Ibid.
12. *Daily Central City Register*, May 21, 1874.
13. *Daily Central City Register*, May 25, 1874.
14. Andrews, p. 73.
15. *Daily Central City Register*, May 25, 1874.
16. *Daily Central City Register*, May 22, 1874.
17. *Rocky Mountain News*, May 2, 1896.
18. *Rocky Mountain News*, May 28, 1863.
19. *Weekly Commonwealth and Republican*, October 23, 1863.
20. Interview with Edward Chase by Thomas F. Dawson, Colorado Historical Society, July 11, 1921.
21. Luckraft letters, April 28, 1896.
22. *Rocky Mountain News*, May 2, 1896.

Chapter Two

1. Jerome C. Smiley, *History of Denver*, p. 369.
2. William Hepworth Dixon, *New America*, p. 92.

3. Smiley, p. 369.
4. *Weekly Commonwealth and Republican*, November 6, 1862.
5. Smiley, p. 339.
6. Isabella Bird, *A Lady's Life in the Rockies*, p. 137.
7. Robert L. Perkin, *The First Hundred Years*, p. 209.
8. *Weekly Rocky Mountain News*, December 4, 1862.
9. David F. Halaas, *Boom Town Newspaper*, p. 91.
10. *Weekly Commonwealth and Republican*, November 20, 1862.
11. *Weekly Commonwealth and Republican*, October 30, 1862.
12. Denver City Council meeting of April 16, 1863, cited in *Rocky Mountain News*, April 23, 1863.
13. *Weekly Rocky Mountain News*, November 6, 1862.
14. *Weekly Commonwealth and Republican*, November 6, 1862.
15. *Weekly Commonwealth and Republican*, February 19, 1863.
16. *Weekly Rocky Mountain News*, April 23, 1863.
17. *Rocky Mountain News*, April 20, 1863.
18. Chapter VI, Section 2, Charter and Ordinances of the City of Denver, 1862.
19. *Weekly Rocky Mountain News*, April 23, 1863.
20. Ibid.
21. Ibid.
22. *Weekly Commonwealth and Republican*, April 23, 1863.
23. Ibid.
24. Interview with Edward Chase by Thomas F. Dawson, Colorado Historical Society, July 11, 1921.
25. *Weekly Rocky Mountain News*, April 23, 1863.
26. *Rocky Mountain News*, April 22, 1863.
27. Clara V. Witter, *The Trail* 18, August 1925, p. 5.
28. Ibid., p. 7.
29. *Weekly Rocky Mountain News*, April 30, 1863.
30. *Weekly Commonwealth and Republican*, April 23, 1863.
31. *Weekly Rocky Mountain News*, April 23, 1863.
32. *Miner's Register* (Central City), April 21, 1863.
33. *Rocky Mountain News*, April 19, 1923.
34. *Rocky Mountain News*, April 30, 1863.
35. *Weekly Commonwealth and Republican*, May 14, 1863.
36. Amendment to Chapter Six of the Denver City Ordinances. The ordinance appears in its entirety in *Rocky Mountain News*, April 22, 1863.

37. Amendment to Chapter Six of the Denver City Ordinances, 1863.

38. *Weekly Commonwealth and Republican,* April 23, 1863.

39. *Weekly Commonwealth and Republican,* April 30, 1863.

40. *Rocky Mountain News,* April 23, 1863.

41. *Weekly Commonwealth and Republican,* April 23, 1863.

42. *Rocky Mountain News,* May 28, 1863.

43. *Weekly Commonwealth and Republican,* May 21, 1863.

44. William B. Vickers, *History of the City of Denver, Arapahoe County and Colorado,* p. 201.

CHAPTER THREE

1. Jerome C. Smiley, *History of Denver,* pp. 485–486.

2. *Rocky Mountain News,* March 16, 1894.

3. Ibid.

4. *Denver City Directory,* 1894.

5. Smiley, p. 918.

6. Clark Secrest, *Hell's Belles,* p. 170.

7. Minutes of meetings, Denver Fire and Police Board, April 20, 1894, p. 323.

8. Ibid.

9. Minutes of meetings, Denver Fire and Police Board, January 18, 1893, p. 255.

10. Smiley, p. 626.

11. *Denver Republican,* March 18, 1894.

12. Ibid.

13. *News,* March 19, 1894.

14. *The Denver Times,* October 8, 1902.

15. *Republican,* March 18, 1894.

16. *The Times,* March 19, 1894.

17. *News,* March 22, 1894.

18. *News,* March 23, 1894.

19. Ibid.

20. Ibid.

21. Ibid.

22. Ibid.

23. Ibid.

24. *Republican,* March 26, 1894.

25. *News,* March 26, 1894.

26. Minutes of meetings, Denver Fire and Police Board, March 28, 1894, p. 318.

27. *The Denver Post,* April 27, 1917.

28. *News,* March 21, 1894.

CHAPTER FOUR

1. *The Denver Times,* March 25, 1895.

2. *Colorado Graphic,* September 17, 1887.

3. Letter from Marion Cook, May 10, 1883, Colorado Historical Society archives.

4. *Rocky Mountain News,* March 24, 1895.

5. *The Times,* March 25, 1895.

6. *Denver Republican,* March 25, 1895.

7. *The Times,* March 25, 1895.

8. *News,* March 25, 1895.

9. *News,* March 24, 1895.

10. Ibid.

11. Ibid.

12. Smilax is a small-leafed vine frequently used as a garland. It is more commonly known today as foxtail.

13. *News,* March 29, 1895.

14. *Republican,* March 29, 1895.

15. *News,* March 29, 1895.

16. *Republican,* March 25, 1895.

17. Ibid.

18. *Republican,* March 29, 1895.

19. *News,* March 25, 1895.

20. *The Times,* March 25, 1895.

21. *Republican,* March 25, 1895.

22. Ibid.

23. *News,* March 24, 1895.

24. *Republican,* March 28, 1895.

25. *Republican,* March 26, 1895.

26. *The Denver Post,* August 15, 1955.

27. Taped interview with Robert Nickerson by Dick Kreck, March 7, 1998.

28. Ibid.

29. *The Post,* April 20, 1969.

30. *The Post,* September 25, 1981.

31. Letter to the Denver Civil Service Commission from Nathan Biffle, May 5, 1942.
32. *The Post,* July 18, 1938.
33. *News,* October 19, 1966.

CHAPTER FIVE
1. *Denver Republican,* August 19, 1895.
2. Ibid.
3. *The Evening Post,* August 19, 1895.
4. *Republican,* August 19, 1895.
5. *Rocky Mountain News,* December 28, 1932.
6. *The Denver Times,* August 19, 1895.
7. *News,* August 20, 1895.
8. *The Times,* August 19, 1895.
9. *The Evening Post,* August 19, 1895.
10. *Republican,* August 19, 1895.
11. *The Times,* August 22, 1895.
12. *The Times,* August 20, 1895.
13. *The Evening Post,* August 19, 1895.
14. *News,* December 28, 1932.
15. *The Times,* August 19, 1895.
16. *The Evening Post,* August 22, 1895.
17. Ibid.
18. Ibid.
19. *The Times,* August 24, 1895.
20. *The Evening Post,* August 19, 1895.
21. Ibid.
22. *The Evening Post,* August 24, 1895.
23. *The Times,* August 27, 1895.
24. *Republican,* August 22, 1895.
25. *Republican,* August 23, 1895.
26. *Republican,* August 22, 1895.
27. *Republican,* August 21, 1895.
28. *The Evening Post,* August 27, 1895.
29. *Republican,* August 28, 1895.
30. *The Times,* August 29, 1895.
31. *The Times,* August 23, 1895.
32. *Republican,* August 30, 1895.
33. *The Evening Post,* August 28, 1895.

34. Jerome C. Smiley, *History of Denver,* p. 894.

35. *The Times,* January 31, 1901.

36. Ibid.

37. *The Evening Post,* October 18, 1895.

38. Interview with spokesperson for the University of Michigan–Ann Arbor's medical school by Dick Kreck, May 23, 1994.

39. *Republican,* August 30, 1895.

40. Ibid.

41. *The Evening Post,* August 22, 1895.

42. *The Times,* January 31, 1901.

43. *The Denver Post,* August 20, 1924.

CHAPTER SIX

1. Bill Hosokawa, *Thunder in the Rockies,* p. 17.

2. Gene Fowler, *Timber Line,* p. 95.

3. Ibid., p. 203.

4. Ibid., p. 99.

5. H. Allen Smith, *To Hell in a Handbasket,* p. 171.

6. Edwin P. Hoyt, *A Gentleman of Broadway,* p. 58.

7. *The Evening Post,* October 31, 1895.

8. Hosokawa, p. 26.

9. Ibid., p. 15.

10. Ibid., p. 130.

11. Fowler, p. 146.

12. *George's Weekly,* September 25, 1903.

13. Ibid.

14. *Rocky Mountain News,* September 22, 1904.

15. *The Post,* October 4, 1904.

16. *News,* September 23, 1904.

17. *The Denver Times,* September 21, 1904.

18. *News,* October 4, 1904.

19. Ibid.

20. *The Denver Post,* October 3, 1904.

21. Ibid.

22. Western Chemical Manufacturing Co. guidelines, *The Post,* September 26, 1904.

23. *News,* September 23, 1904.

24. *The Times,* September 21, 1904.

25. *The Post,* October 6, 1904.

26. *The Times*, September 22, 1904.

27. *News*, October 4, 1904.

28. *News*, September 23, 1904.

29. *Denver Republican*, September 23, 1904.

30. *News*, September 22, 1904.

31. Ibid.

32. *News*, September 26, 1904.

33. *The Times*, September 26, 1904.

34. *The Post*, September 21, 1904

35. *Republican*, October 22, 1904.

36. *The Post*, October 6, 1904.

37. *The Post*, September 22, 1904.

38. *The Times*, September 23, 1904.

39. *News*, September 23, 1904.

40. *The Post*, September 24, 1904.

41. Ibid.

42. *The Times*, September 26, 1904.

43. *The Post*, October 4, 1904.

44. *The Post*, October 5, 1904.

45. *The Times*, March 23, 1894.

46. *News*, April 6, 1923.

47. Ibid.

CHAPTER SEVEN

1. *The Denver Times*, September 8, 1908.

2. *The Denver Post*, September 8, 1908.

3. *Rocky Mountain News*, September 9, 1908.

4. *Denver Republican*, September 9, 1908.

5. *The Times*, September 8, 1908.

6. *Republican*, September 8, 1908.

7. *The Times*, September 8, 1908.

8. *The Times*, September 9, 1908.

9. *News*, September 9, 1908.

10. *The Post*, September 8, 1908.

11. *The Post*, September 9, 1908.

12. *The Times*, September 9, 1908.

13. *News*, September 9, 1908.

14. *News*, September 10, 1908.

15. *Republican*, September 9, 1908.

16. *The Post*, September 9, 1908.
17. *The Post*, September 8, 1908.
18. *News*, September 10, 1908.
19. *The Post*, September 9, 1908.
20. *The Times*, September 8, 1908.
21. *The Post*, September 10, 1908.
22. Ibid.
23. *Republican*, September 12, 1908.
24. *The Post*, September 9, 1908.
25. *The Post*, September 8, 1908.
26. *The Post*, September 13, 1908.
27. *The Post*, February 20, 1951.
28. Interview with retired fire chief Myrle Wise by Dick Kreck, July 16, 1998.
29. *The Post*, September 10, 1908.

CHAPTER EIGHT
1. *The Denver Post*, September 26, 1943.
2. Thomas Noel and Stephen J. Leonard, *Denver: Mining Camp to Metropolis*, p. 228.
3. Michael C. C. Adams, *The Best War Ever*, p. 123.
4. John F. Stover, *American Railroads*, p. 203.
5. Ibid., p. 207.
6. Ronald H. Bailey, *The Home Front: USA*, p. 160.
7. Joseph R. Rose, *American Wartime Transportation*, p. 70.
8. R. C. Farewell, *Rio Grande Secret Places*, p. 84.
9. Edward T. Bollinger, *Rails That Climb*, p. 47.
10. *Boulder Daily Camera*, September 21, 1943.
11. Harry Hawes, "The Reopening of Tunnel 10," *Trains* magazine, February 1944, p. 12.
12. Ibid., p. 13.
13. *The Post*, September 21, 1943.
14. Bollinger, p. 272.
15. *Rocky Mountain News*, September 22, 1943.
16. Ibid.
17. Ibid.
18. Interview with Jack Jaynes by Dick Kreck, September 12, 1998.
19. Interview with Charlie Matty by Dick Kreck, August 5, 1998.

20. Ibid.
21. *The Post,* November 22, 1943.
22. *The Post,* December 12, 1943.
23. Ibid.
24. Bollinger, p. 273.
25. Hawes, p. 16.
26. Self-quoted in speech by A. E. Perlman to American Society of Military Engineers, Salt Lake City, February 3, 1944.
27. *News,* September 30, 1943.
28. Bollinger, p. 273.

CHAPTER NINE

1. Interview with Robert Hyatt by Dick Kreck, 1993.
2. Coroner's inquest, July 20, 1944.
3. Interview with Frank Devine by Dick Kreck, 1993.
4. *Rocky Mountain News,* July 17, 1944.
5. *The Denver Post,* July 17, 1944.
6. Coroner's inquest, July 19, 1944.
7. Interview with Laurette Grimsley Collins by Dick Kreck, 1994.
8. Ibid.
9. Ibid.
10. Interview with Robert Hyatt by Dick Kreck, 1994.
11. Ibid.
12. Interview with Robert Hyatt by Dick Kreck, 1993.
13. Ibid.
14. Ibid.
15. Interview with Jack Franklin by Dick Kreck, 1993.
16. Interview with Jack Jaynes by Dick Kreck, 1993.
17. Interview with Lillian Lally by Dick Kreck, 1993.
18. Interview with Jack Franklin by Dick Kreck, 1993.
19. Interview with Jack Jaynes by Dick Kreck, 1993.
20. Interview with Myrle Wise by Dick Kreck, 1993.
21. *The Post,* July 17, 1944.
22. Interview with Frank Devine by Dick Kreck, 1993.
23. Interview with Myrle Wise by Dick Kreck, 1993.
24. Ibid.
25. Coroner's inquest, July 19, 1944.
26. Ibid.

27. Ibid.

28. Ibid.

29. *The Post*, July 18, 1944.

30. Interview with Laurette Grimsley Collins by Dick Kreck, 1994.

31. *The Post*, July 20, 1944.

32. *The Post*, October 13, 1945.

33. Denver District Court documents filed April 25, 1947.

34. *The Post*, July 20, 1944.

35. Interview with Ed Lowery Jr. by Dick Kreck, 1994.

CHAPTER TEN

1. *The Denver Post*, February 18, 1951.

2. Ibid.

3. *Rocky Mountain News*, February 18, 1951.

4. Interview with Ira Tanner Jr. by Dick Kreck, February 4, 1998.

5. Interview with Jim Jordan by Dick Kreck, November 24, 1998.

6. *News*, March 2, 1951.

7. Interview with Bill Peery by Dick Kreck, February 1998.

8. *The Post*, February 18, 1951.

9. *News*, February 18, 1951.

10. Ibid.

11. Ibid.

12. Ibid.

13. Ibid.

14. Interview with Morris Engle by Dick Kreck, May 21, 1998.

15. *News*, February 18, 1951.

16. *News*, February 19, 1951.

17. Interview with Stan Sorenson by Dick Kreck, February 1998.

18. Ibid.

19. *News*, February 19, 1951.

20. *News*, February 18, 1951.

21. Ibid.

22. Interview with Leroy Newton by Dick Kreck, February 2, 1998.

23. *News*, March 2, 1951.

24. Tom Noel, *The Denver Athletic Club, 1884–1894*, p. 64.

25. *The Post*, February 20, 1951.
26. *News*, March 2, 1951.

CHAPTER ELEVEN

1. *Rocky Mountain News*, July 12, 1961.
2. Ibid.
3. Ibid.
4. Ibid.
5. *The Denver Post*, July 18, 1961.
6. Interview with Foy Wilkerson by Dick Kreck, December 12, 1998.
7. Ibid.
8. *News*, July 12, 1961.
9. *The Post*, September 20, 1961.
10. *The Post*, July 11, 1961.
11. *The Post*, July 12, 1961.
12. Ibid.
13. *The Post*, September 20, 1961.
14. Interview with Foy Wilkerson by Dick Kreck, December 12, 1998.
15. Ibid.
16. *News*, July 13, 1961.
17. *The Post*, September 24, 1961.
18. *The Post*, July 12, 1961.
19. *News*, July 14, 1961.
20. Interview with George Augusto by Dick Kreck, October 10, 1998.
21. *News*, July 14, 1961.
22. Ibid.
23. Ibid.
24. Interview with George Augusto by Dick Kreck, October 10, 1998.
25. Interview with Joe Keelan by Dick Kreck, October 8, 1998.
26. *The Post*, August 23, 1962.
27. Report of the Civil Aeronautics Board in *The Post*, July 20, 1962.
28. Interview with Foy Wilkerson by Dick Kreck, December 12, 1998.
29. *The Post*, September 6, 1962.

CHAPTER TWELVE

1. *The Denver Post,* October 29, 1975.
2. Ibid.
3. *Commonwealth and Republican,* November 6, 1862.
4. Interview with Jim Jordan by Dick Kreck, November 24, 1998.
5. *Rocky Mountain News,* July 26, 1971.
6. Interview with Carl Whiteside by Dick Kreck, December 16, 1998.
7. Ibid.
8. *The Post,* September 29, 1976.
9. *The Post,* June 20, 1975.
10. *The Post,* November 1, 1975.
11. Interview with Jim Jordan by Dick Kreck, November 24, 1998.
12. *The Post,* June 20, 1975.
13. Ibid.
14. Ibid.
15. *The Post,* October 29, 1975.
16. Ibid.
17. Interview with Jim Jordan by Dick Kreck, November 24, 1998.
18. Ibid.
19. Interview with Carl Whiteside by Dick Kreck, December 16, 1998.
20. *The Post,* October 30, 1975.
21. *The Post,* June 14, 1975.
22. *The Post,* October 30, 1975.
23. *The Post,* October 29, 1975.
24. *Cervi's Journal,* November 11, 1971.
25. *The Post,* November 4, 1975.
26. Interview with Carl Whiteside by Dick Kreck, December 16, 1998.
27. Interview with Jim Jordan by Dick Kreck, November 24, 1998.

BIBLIOGRAPHY

ARTICLES

Buys, Christian J. "Of Frozen Hydrants and 'Drunken Sons of Bitches.'" *Colorado Heritage* magazine, Colorado Historical Society, Summer 1997.

Hawes, Harry. "The Reopening of Tunnel 10." *Trains* magazine, February 1944.

Witter, Clara V. "A Pioneer Woman's Story." *The Trail* 18, Colorado Historical Society, August 1925.

BOOKS

Adams, Michael C. C. *The Best War Ever* (Baltimore and London: Johns Hopkins University Press, 1994).

Andrews, Ralph W. *Historic Fires of the West* (Seattle: Superior Publishing Co., 1966).

Bagley, Clarence B. *History of Seattle: From the Earliest Settlement to the Present Time*, vol. 1 (Chicago: S. J. Clarke Publishing Co., 1916; out of print).

Bailey, Ronald H. *The Home Front: USA* (Alexandria, Va.: Time-Life Books, 1977).

Barker, Bill, and Jackie Lewin. *Denver: An Insider's Look at the High, Wide and Handsome City* (New York: Doubleday & Co., Inc., 1963).

Billington, Ray Allen. *Westward Expansion: A History of the American Frontier* (New York: The Macmillan Co., 1967).

Bird, Isabella. *A Lady's Life in the Rockies* (New York: Ballantine Books, 1973).

Bollinger, Edward T. *Rails That Climb* (Golden: Colorado Railroad Museum, 1979).

Bronson, William. *The Earth Shook, the Sky Burned* (New York: Doubleday & Co., Inc., 1959).

Brown, Robert L. *Cripple Creek Then and Now* (Denver: Sundance Publications, 1991).

Current, Richard N. *The History of Wisconsin,* vol. 3, *The Civil War Era, 1848–1873* (Madison: State Historical Society of Wisconsin, 1976).

Denver Fire Department. *Denver Fire Department 1866–1991: A 125-Year Tradition* (Denver: Denver Fire Department, 1992).

Dixon, William Hepworth. *New America* (Philadelphia: J. P. Lippincott, 1876).

Downing, Sybil, and Robert E. Smith. *Tom Patterson: Colorado Crusader for Change* (Niwot: University Press of Colorado, 1995).

Farewell, R. C. *Rio Grande Secret Places,* vol. 1 (Golden: Colorado Railroad Museum, 1997).

Feitz, Leland. *A Quick History of Victor* (Colorado Springs: Little London Press, 1969).

Firemen's Mutual Benefit Association. *Fire Service of Denver* (Denver: Firemen's Mutual Benefit Association, 1890).

Forrest, Kenton. *Denver's Railroads* (Golden: Colorado Railroad Museum, 1986).

Fowler, Gene. *Timberline: A Story of Bonfils and Tammen* (Garden City, N.Y.: Garden City Books, 1951).

Genthe, Arnold. *As I Remember* (New York: Reynal & Hitchcock, 1936).

Goodstein, Phil. *Denver Streets* (Denver: New Social Publications, 1994).

Grimstad, Bill, and Raymond L. Drake. *The Last Gold Rush: A Pictorial History of the Cripple Creek & Victor Gold Mining District* (Victor, Colo.: Pollux Press, 1983).

Halaas, David F. *Boom Town Newspapers: Journalism on the Rocky Mountain Mining Frontier, 1859–1881* (Albuquerque: University of New Mexico Press, 1981).

Hornby, William H. *Voice of Empire* (Denver: Colorado Historical Society, 1992).

Hosokawa, Bill. *Thunder in the Rockies: The Incredible Denver Post* (New York: William Morrow, 1976).

Hoyt, Edwin P. *A Gentleman of Broadway* (Boston and New York: Little, Brown, 1964).

Johnson, Rev. Edward. *History of the Great Fires in Chicago & the West* (New York: H. S. Goodspeed & Co., 1871).

Lowe, David. *Lost Chicago* (New York: Wings Books, 1975).

Miller, Jeff. *Stapleton International Airport: The First Fifty Years* (Boulder, Colo.: Pruett Publishing, 1983).

Noel, Thomas. *The City and the Saloon* (Lincoln: University of Nebraska Press, 1996).

———. *The Denver Athletic Club, 1884–1894* (Denver: Denver Athletic Club, 1983).

———. *Denver's Larimer Street: Main Street, Skid Row and Urban Renaissance* (Denver: Historic Denver Inc., 1981).

Noel, Thomas, and Stephen J. Leonard. *Denver: Mining Camp to Metropolis* (Niwot: University Press of Colorado, 1990).

Perkin, Robert L. *The First Hundred Years: An Informal History of Denver and the Rocky Mountain News* (Garden City, N.Y.: Doubleday, 1959).

Representative Men of Colorado, 1858–1902 (New York and Denver: Rowell Art Publishing Co., 1902).

Rose, Joseph R. *American Wartime Transportation* (New York: Thomas Y. Crowell Co., 1953).

Satterfield, Archie. *The Home Front: An Oral History of the War Years in America* (New York: Playboy Press, 1981).

Secrest, Clark. *Hell's Belles: Denver's Brides of the Multitudes* (Denver: Hindsight Historical Publications, 1996).

Smiley, Jerome C. *History of Denver* (Denver: Sun Publishing, 1901).

Smith, H. Allen. *To Hell in a Handbasket* (Garden City, N.Y.: Doubleday, 1962).

Stover, John F. *The Life and Decline of the American Railroad* (New York: Oxford University Press, 1970).

———. *American Railroads* (Chicago: University of Chicago Press, 1961).

Taylor, Robert Guilford. *Cripple Creek Mining District* (Palmer Lake, Colo.: Filter Press, 1973).

Vickers, William B. *History of the City of Denver, Arapahoe County and Colorado* (Chicago: O. L. Baskin & Co., 1880).

Wharton, Junius E. *History of Denver from Its Earliest Times* (Denver: Byers and Dailey, 1866).

NEWSPAPERS

Boulder Daily Camera
Cervi's Journal
Chicago Tribune
Colorado Springs Gazette
Daily Central City Register
The Denver Post

Denver Republican
The Denver Times
The Evening Post
George's Weekly
Helena (Montana) *Daily Herald*
Miner's Register (Central City)
Rocky Mountain News
Weekly Commonwealth and Republican
Weekly Rocky Mountain News

MANUSCRIPTS

Copy of a letter to the Denver Civil Service Commission from Capt. Nathan Biffle, May 5, 1942. In the author's possession.

Edward Chase interviewed by Thomas F. Dawson, July 11, 1921. Colorado Historical Society, Denver.

Letter from Marion Cook, May 10, 1883. Colorado Historical Society, Denver.

Minutes of meetings, Fire and Police Board of Denver, vol. 2 (1893–1894). Western History Department, Denver Public Library.

Copy of official proclamation naming Nathan Biffle an honorary chief from Chief Richard Gonzales, April 15, 1997. In the author's possession.

Julie Luckraft letters, archives. Colorado Springs Pioneers Museum.

Speech by A. E. Perlman, assistant to the president of the Denver & Salt Lake Railway, to the Utah section of the American Society of Civil Engineers, Salt Lake City, February 3, 1944. Denver & Rio Grande Western Railroad Collection, Colorado Historical Society, Denver.

INTERVIEWS

Retired firemen George Augusto, Terry Brennan, Dan Day, Frank Devine, Jack Franklin, Robert Hyatt, Jack Jaynes, Jim Jordan, Joe Keelan, Charlie Matty, Leroy Newton, Bob Nickerson, Stan "Smokey" Sorensen, Foy Wilkerson and retired chief Myrle Wise.

Also, Judge Richard T. Spriggs of Denver District Court, federal judge John Kane, Colorado Bureau of Investigation director Carl Whiteside and former *Denver Post* reporter Cindy Parmenter.

Anthony Mulligan, the focus of Chapter Twelve, on union-related arson fires, declined in 1999 to be interviewed.

INDEX

(*Note:* Page numbers in boldface indicate photographs or illustrations.)